Experiencing
the Holocaust

**Novels, Nonfiction Books, Short
Stories, Poems, Plays, Films & Music**

EXPERIENCING
ERAS &
EVENTS

Experiencing the Holocaust

Novels, Nonfiction Books, Short Stories, Poems, Plays, Films & Music

Judy Galens
Sarah Hermsen, Editor

Volume 2:
Short Stories
Poems
Plays
Films
Music

Detroit • New York • San Diego • San Francisco • Cleveland • New Haven, Conn. • Waterville, Maine • London • Munich

Experiencing the Holocaust
Judy Galens

Project Editor
Sarah Hermsen

Editorial
Elizabeth Grunow, Allison McNeill, Diane Sawinski

Permissions
Margaret Chamberlain

Imaging and Multimedia
Dean Dauphinais, Robert Duncan

Product Design
Tracey Rowens

Composition
Evi Seoud

Manufacturing
Rita Wimberley

LIBRARY OF CONGRESS CATALOGING-IN-PUBLICATION DATA

Galens, Judy, 1968–
Experiencing the Holocaust : novels, nonfiction books, short stories, poems, plays, films & songs / Judy Galens ; Sarah Hermsen, editor.
p. cm.—(Experiencing eras and events)
Includes bibliographical references and index.
ISBN 0-7876-5414-0 (set : alk. paper)
1. Holocaust, Jewish (1939–1945)—Literary collections. 2. Holocaust, Jewish (1939–1945)—Personal narratives. [1. Holocaust, Jewish (1939–1945)—Literary collections. 2. Holocaust, Jewish (1939–1945)—Personal narratives.] I. Hermsen, Sarah. II. Title. III. Series.
PN6071.H713 G35 2003
808.8'0358—dc21
2002004491

Printed in the United States of America
10 9 8 7 6 5 4 3 2 1

Contents

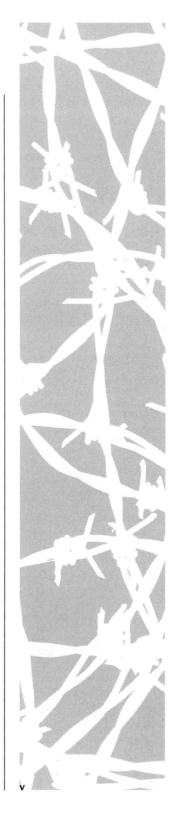

Volume 1

Volume 2

Reader's Guide

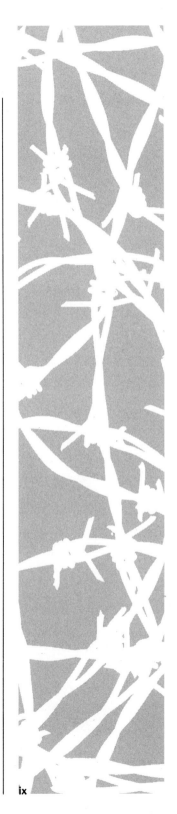

The Holocaust took place before and during World War II (1939–45) when German leader Adolf Hitler and his Nazi Party sought to systematically destroy Europe's Jews, political opponents of Nazism, and other people whom Hitler considered undesirables, such as Roma (Gypsies), homosexuals, and the mentally and physically disabled. *Experiencing the Holocaust: Novels, Nonfiction Books, Short Stories, Poems, Plays, Films, and Music* is a two-volume reference set that provides detailed information on twenty-three creative works, appropriate for young-adult audiences, about the Holocaust. Many of the works were written by people who were alive during the Holocaust era: victims, survivors, witnesses, and bystanders. Some of these works, like *The Diary of a Young Girl*, were written during the Holocaust and reflect daily experiences in an extraordinary time. Others, including Ruth Minsky Sender's memoir *The Cage*, were written many years later, after decades of painful reflection. Some of the works in this set were created by the children of survivors, people who spent their lives far from Hitler's Europe and yet grew up constantly under its shadow. And finally, a number of the pieces discussed in *Experiencing the Holocaust* were crafted by people who have no direct link to the Holocaust but who have been moved to address these events of unparalleled tragedy and gross inhumanity.

Experiencing the Holocaust will help students understand the complexities of the Holocaust era through examinations of important works of literature, film, and music. Such works offer personal perspectives on a subject that can be daunting in its enormity. The statistics and bare facts of the Holocaust can be overwhelming, but the stories of individuals as rendered on the page or screen—their suffering, desperation, and determination—can give students fresh insights and deeper understanding of the time. Through the study of these works, students can explore specific events, issues, personalities, and themes associated with the Nazis' attempt to destroy European Jewry. Each of the books, poems, plays, and other works in this set—many of which are commonly taught in today's classrooms—addresses significant aspects of the Holocaust, including the widespread anti-Semitism in pre-war Germany; the imprisonment of Jews and others in ghettos and in concentration camps; the mass murders of Jews and other prisoners in death camps; resistance efforts in the ghettos and camps; courageous rescues undertaken by individuals and communities; and the plight of the Jewish refugees in the aftermath of the Holocaust.

Each essay in *Experiencing the Holocaust* is supplemented with informative sidebars that offer additional insight into the people, places, and happenings of the Holocaust. Other features of this set include a timeline listing important events of the Holocaust era; a words to know section defining terms used throughout the set; a bibliography of general Holocaust sources, including notable Internet sites; and a comprehensive subject index.

Organization of *Experiencing the Holocaust*

The twenty-three essays included in *Experiencing the Holocaust* are arranged by genre. Each of the seven main genre sections contained in the set—novels, nonfiction books, short stories, poems, plays, films, and music—begins with an overview of Holocaust-related works of that genre and also includes an annotated list of additional notable titles. Some of these works are intended for a general audience, but many are specifically directed at young adults. Following the overview essay that begins each genre section—with the exception of the music section—two to six essays provide detailed analysis of specific works in that genre. Some of the essays contain excerpts from the works being examined. All of the essays include the following sections:

- Identification and summary of the work

- Biographical information on the author or director of the work

- A brief chronology of historical events relating to the work

- Historical background on the issues and events highlighted in the work, providing a larger context in which to view the work

- Plot and character summary or, for poems and nonfiction books, an analysis of subject matter

- Major themes and stylistic characteristics of the work

- Research and activity ideas that explore different facets of the work

- Guide to sources—books and Web sites—containing additional information on the work and the events it addresses

The music genre section is an extended overview of Holocaust-related music, including specific composers, orchestral pieces, and protest songs.

Inclusion Criteria

A number of criteria were considered in the selection of titles to be featured in *Experiencing the Holocaust*. Included are several of the world's most significant works about the Holocaust—such as Anne Frank's *The Diary of a Young Girl* and Elie Wiesel's memoir *Night*—that are suitable for students. Many of the works discussed in this set feature young characters, offering students protagonists with whom they can readily identify. Presenting a wide variety of viewpoints was another important factor in deciding which works to include. The pieces discussed in *Experiencing the Holocaust* explore the era from the perspective of men and women, young and old, victims and survivors, rescuers and bystanders. While the Holocaust is studied primarily as a tragedy of the Jewish people, several million others, including non-Jewish Poles, Roma (Gypsies), and Jehovah's Witnesses, were persecuted and murdered by the Nazis, and their experiences are addressed here as well.

Finally, *Experiencing the Holocaust* was compiled with the intention of exploring a broad spectrum of issues and events associated with the Holocaust era. For example, subjects addressed in this set include the hiding of a Jewish boy at a Catholic school in France (Louis Malle's film *Au Revoir Les Enfants*); a Jew passing as a Christian in Nazi-held Poland (Rose Zar's memoir *In the Mouth of the Wolf*); the horrifying presence of the crematoria in the Nazi death camps (Nelly Sachs's poem "O the Chimneys"); England's extraordinary but flawed program to rescue thousands of Jewish children (the documentary film *Into the Arms of Strangers*); and the postwar illegal immigration to the region that became the state of Israel (Carol Matas's novel *After the War*).

Special Thanks

The author and editor would like to thank Pam Aue for her contributions to *Experiencing the Holocaust*.

Comments and Suggestions

We welcome your comments on *Experiencing the Holocaust*. Please send correspondence to: Editor, *Experiencing the Holocaust*, U•X•L, 27500 Drake Road, Farmington Hills, Michigan, 48331-3535; call toll-free: 800-877-4253; fax to: 248-699-8097; or send e-mail via http://www.gale.com.

Advisory Board

Special thanks are due to U•X•L's *Experiencing the Holocaust* advisors for their invaluable comments and suggestions:

Sara Brooke, Librarian, Ellis School,
Pittsburgh, Pennsylvania

Peter Butts, Media Specialist, East Middle School,
Holland, Michigan

Peter J. Fredlake, United States Holocaust
Memorial Museum (USHMM) Mandel Fellow, Mingus
Union High School, Cottonwood, Arizona

Marolyn Griffin, School Librarian, Desert Ridge
Middle School, Albuquerque, New Mexico

Friedell Kert-Wolson, Detroit Middle School English Teacher-
Retired and Docent, Michigan Holocaust Memorial Center,
Detroit, Michigan

Introduction

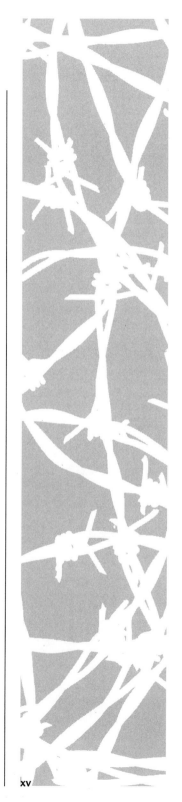

The Holocaust—the campaign of Adolf Hitler (1889–1945) and Nazi Germany to systematically murder the Jews of Europe—was a modern-day tragedy of massive proportions. The word "holocaust" means complete destruction, often by fire; when written with a capital "H," the Holocaust refers to the devastation of European Jewry in the 1940s. Of approximately nine million Jews living in Europe before World War II (1939–45), only three million were still alive by the war's end. In other words, two out of three European Jews died at the Nazis' hands. A number of other groups were targeted for persecution by the Nazis, including Roma (Gypsies), Poles and others of Slavic ancestry, homosexuals, the physically and mentally disabled, political opponents of Nazism, and Jehovah's Witnesses, a religious group that refused to swear allegiance to the German state. In all, the Nazis murdered some eleven million men, women, and children simply because of their heritage or beliefs.

Hitler's Rise to Power

Throughout the early 1920s, Germany was still reeling from its defeat in World War I (1914–18). The war had resulted in a huge loss of life, with some two million German soldiers being killed in the conflict. The victors in the war (the Allied forces, including such nations as Great Britain, France, and, later, the United States) had forced Germany to sign the Treaty of Versailles. This treaty prevented Germany from having a powerful military and mandated that some German territory be assigned to other nations, including a section of eastern Germany that became part of Poland. The treaty also required Germany to pay large fines to the Allied nations, sums the weakened nation could barely afford. German officials were given little choice but to sign the treaty, and for German citizens it was a bitter end after years of devastating war and hardship. With millions of Germans out of work, poverty became widespread, and many suffered from a sense of humiliation that their once-great nation had been brought to its knees by its enemies.

Hitler, who had been born and raised in Austria but fought in the German army during World War I, was particularly devastated by his adopted country's loss in the war. Desperate for someone to blame, Hitler focused on the Jews as Germany's primary enemy. Although they made up less than 1 percent of the population in Germany, Hitler believed the Jews possessed great power and were responsible for the nation's ills. Tapping into a long tradition of anti-Semitism, or hatred of Jews, in Germany and elsewhere, Hitler thought of Jews as untrustworthy and evil. He was convinced that Jews plotted to take over international banks and thus dominate the world. To back up this claim, Hitler and other anti-Semites pointed to a booklet called *The Protocols of the Elders of Zion*. Initially published in Russia in 1903, *Protocols* supposedly documented a Jewish conspiracy to take over the world. In spite of the fact that the booklet was determined to be a complete fake, many people believed it was a genuine document revealing an actual plot for world domination. Some continue to believe that even today.

Leader of the Nazi Party

Armed with a convenient scapegoat (a person or group who unfairly shoulders the blame for a problem) in the

Jewish people and determined to do a better job than the existing government at improving Germany's situation, Hitler decided to become involved in politics. In 1919 he joined a small political group known as the German Workers' Party; he soon became the party's leader and renamed the group the National Socialist German Workers' Party, or Nazi Party. The aim of the Nazi Party was to rebuild Germany by asserting the superiority of the Aryan race, a racial category, not generally accepted, that consists of white Christians of Germanic or Nordic descent. The Nazis also planned to "purify" the nation, ridding it of undesirable elements such as the Jews. The Nazis considered Jews to be members of a different race; therefore, they declared, Jews could not be citizens of Germany.

Initially, many Germans dismissed Hitler as a disturbing madman who could never appeal to enough citizens to become an elected official. But Hitler's popularity steadily grew. A powerful and charismatic speaker, he worked crowds of onlookers into a frenzy with his passionate cries for a renewed Germany. He promised to create new jobs and revive the economy, giving hope to German citizens. He stated over and over that pride in and loyalty to the fatherland, as he referred to Germany, would be instrumental in rebuilding the nation. This intense loyalty to one's country—and, in extreme cases, the belief that one's country is superior to all others—is known as nationalism, which was the defining principle of the Nazi Party. Hitler restored confidence to many German citizens by preaching that they were part of a so-called master race—the Aryan race—that deserved to lead the world. Hitler also achieved success

Hitler's charismatic and powerful speeches often worked crowds into a frenzy and helped spread anti-Semitism throughout Germany. *Reproduced by permission of AP/Wide World Photos.*

through physical intimidation. He created a military branch of the Nazi Party called the *Sturmabteilung,* or SA. The members of the SA, also known as the Storm Troopers or the Brownshirts, provided security at meetings and rallies, never hesitating to use violence to silence the opposition.

In 1923 the Nazis attempted to overthrow the German government in what came to be known as the Beer Hall Putsch (the attempt began in a Munich beer hall; the word *putsch* is German for an attempted overthrow). Hitler was convicted of treason, or betrayal of one's country, and spent nearly nine months in jail. During his imprisonment, he wrote a book called *Mein Kampf* ("My Struggle"), in which he aired his views about many things, particularly his obsessive and violent hatred of Jews.

Nazis in power

While the Nazi Party steadily grew, it remained fairly small and politically insignificant throughout the 1920s. Hitler knew that in order to achieve real power, he would have to secure the allegiance of the masses. His radical ideas played on the insecurities of a population that felt angry, fearful, and desperate, but a brief period of prosperity in Germany in the mid-1920s stalled his efforts to win widespread support. With the U.S. stock market crash and consequent Great Depression beginning in 1929, however, Germany was again plunged into economic turmoil, and the fortunes of the Nazi Party improved. In the 1928 national elections, the Nazi Party received less than one million votes and won 12 seats in the German parliament, or Reichstag. In special elections just two years later, 6.5 million people voted for the Nazis, and they won 107 seats.

During the 1932 election campaign, Hitler traveled from city to city. He gave fiery speeches during which he repeated the goals and beliefs of the Nazis over and over again. He reasoned that even ideas considered outrageous to the general population would, with repetition, become commonly accepted. While a significant part of the population still found Hitler's ideas repellant, many others believed he could return the nation to its former glory. The ranks of the Storm Troopers continued to swell, and they used brutality to quiet opposing voices. The 1932 elections revealed a deeply divided nation: the Nazis earned more than one-third of the vote, but no single party received enough votes to govern Germany. Paul von Hindenburg, the German president and leader of the powerful Social Democrats Party, became convinced that the Nazis could be useful allies, and he appointed Hitler chancellor of Germany (a position akin to prime minister).

Once Hitler gained a position of power within the government, he moved swiftly to seize even greater power. By imprisoning and intimidating his political opponents in the Reichstag, he was able to pass legislation called the Enabling Act. This act gave Hitler the power to abolish the existing government and to pass laws on his own, essentially making him the all-powerful dictator of Germany. Hitler banned all other political parties, abolished labor unions, installed Nazis as governors of the German states, and took control of the news media. Many formerly prominent members of opposing political parties were sent to Dachau and other concentration camps, large prisons where inmates were forced into manual labor. Conditions in the camps were horrible: food was scarce, the barracks where prisoners slept were crowded and filthy, and the guards were brutal. Concentration camps were guarded at first by the Storm Troopers of the SA and later by the elite military unit known as the SS (short for the German word *Schutzstaffel*).

Hitler's Early Years As Leader: 1933–38

Calling himself the Führer (the German word for "leader"), Hitler immediately put into motion policies that would accomplish his goals: alienating Jews from German society and making Germany economically and militarily stronger. He was obsessed with greatly expanding the German empire, or *reich*. He described his rule as a continuation of Germany's proud and powerful past, and he spoke of the German nation under his leadership as the Third Reich.

Persecution of the Jews

Hitler had carefully planned his persecution of Germany's Jews. While violence was a significant part of his harassment of Jews, he planned to primarily use the legal system and a campaign of propaganda (information, and sometimes misinformation, used to persuade people to a certain point of view) to outlaw their very existence. Hitler intended to turn Jews—many of whom were highly assimilated, or blended, into the larger society—into the "other," a group that did not fit in with other Germans. He portrayed them as foreigners and enemies of the state, repeatedly asserting that Jews were filthy, monstrous, and untrustworthy. Hitler cultivated a climate of hostility, fear, and hatred toward Jews, and it became difficult for Jewish people even to walk down a street without being harassed, spit upon, or beaten.

Hitler began passing anti-Jewish laws soon after becoming chancellor. First he prevented Jews from holding official government positions, including teaching jobs. Strict quotas in schools and universities kept Jewish student enrollment to a minimum. Jews were barred from the legal and medical professions and many other occupations. The police made it clear that they would not protect Jewish citizens or business owners from random beatings or riots, which were conducted regularly by members of the Storm Troopers. On April 1, 1933, the Nazis staged a nationwide boycott of Jewish-owned businesses. In 1935 several laws were passed to further deny German Jews their basic rights. Originating in the German city of Nuremberg and known collectively as the Nuremberg Laws, these policies stripped Jews of their German citizenship, denied them the right to vote, and prohibited their marriage to non-Jews. Additional laws over the next few years forced Jewish business owners to sell their businesses to Aryans at sharply reduced prices in a policy known as Aryanization. By the end of the 1930s, all German Jews were required to identify themselves as Jews by carrying special identification cards. In 1941 they were forced to sew a yellow six-pointed star, a centuries-old symbol of Judaism called the Star of David, onto their clothing.

As a result of the swift and brutal changes in Germany, Jews struggled to earn a living and feared for their personal safety. At the time, German policy was based on creating a hostile environment for the Jews, eventually forcing all of them to leave Germany. Tens of thousands did flee, concerned that the situation would only worsen. Many Jews stayed, however, convinced that circumstances would improve and that the international community would pressure the German government to treat the Jews better. No significant pressure came

from other countries, however, and in the absence of any real opposition from the rest of the world, Hitler pressed on with his plans.

Hitler Youth saluting the swastika at a harvest celebration parade in Germany, 1935. *Reproduced by permission of Art Resource.*

Reconstructing Germany: The Hitler Youth and other measures

The totalitarian, or absolutely powerful, government of Nazi Germany held the nation in a tight grip. Hitler wanted to control every aspect of citizens' lives: where they worked, what they did, how they were entertained and informed, and even what they thought. Hitler allowed the public to view only certain kinds of art and to listen to only certain kinds of music, namely traditional works that glorified Germany. Anything modern or experimental was considered dangerous and described by Hitler as "degenerate," which describes something corrupt and immoral. The government controlled radio stations and newspapers, forcing them to repeat Nazi propaganda and to silence any government criticism. The Nazis encouraged citizens to report to the government any traitors—anybody who disagreed with the government's policies—creating an atmosphere of mistrust and suspicion among the people. Children were told to spy on their parents and teachers, and adults were told to watch their coworkers, neighbors, and relatives. Any citizen who dared criticize the government could be reported, facing possible arrest and deportation to a concentration camp.

One of Hitler's most ambitious plans for controlling the population was the network of Nazi youth groups for Christian children of all ages, primarily the *Hitlerjugend,* or Hitler Youth, for boys, and the *Bund Deutscher Mädel,* or League of German Girls, for girls. Separate organizations existed for younger children, including the *Jungvolk,* meaning "young people," for boys aged ten to fourteen. Membership in these groups was voluntary at first, but by 1936 all other youth groups had been outlawed, and by 1939, all children were required to join the Nazi youth organizations. Like many youth groups, the Hitler Youth and League of German Girls emphasized physical strength and outdoor activity: members went hiking and camping and played a number of sports. Unlike typical youth groups, however, the boys in the Hitler Youth were also trained in weapons and taught military-style discipline. And the children in these organizations were schooled in Nazi beliefs from a very young age. They were told repeatedly of the honor of serving their nation and their Führer, of the importance of the Reich over all other things, and of the necessity of defeating the enemies of the Reich, including those within the country's borders, such as the Jews. In essence, the Hitler Youth was grooming a nation of boys to be a mighty army of the future, and the League of German Girls was training young women to be the wives of those soldiers and the mothers of the next generation of fighters.

The Hitler Youth represented the next generation of the German military, but Hitler also invested considerable effort in rebuilding the current generation's armed forces. In direct violation of the Treaty of Versailles, Hitler began to expand the country's military by the mid-1930s, gradually transforming the German military into a powerful, modern force populated by men who were prepared to die for the Führer. Hitler intended to use Germany's military to achieve his aim of territorial domination in Europe. He planned to expand the German empire to include countries like Austria and Czechoslovakia, both of which had large numbers of citizens with German ancestry. He also intended to recapture territory, including western Poland, that had been lost during World War I. Hitler often spoke of the need to acquire territory to provide the superior German "race" with greater *Lebensraum,* or "living space." Germany had become too crowded, and Hitler intended to dominate the citizens of other countries, taking over their land and forcing them to work for and serve the German people. Hitler also planned to conquer parts of the Soviet Union, a nation he despised for its communist doctrine, a system he closely associated with the Jewish people. In addition to garnering new territory for the German people, Hitler's domination of Poland and the western regions of the Soviet Union would also put Europe's largest population of Jews under his control, giving him the ability to dispose of that population as he saw fit.

Kristallnacht: A Turning Point

In 1938 Hitler put into motion his plans to expand the German empire. He forcibly annexed, or took over, Austria in March, an event known as the *Anschluss.* In September he conquered the Sudetenland, a region of Czechoslovakia and six months later he would take control of the rest of that country. That year also marked a turning point in his treatment of Jews. During the autumn of 1938, the Nazis rounded up eighteen thousand Jews of Polish origin, regardless of how many years they had been living in Germany, and forced them to return to Poland. They were stopped at the border, however, as Poland refused them entry. Stuck in limbo at a temporary camp at the Polish-German border, thousands of Polish Jews endured miserable conditions. Among them were the Grynszpan family, and when their son Herschel, who was living in Paris at the time, heard about their plight, he decided to take action. Hoping to call attention to the injustice of the Germans' treatment of these Polish Jews, Herschel Grynszpan went to the German embassy in Paris and shot Ernst vom Rath, a low-level German official. When vom Rath died of his wounds on November 9, Hitler's government used the shooting as justification to launch vicious riots against the Jews, riots that actually had been planned long before.

On the night of November 9, throughout Germany and Austria, gangs of Nazis attacked Jewish communities, taking people from their homes and beating them in the streets. Jewish businesses and apartments were vandalized and numerous synagogues were burned. Nearly one hundred Jews were murdered that night, and, regardless of the fact that the Jews were the victims of the attacks, nearly thirty thousand Jewish men were arrested and sent to concentration camps. The massive quantities of broken glass resulting from these pogroms, or riots, led the Nazis to refer to the event as *Kristallnacht,* which translates as "crystal night" and is often referred to as the "Night of Broken Glass." To further humiliate and punish the Jews, the Nazi leaders ordered the Jewish community to pay a fine for vom Rath's death and to repair the damage from the riots at their own expense. Even the most optimistic Jews could no longer hope for a continued existence in Germany. The brutality of *Kristallnacht* and the government's obvious support of such actions signalled the end of the Jewish community in Germany and Austria.

World War II Begins

As Hitler prepared for the war that he viewed as a necessary means to expand the German empire, the rest of the world watched with growing apprehension, wanting to stop Hitler but fearful that challenging him would lead to another major world war. Great Britain and France, allies of Poland, had said they would defend Poland if Hitler invaded, and on September 1, 1939, that threat became a reality. Backed by the might of the newly refurbished German army, Hitler invaded Poland using a strategy known as *blitzkrieg,* or "lightning war," attacking Poland simultaneously on the ground and from the air. Two days later, Britain and France declared war on Germany, marking the beginning of World War II. Neither Britain nor France sent troops to aid the Polish army, however, and Poland fell to Germany by the end of September.

According to an agreement made earlier between Germany and the Soviet Union, Germany occupied the western part of Poland, while the Soviet Union took over the eastern part. Of the area occupied by Germany, one section was incorporated into the Reich. It was considered part of Germany and was intended as land where German citizens could live. Another section, known as the Generalgouvernement, was governed by an administration set up by the Nazis. The Generalgouvernement was to be the location all the Polish Jews would be deported to, and those deportations began within months of the September invasion. The German occupation of Poland was particularly brutal. The Nazis sought to wipe out all traces of Polish culture and to prevent the Poles from organizing a resistance force. To that end, the Germans murdered numerous prominent Polish citizens: politicians, teachers, doctors, writers, and others. The Nazis considered the Poles, most of whom were of Slavic ancestry, inferior to the Aryans; Poles of German ancestry were treated far better. The most vicious treatment, however, was reserved for the Polish Jews, who were regarded by the Nazis as less than human.

Ghettos

Soon after invading Poland, Nazi officials ordered that the Jews of that nation were to be concentrated in major cities located near railway lines, and they would be housed in small, poor neighborhoods of those cities. These neighborhoods, known as ghettos, were usually sealed, meaning they were closed off to the outside world, surrounded by walls and guarded by police and Nazi troops. The Jews living in the ghettos could not leave and Poles living on the outside could not come in without special permission. Several hundred thousand Polish Jews were uprooted from their homes, forced to leave behind everything they could not carry, and transported to the closest ghetto. The first ghetto in Poland was established in the city of Piotrkow in October 1939. The two largest ghettos in Poland were established the following year, with the Lodz ghetto sealed in the spring of 1940 and the Warsaw ghetto sealed in November.

The ghettos were desperate, poverty-stricken, overcrowded places that Nazi propaganda minister Joseph Goebbels referred to as "death boxes." In the Warsaw ghetto, six or seven people lived in each room of each apartment. The Lodz ghetto housed nearly 200,000 people in a 1.5-square-mile area. In these and other highly populated ghettos, thousands of people had no shelter at all and were left to freeze on the streets during Poland's harsh winters.

With massive overcrowding came numerous other problems: plumbing systems broke down, cleanliness became virtually impossible to achieve, and disease spread rapidly. The Nazis controlled the amount and type of food allowed into the ghettos, allowing barely enough for each person to stay alive. Many thousands died from diseases such as typhus and dysentery, from starvation, and from exposure to the cold. More than 40,000 people in the Lodz ghetto alone—one in five residents—died from those conditions, many of them children or elderly people. In spite of the horrible conditions of life in the ghetto, the residents attempted to continue a somewhat normal existence, secretly setting up schools for the children, putting on theatrical performances, and celebrating Jewish holidays—all of which had been forbidden by the Nazis.

In most ghettos, the Nazis ordered the establishment of a *Judenrat,* or Jewish council, to act as a sort of government body and to ensure that all Nazi policies were carried out. The *Judenräte* usually included influential Jewish citizens, such as doctors, rabbis, and business leaders. The councils established clinics and hospitals, distributed food rations to residents, and dealt with housing issues. They also transmitted requests and complaints from the Jews to the Nazis, most of which were ignored. Their most difficult task, however, involved fulfilling the Nazis' demands to provide names of residents to be sent for forced labor at the Nazi prison camps. After 1940, the *Judenräte* were ordered to turn over members of their community, who would then be sent away from their families to distant camps. Most *Judenrat* members struggled with the situation. Some felt that giving the Nazis a steady flow of workers was a necessary compromise in order to protect the rest of the community; some acted out of self-interest, providing names of others in an attempt to save themselves or their families; others felt it was reprehensible to turn human beings over to the Nazis and refused to cooperate. Those council members who failed to comply were usually killed by the Nazis.

Nazi Camps and the Final Solution

Throughout 1940 and into 1941, the German military machine seemed unstoppable. In 1940 Hitler invaded one country after another—including Denmark, Norway, the

Netherlands, and France—and in each of those nations, harsh anti-Jewish policies were enacted. In early 1941 Germany invaded Greece and Yugoslavia and prepared for its massive invasion of the Soviet Union that would come in the summer of that year. However, not all of Germany's resources were devoted to the war against enemy nations: the Nazis spent considerable time and effort on the war against the Jews as well, building more and more concentration camps to imprison them in Germany, Poland, and elsewhere. While the concentration camp system originally imprisoned political opponents of Nazism, after the start of World War II it became a prison system primarily for those the Nazis deemed racially inferior. The Jews were the most despised group and the most widely persecuted, but the Nazis also targeted Roma, Soviet and Polish prisoners of war, homosexuals, Jehovah's Witnesses, and others.

Upon arriving at a concentration camp, prisoners were forced to give up their clothing, shoes, and any other personal belongings in exchange for ill-fitting prison uniforms and mismatched shoes. Their heads were shaven and, in camps such as Auschwitz, an identifying number was tattooed onto their arms. They slept in barracks filled with row upon row of bunk beds; some had blankets and mattresses, some did not. Their meager diet consisted of watery soup, stale bread, and a coffee-like drink. They were given just enough food to gradually starve to death. Every moment of a prisoner's day was orchestrated by the SS. The guards forced the prisoners to stand for long periods of time, enduring endless roll calls. The guards devised meaningless tasks for the prisoners, such as marching to a distant point and back again, or moving a pile of rocks from one spot to another. Any sign of fatigue or a failure to follow the rules was punished severely by beatings, withdrawal of food, or even death.

Concentration camp prisoners were forced to perform physically demanding labor, including working on construction projects, in rock quarries, or for German businesses, particularly industries that manufactured weapons and other products used in war. Having prisoners perform hard labor achieved two goals: it relieved the labor shortages in Germany that had resulted from the drafting of German men into the army, and it served to humiliate and weaken the prisoners. Thousands died from overwork and exhaustion, while thousands more died of starvation and disease. Estimates of the number of prisoners who died in concentration camps, not including those murdered in the gas chambers of the death camps, range from 500,000 to 800,000.

Death camps
While the high death rate in the ghettos and camps continually reduced the population of Jews in Europe, Nazi officials sought a "solution" to what they referred to as the "Jewish question," or the "Jewish problem": how to eliminate the entire population of European Jews in a relatively short period of time. During the summer of 1941, the plan known as the Final Solution was put into motion. The first stage of the Final Solution involved mobile killing squads, called *Einsatzgruppen,* that were deployed during the invasion of the Soviet Union. Following behind the German military units, the *Einsatzgruppen* entered a Soviet town, rounded up the Jews and other people considered undesirables, and shot them, burying the bodies in large pits. These executions went on for nearly two years, and in all, the *Einsatzgruppen* killed approximately 1.25 million Jews and hundreds of thousands of others.

While the mobile killing squads were fairly effective, the Nazi leadership sought another method of mass murder that would be more efficient and less psychologically taxing on the murderers. The Reich's Euthanasia Program, which, beginning in 1939, had used poisonous gas to kill physically and mentally disabled Germans, had paved the way for the construction of what the Nazis termed extermination centers: camps built for the express purpose of killing large numbers of prisoners on a daily basis. Overseen by Nazi official Reinhard Heydrich, construction of the death camps began in the fall of 1941, shortly after a successful gassing experiment, using the deadly gas Zyklon B, at Auschwitz. In January 1942, at the Wannsee Conference, Heydrich explained the details of the Final Solution to various government officials, all of whom fully supported the plan.

Four camps—Chelmno, Belzec, Sobibor, and Treblinka—were built specifically as killing centers, and concentration camps such as Auschwitz and Majdanek were expanded to include gassing facilities and crematoria, or large ovens, used for burning dead bodies. All were located in Poland. Prisoners arrived at such camps by the trainload, coming from ghettos,

concentration camps, and transit camps (temporary facilities where prisoners were housed until they could be deported elsewhere) from all over Europe. Regardless of age, gender, or physical ability, nearly every prisoner arriving at a death camp was sent to the gas chambers. The only "permanent" prisoners in death camps were those known as *Sonderkommandos*, prisoners forced to assist in the gassings and in the burning of bodies. In many cases, the gas chambers were disguised to look like shower rooms in an attempt to deceive the prisoners for as long as possible. At the death camp section of the Auschwitz complex, known as Birkenau or Auschwitz II, approximately 1.5 million Jews were murdered. In all, some 3.5 million Jews and tens of thousands of Roma, Soviet prisoners of war, and others were killed at death camps.

Gas chamber at the Majdanek concentration camp. The Nazis murdered millions of people in extermination facilities like this one. *Reproduced by permission of the United States Holocaust Memorial Museum.*

Resistance

Many students of the Holocaust have wondered why the Jews did not offer up more resistance, fighting back when the Nazis rounded them up for the ghettos or deported them to the camps. In fact, many did resist, in ways large and small. The most common type of resistance took the form of individuals helping one another to survive, thwarting the Nazis' murderous efforts. Such acts as smuggling medicine into the ghetto or obtaining an extra food ration for a sick prisoner took place on a daily basis and were undertaken at great risk. In the ghettos, Jews resisted the Nazi effort to dehumanize them by holding onto their religious and cultural values, secretly attending a concert or lighting candles on the Jewish Sabbath. Many Jews who escaped from the ghetto system and lived in hiding spent the war years working with underground resistance groups to fight the Nazis or to rescue other Jews. (In addition, thousands of courageous non-Jews who were not part of resistance movements risked their lives to help Jews hide or escape from the Nazis.)

In several instances, residents in ghettos and prisoners in camps organized armed resistance or planned acts of sabotage, destruction of equipment and property. Such incidents took place under extraordinary circumstances: the prisoners were physically and spiritually weakened, they had few weapons and little opportunity to plan and organize, and the outcome was certain to be deadly. In spite of the staggering odds, many Jews engaged in such resistance in an attempt to seek a small measure of revenge, to avoid a passive march to their deaths, or to achieve escape.

The best-known ghetto uprising took place in the Warsaw ghetto in the spring of 1943. A band of resistance fighters, after months of planning, launched an attack on Nazi troops in April. Most of the fighters died, and the ghetto was completely destroyed as the Nazis burned every building. But the fighters knew the alternative was deportation to a death camp, and they hoped to send a message to Jews everywhere that fighting back was a possibility. In several other ghettos, resistance groups managed to smuggle out a number of people who then joined underground movements to fight the Nazis.

Two major escape attempts took place at Nazi death camps. On August 2, 1943, some of the prisoners at Treblinka stole weapons and tried to take over the camp. Amidst the chaos, hundreds of prisoners tried to escape. Most were shot at the fences, and many of those who made it out were caught and killed soon after. Fewer than one hundred survived. At Sobibor, an uprising took place on October 14, 1943. The armed resistance group managed to kill several SS and Ukrainian guards. Hundreds escaped, but, again, most were caught and killed in the vicinity of the camp. Only about fifty people survived the escape and lived to see the war's end. Several hundred people successfully escaped from Auschwitz over the years of its operation, and hundreds died trying. Several *Sonderkommando* prisoners, in an uprising on October 7, 1944, destroyed parts of the camp, including a gas chamber, and then died in battle with the SS guards.

The end of the war

As Germany's fortunes reversed and it became clear that the Allies would win the war, the Nazis undertook a massive effort to achieve their goal of destroying European Jewry and to erase as much evidence as possible of their atrocities. As they fled the camps in late 1944 and early 1945, the Nazi guards forced prisoners to evacuate as well, intending to take surviving prisoners back to Germany where they could then be eliminated. In what came to be known as death marches, prisoners were forced to march great distances without food or water. Anyone who walked too slowly or fell down was shot immediately. In January 1945, more than 65,000 prisoners were marched out of Auschwitz. During several days of travel by foot and on overcrowded cattle cars, more than 15,000 prisoners died.

As the Allies progressed through German-held territories—the Soviet Union from the east and Great Britain and the United States from the west—they liberated the Nazi camps, officially freeing the remaining prisoners. The Allied soldiers were greeted by barely surviving prisoners who had been physically wasted and psychologically devastated by their experiences. In the weeks following liberation, thousands died of malnutrition and disease. The soldiers also found clear evidence—in the form of gas chambers, human remains, and massive amounts of clothing collected from the victims—of mass murder on a scale unmatched in history.

For the survivors of the Nazi camps, the Holocaust did not end with liberation. The horrors they had witnessed and the suffering they had endured would remain with them for many years. In the immediate aftermath of the war, survivors dealt with their physical recovery while at the same time attempting to locate any other surviving family members or friends. Searches for other survivors often yielded tragic news. In addition, Jews from Eastern European countries were left homeless by the war. Numerous Jewish communities were destroyed by the Nazis, and many survivors returned to their hometowns to discover their former residences in rubble, or occupied by locals. Anti-Semitism continued to be a powerful force in Poland and elsewhere, and survivors from those regions knew they faced continued persecution and violence if they tried to return there.

A few survivors successfully immigrated to Western Europe, the United States, or elsewhere in the months after the war. Most, however, were stuck in displaced persons camps, shelters for refugees established by the Allied powers, in Germany. Even after news of the Nazis' atrocities toward the Jews became widely known, most nations refused to relax immigration restrictions to allow more Jewish refugees across their borders. Palestine, which was then controlled by the British, had long been the desired site of a Jewish homeland, but the British tightly controlled immigration there both during and after the war. Desperate to reach Palestine and help in the effort to establish statehood, tens of thousands of Jewish refugees attempted to illegally immigrate there. Once the state of Israel was declared in 1948, immigration was opened to all Jews.

While the trauma of the Holocaust could never be forgotten, many survivors did go on, moving to a new country, finding work, and having children. In the decades immediately following the Holocaust, most survivors tended to remain silent about their ordeals. As they grew older, however, some came to feel an urgent need to document their experiences for future generations. A number of survivors have shared their testimony with Holocaust memorial museums, while others have written memoirs, poems, plays, and other works. In spite of the difficulty of recounting such horrors, these survivors have chosen to speak out, both as a means of releasing painful memories and of ensuring that the terrible inhumanity of the Holocaust can never be forgotten.

Holocaust Timeline

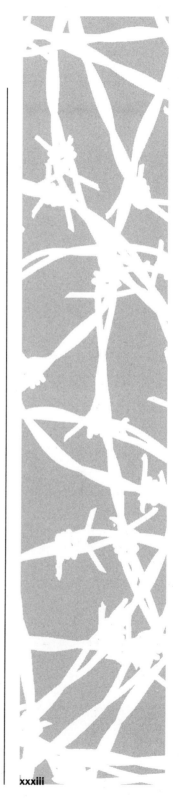

November 9, 1918 The German kaiser (emperor) is overthrown and a republic is proclaimed as the German army faces defeat by the Allies in World War I.

November 11, 1918 The new German government agrees to an armistice, signing the agreement that formally ends World War I.

June 28, 1919 Germany signs the Treaty of Versailles, which takes away territory, severely limits the size of the armed forces, and requires Germany to pay reparations for war damage and admit guilt for causing World War I. Extreme nationalist groups in Germany resent the treaty and blame socialists, communists, and Jews as a result.

September 16, 1919 Adolf Hitler joins the small German Workers' Party in Munich. The party soon changes its name to National Socialist German Workers' Party (NSDAP), called the Nazi Party for short.

October 30, 1922 Benito Mussolini and his Fascist Party march on Rome, then establish a dictatorship in Italy that becomes a model for Hitler.

November 8–9, 1923 In Munich, Adolf Hitler leads the Beer Hall Putsch, the Nazis' attempt to overthrow the government. Police end the rebellion with gunfire, killing sixteen Nazis, injuring others, and arresting Hitler and other Nazi leaders.

1924 Hitler is sentenced to five years in prison for the Beer Hall Putsch, but serves only eight months, using the time to dictate *Mein Kampf* ("My Struggle"), which becomes the Nazi "bible."

1928 The Nazi Party receives about 800,000 votes in national elections, 2.6 percent of the total.

1930 The Nazis receive almost 6.5 million votes in national elections and become the second-largest party in the Reichstag, or German parliament. Members of the SA (the Storm Troopers, or brownshirts), the military wing of the Nazi Party, use violent campaign tactics: they attack opponents, break up meetings, and intimidate Jews.

1932 Paul von Hindenburg, the aged military hero of World War I, is reelected president of Germany. The Nazi Storm Troopers are briefly banned in Germany because of their increased violence during the campaign.

January 30, 1933 Hitler takes office as chancellor of Germany. Von Hindenburg and other powerful conservative politicians believe Hitler can be controlled and that he will be a useful ally against the Communist Party.

February 27, 1933 The Reichstag building is mysteriously set on fire, and Hitler uses the fire as an excuse to declare a state of emergency, revoking many civil rights. Using police powers, Storm Troopers arrest ten thousand opponents of the Nazis, including Communists, and send them to newly established concentration camps.

March 22, 1933 Built to house political prisoners, Dachau, the first concentration camp, is opened near the city of Munich.

March 23, 1933 With many political opponents imprisoned, the Nazis win passage of the Enabling Act, which negates the constitution and gives Hitler dictatorial powers.

April 1933 Hitler enacts the first of the anti-Jewish laws designed to prevent Jews from practicing numerous professions, including jobs in government, medicine, and education. Fifty-three thousand Jews leave Germany in 1933.

April 1, 1933 The Nazis organize a national boycott of Jewish-owned businesses. The boycotts, which officially last one day but continue at the local level for many years, mark the beginning of the Nazis' attempt to economically cripple Germany's Jews.

May 2, 1933 German labor unions are abolished and are replaced by the German Labor Front, run by the Nazis. The Nazis then outlaw the Social Democratic Party (the largest political party before the rise of the Nazis); all other parties are subsequently banned.

May 10, 1933 The Nazis conduct nationwide public book-burnings of works written by Jews, intellectuals, and opponents of Nazism.

May 2, 1934 German president von Hindenburg dies. Hitler combines the office of chancellor and president, naming himself the Führer (leader) of the Third Reich (Empire), controlling the nation with absolute powers.

June 30, 1934 Hitler orders the murder of Ernst Röhm and other leaders of the Storm Troopers, whom both Hitler and the German army fear as possible rivals, in what has become known as the "Night of the Long Knives."

April 1, 1935 The Nazis outlaw the religious practices of Jehovah's Witnesses, a group that has declared political neutrality and refuses to swear allegiance to Germany.

September 15, 1935 The Nazis pass the Nuremberg Laws, which define Jews as a racial group rather than members of a religious community. These laws strip Jews of German citizenship and forbid them from marrying non-Jews.

August 1936 Hitler and the Nazis ease anti-Jewish actions as a result of the Olympic Games being held in Berlin, Germany's capital.

Autumn 1936 Germany and Italy enter into agreements that develop into the Rome-Berlin Axis, a political and military alliance.

March 1938 The German army moves into Austria, uniting the two countries in what is known as the *Anschluss.* Anti-Semitic actions begin immediately: many Austrian Jews are beaten, robbed, fired from their jobs, and arrested.

July 6–15, 1938 Delegates from all over the world attend a conference in Evian, France, to discuss the growing problem of Jewish refugees fleeing Hitler's regime. While acknowledging the scope of the problem and expressing some sympathy for the refugees, the participating nations refuse to change their immigration policies to accept more refugees.

September 29–30, 1938 Hoping to satisfy Hitler's territorial demands and avert another world war, leaders of Great Britain and France meet with Hitler and Mussolini in Munich and agree to give Germany the Sudetenland, a section of Czechoslovakia that was home to many people of German ancestry.

October 1938 Germany expels thousands of Jews of Polish descent. When Poland refuses to accept them, the refugees are left to encamp at the Polish-German border, living in miserable conditions.

November 7, 1938 In Paris, Hershel Grynszpan, a young Jew, shoots and kills Ernst vom Rath, an official at the German embassy, to protest Germany's expulsion of Polish Jews (a group that included his parents).

November 9–10, 1938 The shooting of Ernst vom Rath provides an excuse for the Nazis to launch a series of riots known as *Kristallnacht,* or the "Night of Broken Glass," so named because of the numerous shattered windows. During these organized attacks, thousands of Jews were beaten, nearly one hundred were murdered, synagogues were burned, and Jewish homes and businesses were vandalized. Some thirty thousand Jewish men were arrested and sent to concentration camps.

March 15, 1939 After the region of Slovakia declares independence from Czechoslovakia and allegiance to Nazi Germany, Hitler violates the Munich agreement by taking over the remainder of Czech lands, implementing anti-Jewish measures throughout that country.

August 23, 1939 Nazi Germany and the Soviet Union sign a Non-Aggression Pact, in which the two countries promise not to attack each other and secretly agree to divide Poland and other Eastern European countries between them.

September 1, 1939 Germany invades Poland.

September 3, 1939 World War II begins when Britain and France declare war on Germany in response to the Nazi invasion of Poland. No military assistance is offered to Poland, however, which succumbs to the German military by early October. Germany and the Soviet Union divide Poland, with Germany controlling the western regions and the Soviet Union controlling the east.

September 21, 1939 Reinhard Heydrich, second in command of the SS, the Nazi Party's elite military unit, issues an order for the concentration of all Polish Jews into areas of large cities located near railway lines. These deportations have been described as the first step toward an unnamed "final aim."

September–October 1939 German-controlled Poland is divided into two parts: one part is incorporated into Germany, and the other part, known as the General-gouvernement, or General Government, is to be ruled by a German-appointed administration.

October 1939 Beginning of Nazi Euthanasia (mercy killing) Program, in which tens of thousands (perhaps as many as 275,000) of mentally and physically disabled Germans, including children, are murdered by poisonous gas or injections.

October 8, 1939 The first Jewish ghetto in German-occupied Poland is established, in the town of Piotrkow.

November 1939 Jews in German-occupied Poland are ordered to wear a six-pointed star (the Star of David, a symbol of Judaism) on their clothing at all times.

November 15, 1939 As part of a wave of anti-Jewish policies implemented after *Kristallnacht,* Jewish children are banned from public schools and can only attend all-Jewish schools.

April 30, 1940 The Lodz ghetto in Poland is sealed, imprisoning more than 160,000 Jews in a small area with insufficient housing, food, plumbing, and heat.

April–May 1940 Germany invades Denmark, Norway, Belgium, the Netherlands, and France.

May 20, 1940 The Nazis establish the infamous concentration camp Auschwitz in occupied Poland.

June 13–14, 1940 French troops flee Paris, and German forces enter the city. France signs an armistice, or truce, with Germany. German troops occupy northern France, while a Nazi-friendly French government, located in the city of Vichy, controls the south. Anti-Jewish measures are implemented throughout the western European countries controlled by Germany.

November 15, 1940 The Warsaw ghetto in Poland is sealed, and nearly 350,000 Jews are confined within its walls. The Jews in the ghetto make up about 30 percent of the city's population, and they are forced to live in less than 3 percent of the city's area.

March 1, 1941 Nazi leaders announce plans to build Birkenau (Auschwitz II), the largest Nazi death camp. Construction begins in October.

June 22, 1941 Germany begins Operation Barbarossa, an invasion of the Soviet Union. Mobile killing squads, called the *Einsatzgruppen,* follow behind the army troops, rounding up Jews and other "undesirables" in Soviet villages. The victims, sometimes thousands at a time, are executed by gunfire and buried in mass graves. Over the next two years, the *Einsatzgruppen* would kill well over one million Jews and several hundred thousand others.

July 31, 1941 Hermann Göring, second to Hitler in Nazi hierarchy, gives Reinhard Heydrich the authority "to carry out all necessary preparations…for a total solution of the Jewish question" throughout Nazi-controlled Europe. The plan known as the Final Solution—the campaign to murder every Jew in Europe—is thus set into motion.

September 1941 Jews in Germany are forced to wear the Star of David on their clothing at all times.

September 3, 1941 Nearly 600 Soviet prisoners of war and 250 Poles are the victims of the first murders by poisonous gas at Auschwitz.

September 29–30, 1941 The *Einsatzgruppen* shoot more than 33,000 Jews at Babi Yar, a large ravine outside the city of Kiev, Ukraine.

October 1941 Mass deportations of German and Austrian Jews to ghettos in Poland and the Soviet Union begin.

November 24, 1941 The Nazis begin operation of Terezin, also called Theresienstadt. This "model ghetto" in Czechoslovakia imprisons many Jewish artists and intellectuals and is used to deceive the international community into thinking the Nazis treat the Jews humanely.

December 7, 1941 Japan bombs the U.S. naval base at Pearl Harbor in Hawaii. The United States declares war on Japan the following day.

December 8, 1941 The death camp Chelmno, in the western part of Poland, begins operation. Jews and other prisoners are murdered by poisonous gas in sealed vans.

January 20, 1942 Reinhard Heydrich calls the Wannsee Conference, where the Final Solution is explained to various branches of the German government.

March 17, 1942 Killing operations begin at Belzec, a death camp in Poland. By the end of the year, some 600,000 Jews and other victims are murdered by poisonous gas at Belzec.

May 1942 Operations begin at the death camp Sobibor in Poland, which will ultimately be the site of approximately 250,000 murders by poisonous gas.

May 27, 1942 Reinhard Heydrich is fatally wounded in an attack by Czech resistance fighters.

July–September 1942 Approximately 300,000 Jews are deported from the Warsaw ghetto to death camps and concentration camps.

July 23, 1942 The Treblinka death camp in Poland begins receiving the Jews of Warsaw. Treblinka is the last of four death camps, along with Chelmno, Belzec, and Sobibor, built for the express purpose of exterminating the Jews of Europe. In honor of the assassinated Heydrich, the Nazis refer to the death camp activities as "Operation Reinhard."

January 18, 1943 A group of Jewish resistance fighters in the Warsaw ghetto attack Nazi soldiers as they attempt to round up Jews for deportation. Several Germans and Jews are killed. The resistance fighters spend the next several months preparing for a large-scale uprising.

April 19, 1943 Jewish resistance fighters launch a full-scale uprising against the Germans in the Warsaw ghetto. Though poorly armed and vastly outnumbered, the Jews hold out for several weeks as the ghetto is burned to the ground by Nazi forces.

August 2, 1943 The prisoners at the death camp Treblinka stage an uprising, obtaining weapons and attempting to take over the camp. Hundreds of prisoners flee, but most are caught and killed; only about seventy escape to freedom.

October 1–2, 1943 Germany's attempts to deport Danish Jews are defeated when almost the entire Jewish population of Denmark is safely transported to Sweden with the help of Danish citizens and underground resistance fighters.

October 14, 1943 Hundreds of prisoners at the Sobibor death camp attempt an escape, killing several SS guards in the process. Most of the escapees are caught and killed, with only about fifty surviving.

November 3, 1943 Nazi official Heinrich Himmler launches Operation Harvest Festival, or *Erntefest,* to liquidate (empty out) several forced labor camps near Lublin, Poland. Over the next few days, SS troops and police units kill more than 42,000 Jews at Majdanek, Poniatowa, and Trawniki.

May 15–July 9, 1944 The Germans, after occupying Hungary in March, begin large-scale deportations of Hungarian Jews. By July more than 430,000 Hungarian Jews have been sent to Auschwitz-Birkenau, with approximately half of them being sent immediately to the gas chambers.

July 20, 1944 A small group of German military officers, wishing to end the war, unsuccessfully attempt to assassinate Hitler. Many of them are tortured and executed as a result.

July 23, 1944 The Soviet army enters Lublin in eastern Poland and liberates the nearby Majdanek camp. The Soviets capture much of the camp as well as many documents before they can be destroyed by the fleeing Nazis.

October 6–7, 1944 At Auschwitz-Birkenau, Jewish *Sonderkommando* prisoners (those forced to burn bodies in the ovens, or crematoria) stage a revolt, destroying at least one gas chamber. All the prisoners participating in the battle are killed, and four women prisoners who obtained the explosives are executed in January 1945.

January 18, 1945 As Soviet troops approach, the Nazis begin evacuating Auschwitz-Birkenau. More than 65,000 surviving prisoners are forced on a death march.

January 27, 1945 Troops from the Soviet Union's Red Army liberate Auschwitz-Birkenau. They find more than 7,500 prisoners there—weak and sick, but alive—and the discarded clothing of hundreds of thousands of murdered prisoners.

April 1945 American troops liberate the Buchenwald and Dachau camps in Germany, and British troops free Bergen-Belsen in Germany.

April 30, 1945 Hitler commits suicide with a gunshot to the head in his fortified bunker beneath Berlin.

May 8, 1945 V-E (Victory in Europe) Day: Germany surrenders unconditionally to the Allies.

August 3, 1945 A report by U.S. special envoy Earl G. Harrison reveals the horrid conditions in the displaced persons (DP) camps, the temporary shelters housing primarily Jewish refugees who had survived the war. The report results in improvements in American-run DP camps.

Autumn 1945 The Nuremberg Trials begin. An international military tribunal, with judges from the United States, France, Great Britain, and the Soviet Union, tries twenty-two major Nazi figures from the government and military. Several Nazis are found guilty and sentenced to death.

1946 Hermann Göring, one of the highest Nazi officials to be accused and convicted of war crimes, testifies on his own behalf during the Nuremberg Trials.

May 14, 1948 The State of Israel is established as an independent nation. Over the next three years, nearly 700,000 Jews immigrate to Israel, many coming from Europe's displaced persons camps.

June 1, 1962 Former Nazi official Adolf Eichmann is executed after being found guilty of war crimes for his part in the murder of hundreds of thousands of Jews.

July 4, 1987 Former SS soldier Klaus Barbie is found guilty of crimes against humanity and is sentenced to life in prison.

1992 Human remains found in Brazil are confirmed as those of Nazi doctor Josef Mengele, who performed barbaric experiments on the prisoners of Auschwitz.

1998 The Vatican issues a letter stating that Pope Pius XII, leader of the Catholic Church during the Holocaust, did all he could to save the Jews. Many historians, however, have noted the Catholic Church's failure to strongly protest the Nazis' treatment of Jews, with statements from the Vatican during Hitler's reign focusing primarily on the defense of Jews who had converted to Catholicism.

1998   Swiss banks agree to pay $1.25 billion to Holocaust survivors and their heirs in a legal settlement that found that the banks held onto money deposited by Jews before and during World War II.

1998   Maurice Papon, a former official of the Vichy government in France, is sentenced to ten years in prison for helping the Nazis illegally arrest and deport French Jews.

2002   A federal judge in the United States revokes the citizenship of John Demjanjuk, accused of being a Nazi guard in death camps and forced labor camps during the Holocaust. Over the course of more than twenty years, Demjanjuk's case aroused much controversy. His 1988 conviction in Israel was overturned in 1993.

Words to Know

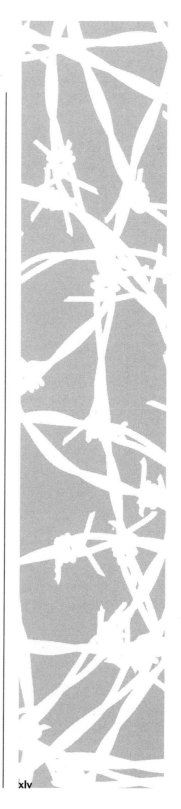

A

Aktion: The German term, often translated as "operation," for the Nazi raids or attacks on Jews; these raids were usually conducted to round up Jews for deportation to a concentration or death camp.

Allies: The nations that banded together to fight against the Axis powers of Germany, Italy, and Japan during World War II. The Allied nations varied throughout the war and included Great Britain, the Soviet Union, the United States, and France.

Anschluss: The term applied to Germany's invasion and annexation (taking over) of Austria in March 1938.

Anti-Semitism: The hatred and persecution of Jews.

Aryan: According to Nazi racial theories, Aryans were white Christians of Germanic or Nordic ancestry. The term carried with it a suggestion of racial superiority; non-Aryans, particularly Jews, were considered racially inferior.

Aryanization: The process of forcing Jews to transfer ownership of their businesses and property to non-Jews.

Axis: The nations of Germany, Italy, and Japan, which fought together during World War II against the Allies. The Axis powers were later joined by Bulgaria, Croatia, Hungary, Romania, and Slovakia.

B

Blitzkrieg: German term meaning "lightning war"; refers to the German military strategy, used with great effect against Poland, of overwhelming the enemy by attacking simultaneously on land and from the air.

Blood libel: A centuries-old false accusation that suggests Jews use the blood of Christian children in some religious rituals. This accusation has been used throughout history to justify anti-Semitic actions.

C

Chancellor: The head of the German government; a position akin to prime minister.

Collaborators: Residents of Nazi-occupied countries who aided the Nazis in controlling the population and rounding up Jews and other victims.

Communism: A political, social, and economic system that places ownership of all business, resources, and property in the hands of the government.

Concentration camps: Large prison camps run by the SS, the elite military branch of the Nazi Party. Concentration camps housed those considered by the German government to be "undesirable" or "enemies of the state": Jews, political prisoners, non-Jewish Poles and Soviets, homosexuals, Roma (Gypsies), and others. Prisoners endured overcrowding, malnutrition, disease, and brutality.

Crematoria: The large ovens used to burn dead bodies in concentration and death camps.

Crimes against humanity: A term referring to horrible crimes—including mass murder, enslavement, and torture—committed against the civilian, or nonmilitary, population of a country.

D

D-Day: June 6, 1944; The day British and American forces landed on the beaches of Normandy in northern France.

Death camps: Complexes built by the Nazis for the express purpose of mass murder. Four camps—Chelmno, Belzec, Treblinka, and Sobibor—were constructed as death camps; existing concentration camps such as Auschwitz and Majdanek were expanded to include mass-murder facilities. Millions of Nazi "enemies," primarily Jews, were killed in the death camps.

Death marches: Forced marches of concentration camp prisoners during the final months of World War II. As Allied forces approached, the Nazis fled the camps, forcing the prisoners to march to distant locations without food, water, or proper clothing.

Deportation: The process by which Nazis forcibly removed people from their normal place of residence to a labor, concentration, or death camp.

Dictator: An all-powerful ruler of a nation; dictators generally rule repressively, depriving citizens of civil rights and severely punishing opponents.

Displaced persons (DPs): People who were forced out of their communities or countries during World War II.

E

Einsatzgruppen: Mobile killing squads made up of SS troops. The *Einsatzgruppen,* following behind the German military during the invasion of the Soviet Union, rounded up Jews and other "undesirables" in towns and villages and shot them, burying the bodies in giant pits.

Emigration: The act of leaving one's country to settle in another.

Euthanasia: The act of killing or allowing the death of a person who suffers from a terminal and painful condition. Nazi Germany's Euthanasia Program, begun in 1939, involved the killing of tens of thousands of people with mental and physical disabilities, people the Nazis felt weakened the "master race."

F

Fascism: A political philosophy or system of government that considers the nation's strength to be far more important than the freedom of its citizens. Fascist governments are dictatorial, tightly controlling the population and suppressing opposition.

Final Solution: The term used by Nazis to refer to the genocide, or complete destruction, of European Jews.

Forced labor: Difficult, back-breaking work done by groups of concentration camp prisoners. Among other tasks, forced-labor prisoners built roads, dug ditches, and constructed camp buildings.

Führer: Pronounced FEW-rha. German term meaning "leader"; Adolf Hitler insisted others refer to him and address him with this term.

G

Gas chambers: Large, sealed rooms, often designed to look like public showers, in which prisoners were murdered by poisonous gas.

Generalgouvernement: Or General Government; an area of Poland occupied by Germany during World War II that was distinct from the region of Poland that had been incorporated into the Third Reich. The Generalgouvernement had its own government, though the leaders were under Adolf Hitler's complete control.

Genocide: The purposeful, systematic destruction of a racial, cultural, ethnic, political, or religious group.

Gestapo: An abbreviation of *Geheime Staatspolizei;* the secret police of Nazi Germany. The Gestapo were renowned for their brutality and viciousness.

Ghettos: Small, run-down sections of cities in German-occupied Eastern European countries where Jews were forced to live, usually behind stone and barbed-wire fences policed by armed guards. Conditions in the ghettos—overcrowding, poor sanitation, insufficient heat and food—led to malnutrition and widespread disease.

Gypsy: A term sometimes used to describe the Roma, people of several different tribes that are believed to have originated in India. Like the Jews, Roma were targeted by the Nazis for complete destruction.

H

Holocaust: Derived from a Greek term meaning complete destruction, generally by fire. The term refers to the period between 1933 and 1945 when Nazi Germany systematically murdered approximately six million Jews and nearly five million others.

J

Jehovah's Witnesses: A religious group persecuted by the Nazis. The religious beliefs of Jehovah's Witnesses prevented them from declaring allegiance to the nation; their refusal to do so made them an "enemy of the state" in the eyes of Adolf Hitler.

Judenrat: "Jewish council"; administrative groups established on Nazi orders in the ghettos. The *Judenräte* (the plural form of the word) were charged with, among other tasks, providing lists of Jews to be deported to concentration camps.

K

Kaiser: The German word for "emperor."

Kapo: A concentration camp prisoner assigned to be in charge of a group of other prisoners on a work detail.

Kristallnacht: "Crystal Night"; often translated as the "Night of Broken Glass." On November 9, 1938, widespread government-sponsored riots directed at Jews began in Germany and Austria. Homes, businesses, and synagogues were destroyed; many Jews were beaten or killed, and 30,000 Jewish men were arrested and sent to concentration camps.

L

Labor camps: Nazi prison camps built with the primary purpose of using prisoners to work as slave laborers. Prisoners worked in factories, in stone quarries, and on construction projects. Some of Germany's largest industries used slave laborers at such camps to produce goods.

Lebensraum: German term meaning "living space." Hitler cited the need for more living space for the German people as one reason for conquering numerous other countries.

Liberation: The freeing of prisoners in concentration camps and death camps. As the Allied armies—from the United States, Great Britain, and the Soviet Union—advanced on German-held territory toward the end of the war, the Nazis retreated. The Allied soldiers came upon one abandoned camp after another, greeted by sick, weak prisoners and abundant evidence of the atrocities committed by the Nazis.

Liquidation: The Nazis' brutal and murderous process of emptying a ghetto, sending all remaining residents to concentration and death camps.

N

Nationalism: Extreme loyalty to a nation, often accompanied by a sense of cultural or racial supremacy over other nations.

Nazi: Member of the National Socialist German Workers', or Nazi, Party. The Nazis pledged their undying loyalty to Adolf Hitler, working to promote the German master race and to eliminate inferior, undesirable elements of society.

O

Occupation: Control of a country by a foreign military power.

P

Partisans: Resistance fighters who conduct secret attacks on a foreign occupying power. During World War II, Jewish and non-Jewish partisans hid out in forests and elsewhere, carrying out raids on Nazi troops and sabotaging military equipment.

Pogroms: Organized and often government-sponsored attacks on a particular group, generally Jews. The term usually refers to raids on Jews during Adolf Hitler's reign and in Russia during the late 1800s and early 1900s.

Propaganda: Spreading information, often misinformation, to persuade people to adopt a certain viewpoint.

R

Rabbi: A Jewish religious leader, often the leader of a congregation.

Refugee: A person forced to leave his or her country to escape persecution.

Reich: Pronounced RIKE. German term meaning "empire."

Reichstag: The German parliament, or lawmaking body.

Resistance: Acts designed to oppose or undermine a foreign occupying army. Resistance took many forms in Nazi-occupied countries, including armed struggle with Nazi troops, smuggling goods or information into sealed Jewish ghettos, or helping Jews to escape Nazi tyranny.

Reparations: Compensation paid by a defeated nation for damage caused to another nation during a war. The Treaty of Versailles forced Germany to pay ample war reparations for having caused World War I.

Resettlement: The Nazi term for forcing Jews into ghettos and concentration camps.

Revisionists: People who distort history, revising widely accepted facts. Holocaust revisionists claim that details about the era—the number of victims and the Nazi methods of mass murder, for example—have been grossly exaggerated.

Righteous gentiles: Gentiles, or non-Jews, who risked their lives to rescue Jews from the Nazis.

S

SA: An abbreviation for *Sturmabteilungen*. The SA, also known as the Storm Troopers or Brownshirts, was a military branch of the Nazi Party that used brutality to quiet opposing voices during Adolf Hitler's rise to power in the early 1930s.

Selektion: The process by which the Nazis decided which prisoners in the concentration camps were fit to work and which would be sent to their deaths in the gas chambers. The term *selektion* also refers to the selection of Jews in the ghettos to be deported to Nazi camps.

Shoah: The Hebrew term for the Holocaust.

Socialism: A political and social system whereby the ownership of property and businesses lies in the hands of the community as a whole.

Sonderkommando: Jewish prisoners in death camps who were forced to dispose of the bodies of people killed in the gas chambers.

SS: An abbreviation for *Schutzstaffel,* or Security Squad. This elite, armed branch of the Nazi Party controlled the police and the intelligence units. Adolf Hitler's personal bodyguards and the camp guards came from the SS.

Star of David: A six-pointed star that has long been a symbol of Judaism.

Storm Troopers: *See* SA.

Swastika: An ancient symbol adopted by the Nazi Party. The black bent-armed cross appeared within a white circle set against a red background on Nazi flags and banners.

Synagogue: A Jewish house of worship.

T

Third Reich: "Third Empire"; a term Adolf Hitler used for the period of his rule. With this term Hitler was attempting to characterize his reign as a continuation of Germany's great military past.

Typhus: A serious and often deadly disease—characterized by a high fever, intense headache, and rash—that flourished in the unsanitary and overcrowded conditions in the ghettos and concentration camps.

U

Underground: Organized networks of people acting to oppose the government or, during wartime, the occupying power.

W

War crimes: Violations of the laws or customs of war.

Y

Yiddish: A language spoken by Eastern European Jews that combines German dialects, Hebrew, and other languages.

Z

Zionism: A movement advocating the return of the Jewish people to their ancestral homeland: the state of Israel (known before 1948 as Palestine).

Zyklon B: A poisonous gas (hydrogen cyanide) used by the Nazis to kill prisoners locked in sealed gas chambers at the death camps.

Experiencing the Holocaust

Novels, Nonfiction Books, Short
Stories, Poems, Plays, Films & Music

Holocaust Short Stories

3

Storytelling has long been a way for the people of an older generation to communicate values and life experience to their children and their children's children. The telling of stories—whether told from the imagination or read from a book—is more than just entertainment, it's a way of bringing to life faraway lands or experiences from the past.

As a literary form, or genre, the short story functions differently from other forms of fiction. Brander Matthews, an American short story writer and literary critic who lived and worked during the late nineteenth and early twentieth centuries, once wrote that a short story typically "deals with a single character, a single event, a single emotion, or a series of emotions called forth by a single situation." This description is particularly true of short stories written about the Holocaust.

Another quality common to short stories about the Holocaust is a sense of fragmentation or isolation. Events may not seem to be related to one another; the character at the center of the story may seem alone in an unfamiliar world; and the story line may not have a clear beginning, middle, and end, as a reader expects in a novel. The structure of the story itself reflects the devastation, degradation, and incomprehensible cruelty of the events portrayed by the writer.

A number of esteemed authors have addressed the Holocaust through short stories, many of which are autobiographical, or based on the author's life; the stories that are not autobiographical are nonetheless based on historical events. Tadeusz Borowski, a well-known writer of Holocaust-related literature, based the stories in his collection *This Way for the Gas, Ladies and Gentlemen* on his experience of Nazi persecution, including imprisonment at Auschwitz. Many of his stories, including the title piece, explore the worst aspects of life in a Nazi camp and are devoid of any sign of hope or redemption. When the war began, Borowski was barely seventeen. By 1940, he was attending underground, or secret, classes, because secondary schools and colleges were not open to Poles or Jews during the German occupation of Poland. His story "Graduation on Market Street" depicts a day in the spring of 1940, when he was taking his final exams as the Nazis began the first major roundups of Jews in the streets of Warsaw.

Ida Fink, whose story "A Scrap of Time" is featured in *Experiencing the Holocaust,* has written a number of Holocaust-related short stories. Focusing on the small details of everyday life, Fink often writes of characters' quests to piece together events of the past and to comprehend the personal tragedies of the Holocaust. The title piece of her collection, "Traces" describes a woman's efforts to collect bits and pieces of information and evidence in an attempt to learn about her sister's disappearance during the Holocaust. Another story in the collection, "The Hand," is a study of the dehumanizing effects of concentration camp life on normal, loving, caring human beings. In this tale, two concentration camp inmates discover that they share a dream of someday scaling a particular mountain peak. What appears to be a bond of friendship and commitment to mutual survival is put to the ultimate test under the worst conditions of physical and mental exhaustion.

"Twilight," a short story written by Shulamith Hareven, appears in the anthology *Facing the Holocaust: Selected Israeli Fiction.* The author depicts one woman's attempt to come to terms with her past and its relationship to her life after the Holocaust. In a dreamlike narrative, the unnamed character visits the city of her birth, now dark and filled with the presence of people she remembers but does not recognize. In one surreal night, she moves through the distant yet familiar territory of her ancestral home: she marries, she bears and then loses a child, and she observes a chilling re-enactment of the deportation to prison camps of festively dressed operagoers. She breaks the spell of the past—temporarily, at least—upon waking to the bright light of her comfortable home in Jerusalem, Israel, surrounded by the sounds and activities of normal life.

Two short stories are featured in *Experiencing the Holocaust.* Ida Fink's "A Scrap of Time" depicts the way the concept of time changed for the people of a Polish town when the Nazis began conducting *aktions*, the violent and terrifying episodes when soldiers rounded up Jews and Poles to be sent away to an unknown location. At first the villagers believe that the destination will be a labor camp, where their loved ones will at least be fed and able to receive packages of food and valuables from home. In the end they learn that those original detainees never arrived at a work camp, having been massacred and buried in a mass grave just a few miles outside of the town.

Bernard Gotfryd's "The Last Morning," published in the collection *Anton the Dove Fancier and Other Tales of the Holocaust,* explores the importance of being a witness to atrocity even when doing so results in excruciating memories. The story depicts the narrator's recollection of the last hours in his family's home before the Nazis took most of his family, including his mother, to a concentration camp. The story poignantly portrays the love of a parent who tries to save the life of her child and the burden of being a survivor who must live with painful memories.

Representative Works of Short Fiction about the Holocaust

Asscher-Pinkhof, Clara. *Star Children*. Detroit, MI: Wayne State University Press, 1986. *Translated into English from Dutch, these brief tales are not short stories in the literary sense but rather brief recollections told from the perspective of child narrators. From events that occurred in the streets of Amsterdam to experiences in the camps of Westerbork and Bergen-Belsen, this collection provides a child's point of view of the Holocaust experience in the Netherlands.*

Borowski, Tadeusz. *This Way for the Gas, Ladies and Gentlemen*. New York: Penguin, 1976. *These twelve short stories explore a range of images and impressions of the Holocaust, based on the author's experiences at Auschwitz. In the title story, the author conveys, in a matter-of-fact way, how unthinkable behavior such as stealing from the pockets of fellow inmates who have died and scrounging for crumbs of moldy food became commonplace among concentration camp inmates dehumanized by Nazi abuse.*

Eliach, Yaffa. *Hasidic Tales of the Holocaust.* New York: Oxford University Press, 1982. *The eighty-nine pieces of this collection are not short stories in the classic sense. They are included here, however, because they represent the tradition of the Hasidic tale, the oral storytelling tradition of the Hasidic Jewish people.*

Fink, Ida. *A Scrap of Time and Other Stories.* Evanston, IL: Northwestern University Press, 1995. *This acclaimed book of short stories depicts life in Poland's Jewish villages before and during the German occupation, providing the small and often tragic details of everyday life during the Holocaust.*

Fink, Ida. *Traces.* New York: Henry Holt, 1997. *A follow-up to* A Scrap of Time, *this collection of twenty-one stories offers further haunting images of life for the Jews in Poland during the Nazi reign of terror.*

Frank, Anne. *Tales from the Secret Annex.* Garden City, NY: Doubleday, 1983. *This book collects Anne Frank's writings other than her famous diary—the short pieces of fiction, personal reminiscences, and essays she wrote during her family's time in hiding from the Nazis. For the most part, the works are brief, juvenile stories or expansions on themes found in her diary entries. In "Cady's Life," the young author writes about the Nazi persecution of Jews from the point of view of a young girl not unlike herself—except that the character is Christian, rather than Jewish.*

Gotfryd, Bernard. *Anton the Dove Fancier and Other Tales of the Holocaust.* Baltimore, MD: Johns Hopkins University Press, 2000 (expanded edition). *Told through the eyes of a teenage boy who lived through the Holocaust, these stories illuminate the contrast between everyday life and the unspeakable realities of what life became under the oppression and cruelty of Nazi persecution.*

Kalman, Judith. *The County of Birches.* Vancouver: Douglas & McIntyre, 1998. *Told from the point of view of a child of Holocaust survivors, the fourteen linked stories in this sophisticated collection explore a Hungarian Jewish family's losses during the Holocaust and their struggle to survive in the aftermath.*

Ramras-Rauch, Gila, and Joseph Michman-Melkman, eds. *Facing the Holocaust: Selected Israeli Fiction.* Philadelphia, PA: Jewish Publication Society, 1985. *This collection contains twelve stories, some of which are excerpts from novels, written by contemporary Israeli writers, including Yehuda Amichai, Aharon Appelfeld, Shulamith Hareven, and Uri Orlev.*

Schmidt, Gary. *Mara's Stories: Glimmers in the Darkness.* New York: Henry Holt, 2001. *These very brief tales are more like folkloric fables than true short stories. The stories are presented as tales told by a woman named Mara to comfort children and others in their concentration camp barracks. The author provides notes at the end of the collection, explaining the origin of each tale.*

"The Last Morning"

Written by Bernard Gotfryd

Bernard Gotfryd was a teenager when World War II (1939–45) and the Holocaust began. Living in eastern Poland, he experienced life in a Jewish ghetto and survived imprisonment in several Nazi concentration camps. For many years after the war ended, Gotfryd considered writing about his experiences. He could not forget the words his mother spoke on the day he saw her for the last time: she told him he had to survive so he could tell the world what the Nazis had done to the Jews. In the early 1980s, Gotfryd, a photojournalist then living in the United States, began to write about his past. In 1990 he collected his short, true stories into the work titled *Anton the Dove Fancier and Other Tales of the Holocaust*. "The Last Morning," one of the stories in that collection, depicts the final hours in which Gotfryd's family lived together in their home before his mother was deported to a concentration camp.

Biography of Author Bernard Gotfryd

Bernard Gotfryd was born May 25, 1924, in Radom, Poland, a city south of Warsaw. He grew up there with his par-

Chronology of Events Relating to "The Last Morning"

May 25, 1924: Bernard Gotfryd is born in Radom, Poland.

January 30, 1933: Adolf Hitler becomes leader of Germany.

September 1, 1939: Germany invades Poland.

Spring 1941: A Jewish ghetto is formed in Radom.

August 16, 1942: Gotfryd's mother is deported from Radom to a Nazi camp; Gotfryd later writes about this day in "The Last Morning."

November 1943: The Radom ghetto is liquidated; Gotfryd is deported to Majdanek, a concentration and death camp.

May 1945: Gusen II, the concentration camp where Gotfryd is imprisoned, is liberated.

May 8, 1945: World War II ends in Europe.

1957: Gotfryd begins working as a photographer and writer for *Newsweek* magazine in the United States.

1990: Gotfryd's collection of autobiographical stories, *Anton the Dove Fancier and Other Tales of the Holocaust,* is published.

ents, Henoch and Sarah, his brother, Michael, and his sister, Hanka. His parents owned a series of businesses, including a dry goods store and a used-furniture business. In September 1939, when Gotfryd was fifteen years old, Poland was invaded by Nazi Germany, sparking the beginning of World War II. In the spring of 1941, a ghetto was established in Radom. All the Jews from the area were forced to live inside the ghetto, a small neighborhood surrounded by barbed-wire fences or concrete walls, and only those with special permission were allowed to travel outside of the ghetto walls. Occasionally the Nazis would conduct roundups, or *aktions,* gathering a certain number of ghetto residents—generally those who did not have work papers—to be deported to concentration camps. Concentration camps were large, Nazi-run prisons where inmates were starved, abused, and forced to perform hard labor. Gotfryd's job as an assistant in a portrait studio enabled him to travel outside of the ghetto and protected him from being deported.

While working in the photography studio, Gotfryd met an attractive young woman who worked for the Polish underground, an illegal organization that fought against the Nazi occupation of Poland. Captivated by the woman and filled with a new sense of purpose, he began secretly helping the underground. Risking his life to do so, Gotfryd supplied his friends in the underground with copies of photographs developed at the studio. The pictures consisted of portraits taken of Nazi officers as well as snapshots of brutal and murderous acts committed by Nazi troops against Jews and other people considered enemies of the Nazi regime.

During the summer of 1942, the ghetto residents began hearing rumors about a large-scale deportation. In August 1942, the deportation took place, and 20,000 Jews, including Gotfryd's mother, were sent from Radom to Nazi camps. As he wrote in "The Last Morning," Gotfryd managed to avoid being deported that day. After the photography studio closed down, he got a job at another studio near the ghetto. He obtained an identification card with a false name from the Polish underground, and a contact in that organization planned for his escape. However, his attempt to escape and go into hiding failed, and the following day, in November 1943, the Radom ghetto was liquidated, or emptied out. The remaining residents, including Gotfryd, were loaded onto cattle cars and transported to Majdanek (sometimes spelled Maidanek or Maidalnek), a concentration and death camp near Lublin, Poland. Death camps were built by the Nazi regime specifically for the task of efficiently murdering large numbers of prisoners at a time.

Before the war's end, Gotfryd was imprisoned in six Nazi camps. His final stretch of imprisonment was in Gusen II, a subcamp of Mauthausen, a concentration camp in Austria. Gusen II was liberated by American soldiers in May 1945. Gotfryd spent the next several months wandering, hoping to find relatives or friends who had survived. While walking down a street in Salzburg, Austria, he ran into his brother. He soon parted from his brother to travel to Poland in search of his sister. After weeks of traveling from one city to the next, Gotfryd finally found his sister and had a tearful reunion with her.

In 1947 Gotfryd immigrated to the United States. He served in the U.S. Army Signal Corps on active duty from 1949 to 1950, and in the reserves from 1950 to 1954. During that period, he married Gina Greenberg, a teacher; they have two children. In 1957 Gotfryd got a job as a photographer at *Newsweek* magazine, a position he would hold for nearly thirty years. Throughout his career he photographed numerous important writers and performers, including such literary giants as James Baldwin and Ralph Ellison. At times he also wrote articles to accompany his photographs.

Many of the writers he photographed, when they learned that he was a survivor of the Holocaust, urged him to write about his experiences. He was particularly encouraged by Primo Levi (1919–1987), an Italian Jewish survivor of the Holocaust who had achieved international recognition for his powerful accounts of life under the Nazi regime. In the early 1980s, Gotfryd decided to begin recording his life experiences. Several of his autobiographical stories were published in magazines, and in 1990 they were collected into the volume *Anton the Dove Fancier and Other Tales of the Holocaust*. Gotfryd dedicated the volume in part to the memory of Levi, who had died in an apparent suicide in 1987. Gotfryd's stories received acclaim from reviewers and fellow writers for their simple yet powerful style. In the introduction to *Anton the Dove Fancier*, Gotfryd wrote that his "episodes" are "about people, some flawed, some good, some evil. More importantly, they are about suffering and the endurance of the human spirit."

Historical Background of "The Last Morning"

Adolf Hitler (1889–1945) became the leader of Germany in January 1933. Capitalizing on the anti-Semitism, or hatred of Jews, that had existed and periodically flourished throughout Europe for centuries, Hitler rallied German citizens behind the notion of Jews as a plague. This plague, Hitler claimed, would prevent the rise of a new German empire unless it could be extinguished. He promoted the idea of a master race, called the Aryan race, that included white Christians of Nordic, or Germanic, descent. The Aryan race, Hitler claimed, had to remain pure and could not be tainted by such undesirables as Jews, blacks, Roma (Gypsies), the physically or mentally disabled, and others. In addition to making emotional speeches in support of racial purity, Hitler promised to alleviate the poverty and unemployment that af-

flicted the nation, and to rebuild Germany into the mighty force it had been before its humiliating defeat in World War I (1914–18).

Soon after taking power, Hitler began implementing laws that reflected his own vicious anti-Semitism. His government called for a one-day boycott of Jewish businesses in April 1933, an action that was the first step in a long-term plan to impoverish German Jews. Over the next several years, Jews were excluded from many professions and from all but exclusively Jewish schools. The Nuremberg Laws of 1935 stripped German Jews of their citizenship and prevented them from marrying non-Jews. In addition to the formal laws, Hitler's government continued to spread misinformation to German citizens, depicting Jews as dangerous, filthy enemies of the German people. Such propaganda encouraged many in German society to humiliate and physically abuse Jewish people.

On November 9 and 10, 1938, Jews throughout Germany and Austria, which Hitler had taken over in March of

Barracks and a guard tower at Majdanek, a Nazi concentration and death camp near Lublin, Poland, where Bernard Gotfryd was imprisoned for a time. *Reproduced by permission of Corbis Corporation.*

that year, became the victims of widespread, government-inspired riots. This event, known as *Kristallnacht,* or "Night of Broken Glass," is seen by many as the beginning of the Holocaust, the systematic destruction of the Jews of Europe. During the riots, homes, synagogues, and businesses were vandalized, looted, and burned. Jews were dragged from their homes into the street and beaten by angry mobs. Tens of thousands of Jews were arrested for the crime of being Jewish and sent to concentration camps. Less than a year later, in September 1939, Germany invaded Poland and, within weeks, brought that nation to its knees. The invasion itself was swift and violent; the six-year occupation of Poland that followed was murderous and devastating.

Poles who were of German descent and who the Nazis viewed favorably cooperated with the occupying forces, but most Poles despised the Nazis and longed for the day when Poland would be a self-governing nation once again. The majority of Poles were of Slavic descent, an ethnic group considered inferior by the Nazis, and the Nazis treated Poles brutally, murdering millions of civilians—Jews and non-Jews—throughout World War II. At best, Poles were treated as second-class citizens in their own country. They struggled to make a living, endured humiliation from German troops, and lived under strict laws that controlled their speech, their school and work environments, and their private lives. The Germans fostered an atmosphere of fear, deprivation, and betrayal in Poland. They deliberately kept many Poles living in poverty, offering rewards of food for information on enemies of Hitler's government, including Jews living illegally outside the ghetto or Poles who dared speak out against Germany. These conditions intensified an already strong hatred of Jews as many Polish citizens sought someone to blame for their misfortunes. In spite of the tight controls Nazi Germany placed on Poland, underground resistance groups formed throughout the country. While their political beliefs and their acceptance of Jews varied, these groups worked toward one goal: secretly fighting against the Nazi regime.

While Poles were treated as inferior by the Nazis, Jews in Poland were treated as less than human. Like the Jews of Germany, Polish Jews also endured restrictive laws and policies designed to strip them of their rights and their property.

Beginning just months after the invasion, the Nazi leadership ordered the formation of Jewish ghettos in cities and towns throughout Poland. Concrete walls and barbed-wire fences surrounded the neighborhoods, and no one could enter or leave without the proper paperwork. Far more people lived in the ghettos than could be accommodated by existing homes and apartments. In some ghettos, it was common for several families to share a single small apartment. With such overcrowding, plumbing systems frequently broke down, and living conditions became unsanitary. Diseases like typhus spread quickly through the ghettos, killing thousands. Jews were forced to work in factories or businesses that were beneficial to the Nazis, but they received little more than small rations of food for their labor. Those who couldn't work were deported to concentration camps or death camps.

As Germany conquered more and more nations throughout Europe, the question of what to do with the millions of Jews being imprisoned took on increasing urgency for

German soldiers tear down a barrier somewhere along the German-Polish border on September 1, 1939. Within weeks of the German invasion, Poland was under German control.
Reproduced by permission of AP/Wide World Photos.

Denying the Holocaust

A common theme running through most Holocaust literature is the importance of bearing witness to the atrocities the Nazis committed. Holocaust survivors sound the call again and again: they must never forget what they saw, and they must tell the world of their experiences so that the world remembers and no one can ever deny that the Holocaust took place.

In spite of abundant physical evidence—photographs, films, barracks and crematoria in Nazi camps, the belongings left behind by the victims—and thousands of eyewitness accounts from survivors, bystanders, liberators, and even the Nazi perpetrators, some people attempt to deny that the Holocaust ever happened. Others acknowledge that the events took place, but insist that the number of victims is exaggerated or that the Nazi leadership never intended to destroy the Jewish population in Europe.

While most people accept the historical facts of the Holocaust, a small number of vocal Holocaust deniers occasionally manage to capture media attention with these outlandish claims, even gaining some measure of acceptance as "historians" or "scholars." Deniers and historical revisionists (those who present

the Nazis. During the summer of 1941, the Nazi leadership devised a plan, known as the Final Solution, to murder every Jew in Europe. Death camps, known by the Nazis as extermination centers, were built to speedily accomplish the murder of trainloads of Jews each day. Many existing concentration camps, such as Majdanek and Auschwitz, also known as Auschwitz-Birkenau, were expanded to include extermination facilities. Generally, these facilities were large gas chambers, designed to look like public showers, in which groups of people were suffocated by poison gas. Dead bodies were buried or burned over open pits or in large ovens called crematoria. By the time Germany was defeated and World War II ended in Europe in May 1945, some six million Jews had been murdered by the Nazis. Five million non-Jews fell victim to the Nazis as well, including Poles, Russian prisoners of war, Roma, Jehovah's Witnesses (a religious group), and many others. European Jewish culture was completely devastated by the Holocaust; two out of every three European Jews were murdered during Hitler's rule.

an altered, or revised, view of history) take advantage of the fact that some people don't want to believe such horrible events ever took place. Revisionists question certain aspects of the Holocaust, claiming, for example, that death camps were never built, in order to cast doubt on the entire body of evidence surrounding the Holocaust.

While the motives of Holocaust deniers vary from person to person, most can be said to be motivated by extreme anti-Semitism. Many are followers of modern-day Nazism or similar movements. Their hope is that, by minimizing the events of the Holocaust, they can return a sense of legitimacy to their own organizations, which are heavily tainted by their association with Hitler's Nazi Party.

The best way to fight against the willful spreading of mistruth is to arm oneself with knowledge of history. In many cases, the efforts of Holocaust deniers and revisionists have had unintended consequences: their baseless claims have encouraged many people to find out more about the Holocaust, to learn the truth and guard against those who deny history as a way to spread hate.

Plot and Characters in "The Last Morning"

In "The Last Morning," Bernard Gotfryd recalls the events of Sunday, August 16, 1942: "the day I saw my mother for the last time." The residents of the Radom ghetto had heard rumors that a large-scale deportation would take place on August 16, and they were quietly and mournfully preparing for the inevitable. Bernard's mother arises early and, as her son watches, goes out to the garden, sits on a bench under the lilac tree, and weeps. Moments later, she returns to the kitchen and begins preparing breakfast for the family from their meager storage of food. Unable to bear the sense of doom in the house, Bernard runs to the center of the ghetto to see what other residents are doing. He notices a poster reminding residents that anyone who is sick, feeble, or disabled must be brought to the hospital. His grandmother, who is recovering from a stroke, must report to the hospital, and Bernard fears the worst; he doesn't know exactly what foul plan the Nazis have devised for the sick, but he suspects that something terrible will happen.

While Bernard's family goes through some of the motions of an ordinary day—cleaning the house, cooking meals—they also prepare for a departure. His mother packs a small suitcase while his father looks through the family photo album and puts in his pocket a picture taken on his wedding day. Friends stop by for tearful goodbyes. In the late afternoon, Bernard's grandmother comes out of her room and announces that she is ready to go to the hospital as ordered. Bernard and his brother agree to walk her there; at the gate of the hospital they part. Upon returning to the house, Bernard and his brother find their mother and her friend weeping inconsolably. Their mother pleads with them to run away, to go into hiding and avoid the deportation. "She begged us," the author recalls, "to stay alive so that we could tell the world what had happened." Taking nothing but their jackets, the brothers leave the house and run to the other side of the ghetto.

Sneaking past the armed guards, Bernard and his brother climb the fence surrounding the ghetto and run to a stable inhabited only by horses and field mice. Finding separate hiding places in the stable, the brothers cover themselves with hay and prepare to wait for the deportation to end. A man, the horses' caretaker, comes in and out several times to tend to the horses; at one point he looks directly at the spot where Bernard is hidden, but he does nothing. When darkness comes, Bernard hears nightmarish sounds coming from the town square. Screams of fear and anguish mix with sounds of gunfire. He can hear people desperately calling out the names of family members, and he knows some of the voices he hears belong to young children. He imagines his mother, his sister, and other relatives trapped in the chaos, and part of him longs to go to them. But he stays where he is, and by dawn the noises have died down.

Through a crack in the stable wall, Bernard can see thousands of people walking down the street, armed Nazi guards keeping them in line. He scans as many faces as he can, looking for his mother or someone else he knows. Suddenly he hears voices below him. The caretaker, in the company of two Nazi guards, climbs to Bernard's hiding space and demands that he come out. The man knows where Bernard's brother is hiding as well, and the two young men are beaten by the guards and taken back to the ghetto. Upon their return to the town square, they see a large cart filled

with naked dead bodies. Among them is their grandmother. Somehow, Bernard and his brother manage to stay in the ghetto for some time, avoiding deportation for several more months. He has seen his mother for the last time, and he doesn't even have a photograph by which to remember her. "Whenever I want to remember her," he writes, "I close my eyes and think of that Sunday in August of 1942 when I saw her sitting in our ghetto garden, crying behind the lilac tree."

The disinfection room in the extermination block of Majdanek concentration camp. Victims were forced to shower in this room before being led to the gas chamber. *Reproduced by permission of Corbis Corporation.*

Style and Themes in "The Last Morning"

"The Last Morning" is a true story, an episode from author Bernard Gotfryd's youth in Nazi-occupied Poland. The tale reads, however, like fiction, with elements of adventure and drama. The events of the story build to a suspenseful climax, and the main character experiences growth and change. Many of the "tales" in Gotfryd's *Anton the Dove Fancier and*

Other Tales of the Holocaust have a similar feel: they are memoirs, but they are written in the style of narrative fiction. Perhaps certain memories could be confronted by the author only through the conventions of storytelling. By treating himself and his loved ones as characters and the events of his life as dramatic incidents, the author may have had an easier time revisiting his traumatic past. Or perhaps Gotfryd chose to use the tools of fiction simply as an effective way to communicate with readers. As he reveals in "The Last Morning," it is vitally important to him for people to understand his experiences. He may have chosen to write this story in the familiar style of fiction to prompt readers to closely analyze his words and their meaning in a way that would not take place with a straightforward essay about his past.

In late summer 1942, when the events of "The Last Morning" took place, Bernard was eighteen years old. He was on the verge of manhood, wanting to be brave and strong in a terrifying situation but fearful of being separated from his family. When his mother asks him to retrieve her suitcase from the attic, Bernard takes a moment alone to hug the suitcase close to his body. Perhaps uncomfortable with openly showing affection to his mother, the teenager instead clings to the suitcase, a symbol of her impending departure. When the time comes to follow the Nazis' order and escort his grandmother to the hospital, Bernard, along with his brother, volunteers to walk her there. He is fulfilling an adult role, sparing his parents the painful task of delivering his grandmother to the Nazis. After dropping her off, Bernard is overcome with sadness. But he fights back his tears in his brother's presence, concerned that his emotions will be interpreted as youthful weakness.

During this time of extreme stress as his family faces separation and a frightening future, Bernard finds that the traditional parent-child roles are not as clearly defined as they once were. He sees his parents alternate between moments of courage and vulnerability. They are only in their forties at the time, but throughout the day there are times when they seem old and weak. His mother longs to take care of him and protect him from the threat posed by the Nazis. She caresses his face as she had done when he was a small boy, and she tucks a sandwich into his jacket pocket. But when Bernard sees his mother crying—alone in the garden and later, hysterically, with a

friend in the house—he sees her as someone who needs protection. She wants to mother him, but when the deportation is about to begin, she begs him to take on an adult role and escape the deadly trap laid by the Nazis and survive on behalf of the rest of the family. Bernard's father is a quiet man who does not show his fear and claims to have stopped thinking about anything at all. He looks through the family's collection of photographs and slips his wedding picture into his jacket pocket. Bernard pretends not to have seen this act that reveals the depths of his father's fear of becoming separated from his wife.

Once Bernard makes the decision to escape the ghetto with his brother, he essentially leaves his childhood behind and assumes a painful and difficult task. His mother has begged him to survive the Nazi atrocities and bear witness to all that has happened. But Bernard soon learns that being a witness carries with it a heavy responsibility. As he hides in the stable that night, he hears the chilling sounds of rifle shots and screaming people, including small children. People

In ghettos throughout Poland, Nazi soliders brutally rounded up Jews for deportation to concentration and death camps. Here, women and children in the Warsaw ghetto are herded toward the railway station.
Reproduced by permission of AP/Wide World Photos.

shout out the names of loved ones, sounds that give Bernard a sense of the chaos and confusion that must be going on in the town square. He is spared the nightmare of being in the midst of the deportation, but he must cope with a sense of guilt and betrayal that he has left the rest of his family there to suffer. He is tortured by his own imagination; he pictures his mother crying out, and he imagines his relatives with their young children being rounded up by the Nazis. He is nearly overcome with emotion—"[f]rightened and burdened with my misgivings"—but he is determined to stay in hiding.

The next morning, after being escorted by Nazi officers back to the ghetto, Bernard can see ample evidence of what went on the night before; destruction and death are everywhere. Amidst the dead bodies, he sees his grandmother's lifeless form. "She seemed to be looking straight at me," he recalls—as if she is accusing him of wrongdoing, now that she is dead and he has survived. As a witness, Bernard must carry with him forever all that he has seen and heard during that day and night. And, to fulfill his mother's request to tell the world what the Nazis did, he feels the need to share his story with others. But while relating his story fulfills his promise to his mother, it brings him no closer to a sense of peace. "All these years I've been talking and telling," he writes, "and I'm not sure if anybody listens or understands me. I myself am not sure if I understand."

Research and Activity Ideas

1) Imagine that you have gone into hiding like Bernard. Write about the experience: How do you feel physically and emotionally? Would you stay in hiding or return to the ghetto to be with your family? If you stayed in hiding, how would you feel when the deportation was over?

2) Write about an episode in your life that you consider a turning point. What led up to this important event, and how did your life change afterward?

3) Read accounts written by people who witnessed the horrors of the Holocaust. Consider that the witnesses to these events include not only victims who survived but also those bystanders who saw what went on and did nothing

to stop it. Choose the viewpoint of survivor or bystander, and write a poem or essay about the feelings of guilt such a person may have experienced after the war.

Where to Learn More About ...

Bernard Gotfryd and "The Last Morning"

Gotfryd, Bernard. *Anton the Dove Fancier and Other Tales of the Holocaust.* New York: Washington Square Press, 1990.

Kaganoff, Penny. "Review of *Anton the Dove Fancier and Other Tales of the Holocaust.*" *Publisher's Weekly* 237 (July 6, 1990): p. 62.

Life in the Jewish Ghettos and Personal Accounts of the Holocaust

Adelson, Alan, and Robert Lapides, eds. *Lodz Ghetto: Inside a Community Under Siege.* New York: Viking Penguin, 1991.

Boas, Jacob. *We Are Witnesses: Five Diaries of Teenagers Who Died in the Holocaust.* New York: Henry Holt, 1995.

Holliday, Laurel. *Children in the Holocaust and World War II: Their Secret Diaries.* New York: Pocket Books, 1995.

"A Scrap of Time"

Written by Ida Fink

Holocaust survivor Ida Fink has written numerous short sto- ries and other works of fiction about the Holocaust. Many of her works are based on her own life experiences, and she often writes about the importance—and the pain—of remem- bering the past. In "A Scrap of Time," the narrator shares a story about "a certain time not measured in months or years." The "scrap of time" described in the title refers to one morning during the narrator's youth, a morning when German Nazi troops conducted what was known as an *aktion* in the small Polish town where the narrator lived. An *aktion* began with or- ders from the Nazis for all the Jewish residents of a ghetto—a small and usually prison-like, walled-in neighborhood where the Jews of a town or city had been forced to live—to report to a central location. Then, from among the group of Jews, the Nazis decided who among them was to be loaded onto cattle cars and taken to a concentration or death camp. Concentra- tion camps were large, Nazi-run prisons where inmates were treated violently and inhumanely; death camps were Nazi camps designed specifically for mass murder. In "A Scrap of Time," the narrator describes the events of the first *aktion* in her town and the tragic consequences for her family.

Chronology of Events Relating to "A Scrap of Time"

January 11, 1921: Ida Fink is born in Zbarez, Poland.

January 30, 1933: Adolf Hitler becomes leader of Germany.

September 1, 1939: Nazi Germany invades Poland.

1941: Fink and her family become residents of a Jewish ghetto.

Mid-1941: Germany begins invasion of territories of Soviet Union; Final Solution is put into place.

1942: Fink escapes the ghetto, spending the rest of the war in hiding.

May 8, 1945: World War II ends in Europe when Germany is defeated.

1948: Fink marries Bruno Fink.

1957: Fink immigrates to Israel.

1959–68: Fink works at Yad Vashem, the Holocaust memorial museum in Israel, recording survivor testimonies.

1987: Fink's collection *A Scrap of Time and Other Stories* is published in Polish and English.

Biography of Author Ida Fink

Ida Fink was born Ida Landau on January 11, 1921, in a town called Zbaraz, which was then part of Poland and is now in Ukraine. Her father, Ludwik, was a physician, and her mother, Franciszka, was a teacher. Fink grew up in Poland, studying music as a young woman at the Lwow (also spelled Lvov) Conservatory, a school for musically gifted students. In September 1939, when Fink was eighteen years old, Poland was invaded by Nazi Germany, an invasion that marked the beginning of World War II (1939–45). Under German occupation, Polish citizens were treated harshly and deprived of many of their rights. The Jews of Poland—and of every nation controlled by Germany—were the targets of especially vicious attacks. A fundamental goal of the Nazi leadership was to rid Europe of the Jewish population, and one of the first steps taken toward this goal was to force Jews to live in concentrated areas known as ghettos. Within two years of the German invasion of Poland, every major Polish city and many smaller ones had a small neighborhood designated as the Jewish ghetto. In 1941 Fink and her family were among those forced to live in such a neighborhood, where activity was restricted, food was scarce, and overcrowding was widespread.

In 1942 Fink escaped the ghetto, spending the rest of the war years in hiding on the Aryan side, the term for the areas outside the ghetto where Jews were forbidden to go. ("Aryan" is the word used by Nazis to describe a so-called superior race of people who are white, Christian, and of Germanic ancestry. The ideal Aryan, according to the Nazi view, was tall, with fair hair and light eyes.) Fink survived the war, and in 1948, three years after the war ended, she married Bruno Fink. Together the Finks had one child, a daughter named Miriam. In 1957 the Finks moved to Israel. There, Fink began working at Yad Vashem, the Holocaust memorial museum, in an effort to document for future generations the experiences of other survivors. Fink did not write of her own experiences until several years after the war had ended; she felt that she needed to wait in order to be able to make sense of what had happened to her.

When she did begin to write about the Holocaust, Fink chose to write fiction instead of factual accounts of her life, though many details of her experiences are incorporated into her works. Most of her writings are short stories, and all of them approach the Holocaust in a realistic, straightforward manner. Writing in Polish, she created several radio plays that were produced in the 1970s and 1980s, and in 1987 she published her first collection of short stories along with a short play, *A Scrap of Time and Other Stories,* for which she won the Anne Frank Prize for Literature. The stories in this work depict everyday life for Polish Jews living under the barbaric rule of the Nazis. Reviewers have praised Fink for her restrained, subtle writing in *A Scrap of Time and Other Stories.* She does not overwhelm readers with graphic details, choosing instead to provide hints and suggestions about the horrors of life under the Nazi regime.

In the early 1990s Fink wrote a novel that was published in English as *The Journey* (1992). This work, which begins in 1942, tells the story of two Jewish sisters and their efforts to live secret lives on the Aryan side. Periodically changing locales and identities, the sisters remain on the run for several years after escaping from a Jewish ghetto. At one point they are imprisoned as non-Jews in a German labor camp; when the camp guards become suspicious that the sisters are actually Jewish, they must escape. Critics again hailed

Soldiers oversee the streets of the Lodz ghetto. In large cities, like Warsaw and Lodz, the ghettos were surrounded by walls and barbed wire. The entrances were closed and guarded, and no resident could leave without permission.
Photography by Paul Mix. Reproduced by permission of the United States Holocaust Memorial Museum.

Fink's understated style, noting her ability to present small details of daily life against a background of terrible tragedy.

Fink published another collection of short stories, *Traces*, in 1997. The stories in this collection, like those in *A Scrap of Time*, depict in a bare style the horrors of life for Polish Jews during the German occupation. The stories' main characters are not noble and heroic; rather they are ordinary, flawed people living under extraordinary circumstances. The title refers to what people leave behind in the memories of those who knew them, or in their possessions and personal items, when their lives are abruptly ended. Fink's works, which have been translated into several languages and appear in numerous collections of short stories, have touched readers and critics alike, valued both for what they say and for what remains unsaid.

Historical Background of "A Scrap of Time"

When Adolf Hitler (1889–1945) came to power in Germany in 1933, his vision for his country involved a re-

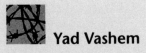

Yad Vashem

Yad Vashem, also known as the Holocaust Martyrs' and Heroes' Remembrance Authority, is a large complex including museums, educational facilities, and monuments to remember the dead. Located in Jerusalem, Israel, Yad Vashem plays a major role in documenting information about the Holocaust and its victims, ensuring that future generations around the world will learn and never forget about this terrible period in human history.

Yad Vashem's primary goals include documenting the events of the Holocaust, collecting survivors' testimonies, and offering memorials to those who died during the Shoah, the Hebrew term often used for the Holocaust. Yad Vashem's archive collection includes nearly sixty million pages of documents, almost 100,000 photographs, reels of film footage, and numerous videotapes of survivor testimonies. The Yad Vashem complex also includes a vast library, an international school for students and for educators who wish to teach others about the Holocaust, and a research center that continues to explore topics related to the Holocaust.

Perhaps the most important part of Yad Vashem is the historical museum. As many as two million people walk through the halls of the museum each year. The museum presents the history of the Holocaust era in chronological order, from Hitler's rise to power in 1933 to the end of the war in 1945. In addition to written ex-

covery from extreme economic hardship and a rebuilding of the nation's military, which had been stripped of its power after Germany's defeat in World War I (1914–18). He intended to build a massive and powerful German empire, which he called the Third Reich ("reich" means empire). To accomplish his goals, Hitler felt it was necessary to control every aspect of German society, to control the very thoughts of his citizens. He believed that the German people would be more likely to support him without question if they felt threatened by, and united against, common enemies. These so-called enemies were numerous and included the physically disabled, people of color, the Roma (commonly referred to as Gypsies), and the Jewish people. Hitler also opposed, and sought to control and imprison, groups whose political or religious beliefs conflicted with his quest for domination. He targeted communists, intellectuals such as university professors, and certain religious groups. Of the many enemies of

planations of various events, the museum also displays artifacts (objects used during that period in history), photographs, and other documents. Yad Vashem also has an art museum that displays works created in the ghettos and Nazi camps as well as art created after the war.

As part of its effort to remember the millions of Holocaust victims, Yad Vashem built the Hall of Names in 1968. The Hall of Names contains millions of "Pages of Testimony." Each page contains information about a Jewish victim of the Holocaust: details about the person's birth, where he or she lived, and the circumstances of his or her death. The purpose of the Hall of Names is to remember the dead as individuals with identities and personal histories rather than as nameless victims.

With the Avenue of the Righteous among the Nations, Yad Vashem honors those non-Jews who, according to the museum's Web site, "acted according to the most noble principles of humanity, risking their lives to help Jews during the Holocaust." Nearly 20,000 people have been given this honor, with each awarded a medal and commemorated as one of the Righteous among the Nations at Yad Vashem. Some saved only a single Jewish life, others saved thousands. All put their own safety aside in order to help those in dire need.

the Third Reich, the Jews were singled out for particularly harsh treatment by the government from Hitler's earliest days in power.

The Nazis begin persecuting Jews in Germany

Within just a few months of becoming leader of Germany, Hitler and his Nazi Party began enacting laws designed to isolate Jews from German society and to strip them of their basic rights. Over the next several years, such laws gradually prevented Jews from holding jobs in most fields, from owning businesses, from shopping in most stores, and from gathering in public places. Jews could not legally own valuables and were barred from studying at universities. Jewish children were forced to attend Jewish schools. In addition to such legal measures, the government also encouraged German citizens to harass and humiliate Jews. Such behavior was considered a show of support for the government, and conversely, befriending or supporting a Jew was thought of as a betrayal. In November 1938, a series of riots later known as *Kristallnacht,* or the "Night of Broken Glass," destroyed thousands of Jewish homes, synagogues, and businesses. Tens of thousands of Jews were arrested and sent to concentration camps. These riots, encouraged by the government, signaled a change for the worse in the treatment of German Jews. After the invasion of Poland and the beginning of World War II in September 1939, ever greater numbers of Jews were arrested and sent to concentration camps for the crime of being Jewish.

The Nazis invade Poland

When Germany invaded Poland and subsequently divided control of that nation with the Soviet Union, Polish Jews in the German-occupied territories were subject to the same persecution, or punishment, that the Jews of Germany had suffered. In a matter of months, the Nazi leadership had begun forcing Polish Jews to live in designated areas called ghettos. In the larger cities, such as Warsaw and Lodz, the ghettos were surrounded by walls and barbed wire. The entrances were closely guarded, and no resident could leave without permission. Conditions in these ghettos were horrible; food was very limited, living spaces were overcrowded, and starvation and disease afflicted thousands. Some ghettos in smaller towns were "open" ghettos; residents were still restricted in what they could do, but there were no walls surrounding the ghetto. Whether living in a large or small ghetto, all residents faced the terror of the occasional *aktion,* when Nazi troops would round up a certain number of people for deportation to the concentration camps. Sometimes those chosen for deportation never made it to the camps; they were instead driven to a remote spot and executed.

The Nazis used various methods of deception to ensure that ghetto residents would cooperate. They told the Jews that they were being sent to labor camps where they would have to work hard but where they would receive plenty of food and adequate housing. Many deportees were forced to write letters to their families back in the ghetto, reporting that they had arrived at a labor camp and that conditions

German soliders advance through the streets of Kharkov in the Ukraine. Nazi troops closely guarded city streets, destroyed Jewish-owned businesses, and arrested millions of Jews for the crime of being Jewish. *Reproduced by permission of AP/World Wide Photos.*

were fine. The reality, as the Jews soon learned, was quite different. Prisoners in the concentration camps were treated like animals. Their heads were shaved; their clothes and personal belongings were taken. Prisoners lived in barracks, sleeping in wooden bunks with no mattresses. Food portions were small, and the menu often consisted of watery soup and stale bread. The guards tortured and murdered inmates on a whim, distributing punishments harshly and unpredictably.

The Final Solution

During 1941, the Nazi leadership began implementing a plan to get rid of every Jew in Europe. While Jews were already dying by the thousands in the ghettos and concentration camps of starvation and disease, this new plan, known as the Final Solution, involved a more systematic method of mass murder. As Germany invaded various territories of the Soviet Union in mid-1941, groups of Nazi troops known as the *Einsatzgruppen,* or Operational Squads, followed behind the army troops and conducted mass executions of Nazi enemies, particularly Jews. These squads rounded up their intended victims—hundreds and sometimes thousands at a time—and shot them. Leaders of the Nazi Party soon concluded that this method of murder was not the best way to accomplish their goal of genocide, the destruction of an entire racial or ethnic group. Shooting people, including women and children, at close range was deemed too psychologically difficult for those in the Operational Squads. In addition, this method was deemed too slow and inefficient, and such operations were difficult to keep a secret from the rest of the population. Beginning in late 1941, the Germans began constructing extermination centers, or death camps, which were built for the express purpose of efficient, impersonal mass murder. Prisoners sent to such camps were usually killed soon after arrival. After being forced to enter sealed rooms that were often designed to look like shower rooms, the victims were then killed by poisonous gas piped into the rooms.

From the earliest days of the ghettos, escaping the Nazi grasp was extremely difficult. Those who managed to leave the ghetto undetected had to find a way to hide out for the duration of the war. Another option for those escaping from the ghetto was to obtain false papers, assume a false identity, and live a secret life as a non-Jew. Jews attempting to survive outside the ghetto faced numerous obstacles, and most who attempted such paths were eventually caught and murdered by the Nazis. Escapes from the camps were even more difficult, and far less successful. Eventually the Nazis murdered six million Jews, two-thirds of the pre-war Jewish population in Europe.

Plot and Characters in "A Scrap of Time"

Ida Fink's "A Scrap of Time" is narrated by a Jewish woman who was a young girl in German-occupied Poland dur-

ing the war. She explains that she has "been digging around in the ruins of memory" to recall the events of a particular day in the town where she lived. She does not name the town or give a calendar date for the day in question. The events of that day, she states, mark the beginning of the residents measuring time in a different way. When the day begins, the residents of the town still discuss events of the past in the usual way, placing them in a given month or year, or around the time of a certain holiday. During the day in question, however, their lives are turned upside-down, and their way of measuring time changes to match their new reality. After this day, the Jews of this town can no longer pretend to live normal, everyday lives. They are victims of Nazi power, the targets of a vicious campaign to wipe out an entire people. From this day forward, the narrator explains, events are described as having taken place before or after a given *aktion,* when Jews were sent away from the town to uncertain destinations.

The town's residents have been given an order to report to the marketplace, the central area of the town, to re-

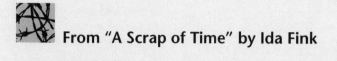

From "A Scrap of Time" by Ida Fink

This beautiful, clear morning that I am digging out of the ruins of my memory is still fresh; its colors and aromas have not faded: a grainy golden mist with red spheres of apples hanging in it, and the shadows above the river damp with the sharp odor of burdock, and the bright blue dress that I was wearing when I left the house and when I turned around at the gate. It was then, probably at that very moment, that I suddenly progressed, instinctively...off on a roundabout route, across the orchard, along the riverbank, down a road we called "the back way" because it wound through the outskirts of town. Instinctively, because that moment I still did not know that I wouldn't stand in the marketplace in front of the town hall. Perhaps I wanted to delay that moment, or perhaps I simply liked the river....

There was the square, thick with people as on a market day, only different, because a market-day crowd is colorful and loud, with chickens clucking, geese honking, and people talking and bargaining. This crowd was silent. In a way it resembled a rally—but it was different from that, too. I don't know what it was exactly. I only know that we suddenly stopped and my sister began to tremble, and then I caught the trembling, and she said, "Let's run

port for duty in a German labor camp. Most people dutifully follow the order, though some older residents decide not to go because they fear they will be unable to perform heavy physical labor. The narrator leaves the house with her sister; they intend to head to the marketplace as ordered, but for some reason they decide to take "a roundabout route, across the orchard, along the riverbank, down a road we called 'the back way' because it wound through the outskirts of town." Because they took the long way to the center of town, they arrive after many other people. They glimpse the marketplace from a distance, seeing crowds of people silently gathered there. Something about the silence and the mood of the people terrifies the girls, and they turn and run away from the marketplace. They sit on a hillside for a long while before returning to their home.

Upon returning, they learn about what happened in the marketplace. They are told that the women had been immediately sent home, and that, from among the men, the

away," and although no one was chasing us and the morning was still clear and peaceful...we ran for a long time until we were high up the steep slope known as Castle Hill—the ruins of an old castle stood on top of it—and on this hillside, the jewel of our town, we sat down in the bushes, out of breath and still shaking....

We sat there for an hour, maybe two, I don't know, because it was then that time measured in the ordinary way stopped. Then we climbed down the steep slope to the river and returned to our house, where we heard what had happened in the marketplace, and that our cousin David had been taken, and how they took him, and what message he had left for his mother.... First we learned that the women had been told to go home, that only the men were ordered to remain standing there, and that the path chosen by our cousin had been the opposite of ours. We had been horrified by the sight of the crowd in the marketplace, while he was drawn towards it by an enormous force, a force as strong as his nerves were weak, so that somehow or other he did violence to his own fate, he himself, himself, himself, and that was what he asked people to tell his mother, and then he wrote it down: "I myself am to blame, forgive me."

Nazis chose seventy-one people to load onto trucks. One of the seventy-one was the narrator's cousin, David. She learns that, by the time the residents had begun to gather, many people knew or suspected that the Nazis were not taking the town's residents to a labor camp. A family friend, spotting David on his way to the marketplace, offers to hide him in his apartment, in a room overlooking the marketplace. David goes with the man, but after some time spent looking out the window at the others gathered below, he chooses to leave his hiding place and join his friends and family in the marketplace. The Nazis question the men lined up in the town square about their professions; those who claim to be tradespeople or skilled laborers, like carpenters, are left behind. Those who report that they are teachers, as David is, or lawyers are told to board the waiting trucks.

As David walks toward the trucks, he shouts out to those left behind, "Tell my mother that it's my own fault and that I beg her forgiveness." He then writes those words down on paper, asking that someone deliver the note to his mother. "Presumably," the narrator states, "he had already stopped believing what all of us still believed later: that they were going to a camp. He had that horrible clarity of vision that comes just before death." The narrator explains that, after that day, postcards arrived from people who had been taken away in the trucks, postcards that confirmed their arrival at a labor camp. The Nazis let it be known that gifts of coffee or other valuables from people in the town would buy news about family members who had been deported. Townspeople could also send packages of food and supplies to their relatives in the camps.

Not until some years later, after the war ended, does the narrator and her family learn the truth about what happened the day that David was deported. While they had suspected something awful had taken place and had even heard rumors about such a tragedy, the family had refused to believe until they heard from someone who had seen it firsthand. A peasant from their town—the same person who had delivered the note to David's mother—eventually tells them that the seventy-one people who had been driven away in trucks that day were taken into the woods a few miles outside of town. After a mass grave had been dug, all seventy-one were shot. David, in a futile last-minute attempt to escape death, had climbed a tree. He "wrapped his arms around the trunk like a child hugging his mother, and that was the way he died."

Style and Themes in "A Scrap of Time"

The style of "A Scrap of Time" gives the sense that the story is autobiographical—recounting events that the author actually experienced—rather than fictional. While the story may be based on author Ida Fink's personal experiences, and is certainly based on actual historical events, it is categorized as fiction. Regardless of the category, however, the narrator gives readers a sense of immediacy—of being there with her, seeing what she sees. The main reason the story seems so intimate is that it is told in the first person, a literary style that means the narrator is also a character in the story, and he or she uses "I" or "we" in telling the tale. In addition, Fink incorporates specific, vivid details about the morning in question, the kinds of details that stand out in the memory of a life-altering event. The narrator remarks that, even many

years later, the memory of that morning "is still fresh." She recalls "a grainy golden mist with red spheres of apples hanging in it, and the shadows above the river damp with the sharp odor of burdock [wild herbs], and the bright blue dress that I was wearing…". The fear she experiences that day etches certain details into her mind that can never be erased and makes the moment seem real to the reader.

"A Scrap of Time" includes many details about sights and sounds and smells, but on the other hand it lacks many larger details. The narrator is unnamed, and the town she lives in is not specified. She does not cite the month or year in which the described event took place. She does not use the word "Nazis," and instead refers to the town's oppressors as "they" or "the authorities." These minimal details about time and place give the story a universal quality; the events in the story could have happened on any given day, in towns all over Poland, the Soviet Union, or many other nations invaded by Nazi Germany.

Prisoners from the Buchenwald concentration camp handcuffed to each other awaiting execution. Many prisoners were taken from ghettos and camps to nearby woods and killed. *Reproduced by permission of the United States Holocaust Memorial Museum.*

An important theme of "A Scrap of Time" is the way perceptions of time—how quickly or slowly it passes, how distant or near certain past events seem—can be altered by a life-changing event. The narrator speaks of two different times, one that "is measured in months and years," and another that is measured by certain traumatic events. During the period discussed in the story, when the town's citizens were murdered by the Nazis, life abruptly changed for the town's residents. The narrator pinpoints the exact moment when her life changed, when "time measured in the ordinary way stopped." After running away from the action taking place in the town center, the narrator and her sister sit on a hillside, watching their house below for signs of a change. She does not know how long they sit their waiting—"an hour, maybe two"—but she does know that it's at that instant that "normal" life has been suspended.

In "A Scrap of Time," Fink juxtaposes, or places side by side, images of this normal, everyday life with information about the horrors committed by the Nazi troops. She writes of the narrator choosing flat stones to skip in the river, a neighbor going outside to beat the dust out of her rugs, and the noises made by chickens and geese and people on market day. She then writes of the Nazis' campaign of deception in which they encourage residents' hopes that their deported family members are still alive and accept bribes to provide false information about those relatives. Such deceptions cover up the atrocity the Nazis committed when they loaded up the townspeople, drove them to the woods, and shot them. The narrator's descriptions of nature and the simple, day-to-day activities of the townspeople, when read by themselves, give a peaceful, serene feeling. But when such details are the background for unspeakable human cruelty, they take on a strange, sad quality. When the narrator and her sister sit atop the hillside overlooking the town, it is as if they have a view of both the past, embodied by the peaceful countryside and the home of their family, and the future, represented by the cruel disregard for human life taking place in the marketplace below.

Research and Activity Ideas

1) In "A Scrap of Time," the narrator's cousin David is taken away by the Nazis and shot in a forest. Before

leaving, he writes his mother a note that says, "I myself am to blame, forgive me." What do you think he means by that? Do you feel that he is to blame for his own death? What do you think went through his mind that day that compelled him to join the other villagers in the town square rather than remain hidden?

2) Research the Jewish ghettos in Poland during World War II, studying the larger ghettos, such as the ones in Warsaw and Lodz, as well as the smaller ghettos. Focus on the details of everyday life and write an essay or short story that includes such details.

3) Think about a significant event in your life, perhaps something that, as described in "A Scrap of Time," made you feel differently about your world. Write about that memory, paying attention to the fact that some details seem very vivid while others have faded over time.

Where to Learn More About ...

Ida Fink and "A Scrap of Time"

"Ida Fink." *Polish Literature.* http://www.polska2000.pl/en/authors/fink_ida.html (accessed on December 17, 2002).

Rittner, Carol, and John K. Roth, eds. *Different Voices: Women and the Holocaust.* New York: Paragon House, 1993.

Jewish Ghettos in Poland

Altman, Linda Jacobs. *The Holocaust Ghettos.* Berkeley Heights, NJ: Enslow Publishers, 1998.

Hoffman, Eva. *Shtetl: The Life and Death of a Small Town and the World of Polish Jews.* Boston, MA: Houghton Mifflin, 1998.

Yad Vashem

Yad Vashem: The Holocaust Martyrs' and Heroes' Remembrance Authority. http://www.yad-vashem.org.il (accessed on January 16, 2003).

Holocaust Poems

Poetry is perhaps the most personal and powerful of all forms of literature. The American poet Edwin Arlington Robinson (1869–1935) died before the Holocaust, yet his description of poetry as "language that tells us...something that cannot be said" seems particularly appropriate in a discussion of Holocaust-related poetry. The realities of the Holocaust have been described as "unspeakable." It is in poetry that some Holocaust survivors, as well as poets in later generations, have found a means of expressing what cannot be conveyed in any other way.

Holocaust poetry may be subdivided into three broad categories. The first contains works written during the Holocaust by victims or survivors. One example of this type of poetry is found in the writings of Hannah Senesh, a young Hungarian Jewish woman who was executed for her attempts to rescue Jews from her homeland. Her poems, including "Blessed Is the Match," were published along with her diary following the war's end.

The second type of Holocaust poetry includes works written after 1945 by survivors of Nazi persecution, whether they survived in hiding or disguised as non-Jews, escaped as refugees to a country safe from Nazi control, or were liberated from concentration camps. Yala Korwin, Nelly Sachs, Abba Kovner, and Primo Levi are representative of these Holocaust poets.

The third general category of poetry related to the Holocaust includes works written in response to the horrors of the era even although the poets themselves were not objects of Nazi persecution. Some of these writers are children of Holocaust survivors, although many are not. American poet William Heyen, for example, was born in the United States to a man who had emigrated from Germany in the 1920s, leaving behind relatives who fought and died for Nazi Germany; Heyen has published multiple collections of Holocaust-related poetry. Russian poet Yevgeny Yevtushenko's famous poem, "Babi Yar," which was first published in 1960 and has since appeared in many anthologies, is another example of Holocaust-related poetry written by someone who did not witness the events of the Holocaust era.

Poets writing about the Holocaust have addressed all facets of the era. The dangerous spread of murderous prejudice in Hitler's Europe—and the plague of apathy that kept good people from protesting such treatment—is the focus of Pastor Niemöller's "First They Came for the Jews." The poet explains that he did not defend the Jews or members of other political or religious groups because he was not part of such groups; when the Nazis came for him, he explains, "there was no one left / to speak out for me." From Paul Celan's "Death Fugue" to Nelly Sachs's "O the Chimneys" to Tadeusz Borowski's "Night over Birkenau," numerous poems have been written about the horrors of the Nazi camps and the murderous campaign known as the Final Solution. Poets including Lily Brett, Primo Levi, and Abba Kovner are among many who have addressed the slow and painful process of piecing together a life after the Holocaust.

Four poems are featured in *Experiencing the Holocaust.* "The Butterfly," by Pavel Friedmann, is one of the best-known pieces of poetry to have survived the Holocaust. Friedmann, however, did not survive and was murdered at Auschwitz in 1944. Written in 1942 at the Terezin concentration camp, this work poignantly illustrates the human need to search for beauty even in the darkest, ugliest places.

"Leaving You," by Lily Brett, is a poem written by the daughter of a Holocaust survivor. The horrific experiences of survivors cast a dark shadow over their lives that often extended to the lives of their children, whether the parents spoke often of their painful past or refused to speak of it at all. This work addresses the complex relationship between a woman and her mother who is a Holocaust survivor. The daughter explains that her powerful identification with her mother's painful memories has made it difficult for her to develop a separate identity.

Poet Nelly Sachs survived the Holocaust by escaping to Sweden in 1940. She left behind a large network of family and friends, most of whom died at the Nazis' hands. Her poem "O the Chimneys" is a psalm-like lament for the millions of Jews and others who were murdered in gas chambers at Nazi death camps, their bodies disposed of in large ovens known as crematories. In this poem, smoke rising from the death camp chimneys is said to be the body of Israel—in other words, the Jewish people—drifting over Earth. Sachs mourns not just the loss of individuals, but the devastation of European Jewry.

Primo Levi's "Shema" was written in 1946, not long after the poet returned to his home in Turin, Italy, after being liberated from Auschwitz in 1945. The title of the poem is taken from the central Jewish prayer of the same name, a prayer that declares the Jewish belief in one God. In "Shema," the poet addresses the world, those "who live safe in your warm houses," demanding that the pain and suffering of Holocaust victims not be forgotten, so that such degradation of human life might never again be allowed to happen.

Representative Poetry about the Holocaust

Borenstein, Emily. *Night of the Broken Glass: Poems of the Holocaust.* Mason, TX: Timberline Press, 1981. *The works in this book, written by a poet whose relatives died during the Holocaust, are arranged under three headings: I Must Tell the Story; May It Never Be Forgotten; and Psalm of Hope.*

Brett, Lily. *After the War: Poems.* Melbourne: Melbourne University Press, 1990. *Part of the "second generation"—she is the child of Holocaust survivors—Lily Brett has written numerous poems addressing the long-ranging impact of the Holocaust not just on survivors but on future generations as well.*

Celan, Paul. *Poems of Paul Celan*. Edited and translated by Michael Hamburger. New York: Persee Books, 1990. *An acclaimed Holocaust poet, Paul Celan survived imprisonment in concentration camps and spent part of the war years in hiding. Many of his poems focus on the tragic, and Celan himself committed suicide at the age of forty-nine.*

Duba, Ursula. *Tales from a Child of the Enemy*. New York: Penguin, 1997. *The story-poems of this collection depict a German girl's experiences of the World War II years (1939–45) and her horror at learning—more than a decade after the war's end—of the Holocaust and her country's responsibility for it.*

Fishman, Charles, ed. *Blood to Remember: American Poets on the Holocaust*. Lubbock, TX: Texas Tech University Press, 1991. *This collection of 256 poems contains the works of nearly two hundred American poets, some of whom are Holocaust survivors.*

Glatstein, Jacob. *I Keep Recalling: The Holocaust Poems of Jacob Glatstein*. Hoboken, NJ: Ktav Publishing House, 1993. *This collection of poems was originally selected and published in 1967 by the Association of Survivors of Bergen-Belsen, a Nazi camp. The poems appear in Yiddish with English translations by Barnett Zumoff.*

Heyen, William. *Erika: Poems of the Holocaust*. New York: Vanguard Press, 1984. *The author of these poems is the son of a non-Jewish German man who immigrated to the United States in 1928. His other family members stayed behind and eventually died as soldiers in the German army during World War II. These works reflect not only the horrors of the Holocaust but also the anguish of a family torn by conflicting loyalties.*

Hyett, Barbara Helfgott. *In Evidence: Poems of the Liberation of Nazi Concentration Camps*. Pittsburgh, PA: University of Pittsburgh Press, 1986. *These poems are derived from the testimony of American and British soldiers who witnessed the horrific conditions of the concentration camps when the Allied military forces, which included the Soviet Union, Great Britain, and the United States, defeated the Germans.*

Korwin, Yala. *To Tell the Story: Poems of the Holocaust*. New York: Holocaust Library, 1987. *Yala Korwin and her sister survived the Holocaust in Poland by passing as non-Jews; other family members were murdered in death camps. The poems in this collection are based on the poet's wartime experiences.*

Kovner, Abba. *My Little Sister and Selected Poems 1965–1985*. Oberlin, OH: Oberlin College, 1986. *Abba Kovner was a leader of the Vilna ghetto resistance group. After the war, he immigrated to Israel, where he lived with other Holocaust survivors on a kibbutz, or settlement, until his death in 1987. This volume collects his major Holocaust poems.*

Kramer, Aaron, ed. *The Last Lullaby: Poetry from the Holocaust*. Syracuse, NY: Syracuse University Press, 1997. *This volume collects poetry written during the Holocaust—in ghettos, concentration camps, forests, and other places where Jews were brutally persecuted by (or in hiding from) the Nazis.*

Krizkova, Marie Rut. *We Are Children Just the Same: Vedem, the Secret Magazine by the Boys of Terezin*. Philadelphia, PA: Jewish Publication Society, 1995. *Poems and other short writings from the Terezin ghetto are collected here, all written by boys between the ages of twelve and fourteen.*

Levi, Primo. *Shema: Collected Poems of Primo Levi.* London: Menard Press, 1976. *This collection contains "Shema" and other poems written by the Jewish Italian author and Holocaust survivor.*

Lifshin, Lyn. *Blue Tattoo.* Desert Hot Springs, CA: Event Horizon Press, 1995. *The poems in this book have been arranged to roughly correspond to the chronology of events of Holocaust history.*

Sachs, Nelly. *O the Chimneys: Selected Poems, Including "Eli," a Verse Play.* New York: Farrar, Straus and Giroux, 1967. *A Nobel Prize-winning poet, Sachs was a German Jewish survivor of the Holocaust.*

Schiff, Hilda, ed. *Holocaust Poetry.* New York: St. Martin's Press, 1995. *This collection of poetry, organized by themes such as "Persecution," "Destruction," and "Afterwards," includes Holocaust-related verses written by well-known poets from around the world.*

Senesh, Hannah. *Hannah Senesh: Her Life and Diary.* New York: Schocken Books, 1983. *This volume contains both the diary and the poetry of a heroic young Hungarian Jewish woman who was killed by a firing squad in 1944 for trying to help Jews escape from Hungary.*

Sutzkever, Abraham. *Selected Poetry and Prose.* Berkeley, CA: University of California Press, 1991. *Sutzkever has been called Israel's foremost Yiddish poet. This collection features works based on the poet's experience as a Holocaust survivor.*

Volavkova, Hana, ed. *I Never Saw Another Butterfly: Children's Drawings and Poems from Terezin Concentration Camp.* New York: Schocken Books, 1993. *This classic of Holocaust literature includes Pavel Friedmann's poem "The Butterfly," as well as numerous other examples of poetry and artwork by young people imprisoned in the Terezin concentration camp, also known as Theresienstadt.*

"The Butterfly"

Written by Pavel Friedmann

Several years after the end of World War II (1939–45), suitcases full of papers were taken off a shelf in the Jewish Museum of Prague, Czechoslovakia. These suitcases had been brought to Prague after the war's end, but their contents had remained unexamined for several years. Inside these suitcases were drawings and writings created by the young inmates of Terezin, a concentration camp that imprisoned over 140,000 Jews between 1941 and 1945. Part of a network of forced-labor prisons established by Germany's Adolf Hitler (1889–1945) and his ruling Nazi Party, Terezin, also called Theresienstadt, was a temporary and miserable home for tens of thousands of Jews young and old. Many of the young inmates expressed their fear, sorrow, and longing for a normal life through art and poetry. Perhaps the most famous example of poetry written in Terezin is the work called "The Butterfly." Written by Pavel Friedmann in 1942, "The Butterfly" recounts the comfort the young man finds in sights of natural beauty—flowers, trees, and a brilliant yellow butterfly—amidst the horror of life in a concentration camp. The poem contains the line "I never saw another butterfly," touching words that serve as the title of a book that includes many of the poems and drawings produced by the children and young adults of Terezin.

Chronology of Events Relating to "The Butterfly"

January 7, 1921: Pavel Friedmann is born in Prague, Czechoslovakia.

March 15, 1939: Germany takes control of Czechoslovakia.

November 1941: City of Terezin converted to Theresienstadt, a concentration camp.

April 26, 1942: Friedmann gets deported to Terezin.

June 4, 1942: Friedmann writes "The Butterfly."

June 23, 1944: The International Red Cross visits Terezin; the visitors are deceived into believing that Jews are treated decently there.

September 29, 1944: Friedmann dies in Auschwitz.

May 1945: Terezin is liberated from Nazi control by the army of the Soviet Union.

1959: A collection of art and poetry created by the young inmates of Terezin, including "The Butterfly," is published for the State Jewish Museum in Prague, Czechoslovakia. A few years later an edition is published in the United States.

Biography of Poet Pavel Friedmann

Few details exist about Pavel Friedmann's life. Most sources list his birthdate as January 7, 1921, and his birthplace as Prague, which was the capital of Czechoslovakia (now the capital of the Czech Republic). Other sources suggest that Friedmann was seventeen years old when he wrote his famous poem in 1942, which would make 1925 the year of his birth. On April 26, 1942, Friedmann was sent to Terezin. There he joined tens of thousands of other Jews crammed into a walled city built to house only a few thousand. Friedmann, like many of the fifteen thousand young people who lived in Terezin at some point during the war, found an outlet for his fear and despair in creative expression: writing poetry. On June 4, 1942, only a few weeks after arriving in Terezin, Friedmann wrote "The Butterfly," a poem that would later become familiar to millions of people as a symbol of the suffering of young people during the Holocaust.

At some time in the next two years, Friedmann, like most of Terezin's inmates, was deported to Auschwitz, a death camp in Poland where more than one million people were murdered in just three years' time. On September 29, 1944, Friedmann died in Auschwitz.

Thanks to the determined efforts of many people, Friedmann's poem—and thousands of other drawings and writings created by Terezin's youthful prisoners—was preserved for future generations. Of the fifteen thousand children under the age of fifteen who passed through Terezin, only about one hundred survived the Holocaust. But many of the individuals who perished will be remembered through their words or drawings, many of which demonstrate their youthful ability to find beauty in the most unlikely places.

Historical Background of "The Butterfly"

The city of Terezin, located northwest of Prague, was founded in 1780 by Joseph II, an Austrian emperor. Built as a fortress to protect the region from northern invaders, Terezin was constructed in the shape of a star. This stark, gray town, with its narrow streets and high walls, sits in contrast to its peaceful surroundings, as described by acclaimed American author Chaim Potok in the foreword to *I Never Saw Another Butterfly:* "a serene world of meadows and low rolling hills and summer butterflies against a distant background of bluish Bohemian mountains." In the years leading up to World War II, Terezin was home to soldiers as well as civilians, with the total number of residents at fewer than four thousand, including about one hundred Czech Jews.

On March 15, 1939, Adolf Hitler led the German army on an invasion of Czechoslovakia. A few months later, with Germany's September invasion of Poland, World War II began. As many historians have pointed out, Hitler and his Nazi Party were conducting two wars at the same time, one against the Allied powers (including the United States, England, and the Soviet Union) and one against the Jewish population of Europe. Hitler's violent hatred of Jews led him to blame them for Germany's troubles—poverty, instability, unemployment—in the years following World War I. And that same hatred became a fundamental part of the Nazi Party's policy. After becoming dictator of Germany in 1933, Hitler immediately began enacting laws that deprived German Jews of their basic rights. His initial plan to force or pressure Jews

into leaving Germany eventually evolved into a brutal plot to eliminate all European Jews.

Terezin: the "model ghetto"

To that end, the Nazis began rounding up Jews in every nation Germany had invaded. Jews were forced to live in neighborhoods surrounded by barbed-wire or concrete walls known as ghettos before being deported to concentration camps, large prisons where they had to perform hard physical labor. Millions of Jews were ultimately taken to death camps, which were designed specifically for mass murder. In November 1941, the Czechoslovakian town of Terezin was converted into a concentration camp that the Germans renamed Theresienstadt. (Some historians refer to Terezin as a ghetto, while others describe it as a concentration camp. Regardless of the description applied to it, Terezin was essentially a prison.)

The Nazis struggled with the problem of how to dispose of the more prominent Jewish citizens—decorated sol-

Millions of children suffered, and more than one million died, in concentration camps such as Auschwitz, shown above. *Reproduced by permission of the United States Holocaust Memorial Museum.*

diers who had fought for Germany in World War I, rabbis and other leaders of the Jewish community, and world-famous artists, writers, and scientists. While these people were Jews and therefore considered less than human by the Nazis, they were also people of some importance who were known to the outside world. The Nazis also understood that the full truth about what went on in concentration camps and death camps could not be revealed to the rest of the world for fear that other world leaders might try to shut them down. So Terezin, it was decided, would be a "model ghetto"; it would be designed to look to any visitors like a fairly comfortable place to live.

The Nazis spread false information about Terezin to Jews in Czechoslovakia and elsewhere. They claimed that Terezin would provide a refuge for certain Jews from the violence of life during wartime. Elderly Jews were told that Terezin would be a retirement home for them. Others were told that Terezin would be a labor camp, but one where inmates were treated decently and kept safe. The Nazis declared that Jews would govern the city, and that no guards from the SS, the elite and brutal Nazi security force, would reside within its walls. The Nazis had people so convinced that Terezin would provide safety that some even paid large sums to gain admittance.

The harsh reality hidden from the world

The reality of Terezin turned out to be quite different from the way it was advertised. As more and more people were transported there, conditions became increasingly crowded. Inmates slept in bunk beds in barracks—plain, drab buildings originally constructed to house soldiers—or, when all the beds were taken, on the hard floor. During the war Terezin held ten times the number of people that the city had been built to accommodate, and such overcrowding resulted in unsanitary conditions that were breeding grounds for disease. The food given to the prisoners was barely enough to keep them alive, and many people slowly starved to death. *I Never Saw Another Butterfly* includes this description of a typical meal in Terezin from fifteen-year-old Petr Fischl: "We stood in a long queue [line] with a plate in our hand, into which they ladled a little warmed-up water with a salty or coffee flavor." Any able-bodied person over the age of fourteen was forced to perform hard labor, working up to fourteen

hours per day and enduring harsh punishments from their Nazi guards if they could not keep up. Many of those who managed to avoid disease and malnutrition died from sheer exhaustion and overwork.

As miserable as the conditions in Terezin were, though, the inmates would rather have endured that suffering than be among the people being transported to Auschwitz,

Terezin (also called Theresienstadt) concentration camp, in Czechoslovakia, where more than 140,000 Jews were imprisoned between 1941 and 1945. *Reproduced by permission of AP/Wide World Photos.*

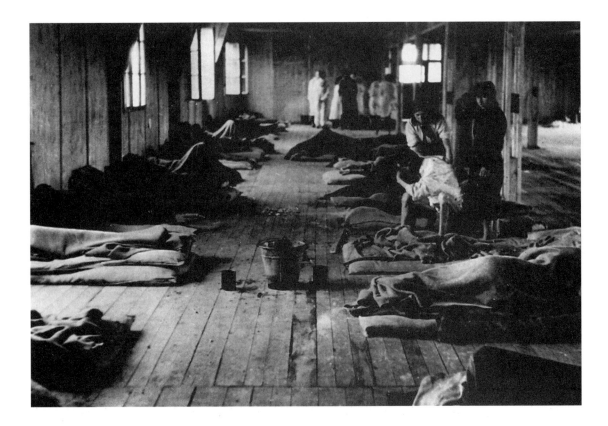

Sick prisoners lay on pallets in a women's camp in Terezin. Few people outside the camp saw how poorly the prisoners were actually treated. *Reproduced by permission of the YIVO Institute for Jewish Research/United States Holocaust Memorial Museum.*

also known as Auschwitz-Birkenau, or other death camps. Every so often the Nazi guards would post a list of the names of Terezin inmates who were to be transported; days later those people—sometimes several thousand of them—would be taken away in railway cars, never to be heard from again. Instead of being the safe haven the Nazis had described, Terezin was merely a place where Jews were temporarily held while room could be made for them at Auschwitz.

Late in 1943, the International Red Cross, a neutral organization designed to help civilian victims of war, submitted a request to investigate the conditions at Terezin. Nine months later, the Nazis agreed. They had used those months to beautify and alter Terezin to fool the Red Cross into thinking that inmates were treated humanely. The Nazis scrambled to transport as many inmates as possible to Auschwitz so the overcrowding in Terezin would be less obvious to the Red Cross. Just in time for the visit from the Red Cross in the summer of 1944, buildings got a fresh coat of paint, disabled

When members of the International Red Cross (the man on the right) visited Terezin to investigate how the prisoners were treated, all evidence of Nazi brutality had been hidden. *Reproduced by permission of the United States Holocaust Memorial Museum.*

and sickly prisoners were ushered out of sight, long-empty shop windows were filled with fresh food. The Red Cross representatives toured the camp, seeing buildings set aside as schools for children, newly furnished apartments for prominent prisoners, and plays performed by the children of Terezin. In truth the Nazis allowed no schools, and living conditions were far worse than the residences seen by the Red Cross. But the organization left Terezin satisfied that the Jews there were treated fairly well. The Nazis completed the deception by producing a movie falsely documenting comfortable conditions for Terezin's inmates, a movie that could be shown to the world to "prove" that the rumors of harsh treatment and mass murder of Jews were untrue. The film described Terezin as Hitler's gift to the Jews.

Artistic expressions

In spite of their nightmarish existence, the inmates of Terezin managed to continue creating works of art and litera-

Friedl Dicker-Brandeis

Friedl Dicker-Brandeis was a Jewish artist, designer, and art teacher living in Prague, Czechoslovakia, when the Nazis came to power in Germany. She had trained at Germany's Bauhaus school, an art and design institute that emphasized the connection between visual arts—painting, sculpture, and so on—and crafts, like woodworking or furniture design. Bauhaus artists sought to bring both beauty and functionality to everyday objects, from teapots to chairs. Dicker-Brandeis designed homes and schools, and she taught children about color and form.

In 1942 Dicker-Brandeis and her husband, Pavel Brandeis, were living in the small rural Czechoslovakian town of Hronov. The order came in December of that year that the town's population of Jews would be rounded up and transported to the concentration camp Terezin, also known as Theresienstadt. Dicker-Brandeis packed her suitcase with the items she considered most important to her survival: art supplies.

At Terezin, Dicker-Brandeis was one of several teachers who conducted se-ture. The many artists and writers living there clung to the idea of holding onto life by writing, drawing, painting—and teaching and encouraging others to do so as well. Such creative activities could serve both as a way of expressing their extraordinary fear and sorrow and as a way to leave behind concrete evidence of their existence. And several of the artistically gifted adults in Terezin realized the importance of sharing their skills with the children living there. Risking their lives—for the Nazis had forbidden such things—these teachers conducted classes and provided art materials to the young inmates. One particularly beloved art teacher in Terezin, Friedl Dicker-Brandeis, spent a great deal of her time instructing students in the basics of drawing. Dicker-Brandeis realized that art offered children a sense of normalcy as well as an outlet for expressing their feelings. Some of the works did express the children's fears, while others reflected the simple pleasures of the life the children had previously known: a visit to a park, a holiday meal with family, or playing with classmates at school.

Several thousand works of art and poetry were created by the young people living in Terezin during World War II.

cret classes for the children. While some teachers exchanged lessons for food, Dicker-Brandeis offered her services for free. She understood the importance of giving the children something to focus on besides their fear, sorrow, and physical suffering. Her students studied color and composition, and created portraits and landscapes. They used art to express their worst nightmares and their fondest memories. Dicker-Brandeis acted as more than just an art teacher: for many of the children, she was a therapist as well, helping them cope with their anxiety by analyzing and discussing their artwork. In *Fireflies in the Dark: The Story of Friedl Dicker-Brandeis and the Children of Terezin,* Susan Goldman Rubin sums up Dicker-Brandeis's contribution: "She lovingly enabled her students to rise above their horrifying situation and find pleasure and dignity through art."

On October 6, 1944, just seven months before the end of World War II, Friedl Dicker-Brandeis was sent by train to Auschwitz-Birkenau, the notorious Nazi death camp. She was murdered there soon after arriving.

Kept hidden from the Nazi guards, these works were preserved throughout the war years. In May 1945 Terezin was liberated, or freed from Nazi control, by the Soviet army. The war in Europe had ended, and the losing German army was forced to retreat. Amidst the confusion following the war's end, suitcases filled with drawings and poems by the young people of Terezin were safely carried to the Jewish Museum in Prague. Years later they were rediscovered, and in the years since they have been displayed in museums and reprinted in many books. They remain as testimony to the many young lives lost during the Holocaust and as painful evidence of the suffering that children endured during the war.

Subject Matter of "The Butterfly"

Pavel Friedmann's "The Butterfly" is a short, fairly simple poem relating his last sighting of a bright yellow butterfly flying in the sky above Terezin. The poet acknowledges that in spite of being "penned up inside this ghetto," he has been able to find some comfort in the beauty of nature. Even

Drawing titled "Hell," by ten-year-old Liliane Frankl, done while she was a prisoner at the Terezin concentration camp.
Reproduced by permission of Corbis Corporation.

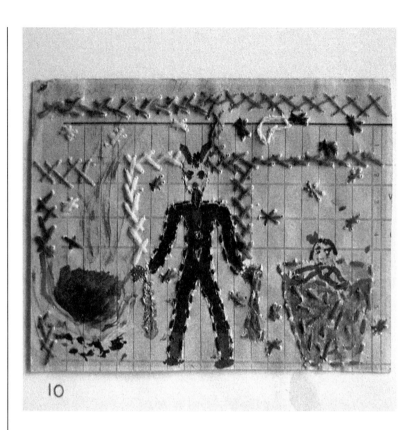

though his life has changed dramatically since coming to Terezin, he appreciates seeing that the rhythms of the natural world continue. "The dandelions call to me," he relates, "and the white chestnut branches in the court."

But the "richly, brightly, dazzlingly yellow" butterfly he spotted that day has not returned, and neither have any other butterflies. Friedmann suggests that such creatures of fragile beauty do not live within the confines of the ghetto.

Style and Themes in "The Butterfly"

"The Butterfly" was written by Pavel Friedmann, a young man who was an inmate of Terezin concentration camp. Friedmann was not a professional poet, and his tragic death at Auschwitz two years after the writing of his famous poem meant that he would never have the chance to develop his gift for poetry or anything else. "The Butterfly" remains significant today not as part of the collection of a major poet but for the insight it gives into the mind of a young person suffering the harsh cruelties of life in a concentration camp, a person who could still find some elements of beauty in that life.

The brilliant yellow butterfly Friedmann describes—"such, such a yellow / Is carried lightly 'way up high"—symbolizes a fragile freedom. A butterfly's wings are delicate, but they are powerful enough to give it flight. The freedom possessed by butterflies, birds, and other wild animals must have filled concentration camp victims both with pleasure and with sorrow over their lost freedom. The butterfly also represents hope. While many inmates of Terezin may have arrived with some hope that they could be safe there, that hope soon evaporated when they learned of the horrible living conditions and of the regular transports carrying people from Terezin to such death camps as Auschwitz. The butterfly Friedmann describes in his poem, like the hope some inmates felt, has left Terezin. It has "kiss[ed] the world good-bye," and Friedmann explains that he "never saw another butterfly."

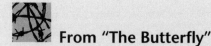

From "The Butterfly"

The last, the very last,
So richly, brightly, dazzlingly yellow.
   Perhaps if the sun's tears would sing
    against a white stone....
Such, such a yellow
Is carried lightly 'way up high.
It went away I'm sure because it wished to
   kiss the world good-bye.
For seven weeks I've lived in here,
Penned up inside this ghetto.
But I have found what I love here.
The dandelions call to me
And the white chestnut branches in the
   court.
Only I never saw another butterfly.
That butterfly was the last one.
Butterflies don't live in here,
   In the ghetto.

Research and Activity Ideas

1) Why do you think butterflies, as Pavel Friedmann says in his poem, "don't live in here, in the ghetto"?

2) Imagine that you have been taken from your home and placed in a concentration camp. Think about what you would miss about your house or neighborhood, and think about what would most frighten you or upset you about life in the concentration camp. Write a poem or draw a picture expressing your feelings.

3) Compare Pavel Friedmann's "The Butterfly" with another poem from *I Never Saw Another Butterfly:* "On a Sunny

Evening," an anonymous poem "written by the children in Barracks L318 and L417." What themes do both poems share, and how are these themes expressed?

4) Research the Terezin concentration camp, studying the events surrounding the visit of the International Red Cross in 1944. How do you think the inmates felt when they heard the Red Cross would be visiting? How is it possible that the Red Cross only saw what the Nazis wanted them to see instead of seeing the truth about how inmates lived in Terezin?

Where to Learn More About …

Friedl Dicker-Brandeis

Rubin, Susan Goldman. *Fireflies in the Dark: The Story of Friedl Dicker-Brandeis and the Children of Terezin.* New York: Holiday House, 2000.

Terezin Concentration Camp

"1944: Desperate Acts." *The Holocaust Chronicle.* http://www.holocaustchronicle.org/staticpages/536.html (accessed on December 18, 2002).

Auerbacher, Inge. *I Am a Star: Child of the Holocaust.* New York: Prentice-Hall, 1986.

Troller, Norbert. *Theresienstadt: Hitler's Gift to the Jews.* Translated by Susan E. Cernyak-Spatz. Chapel Hill: The University of North Carolina Press, 1991.

Volavková, Hana, ed. *I Never Saw Another Butterfly: Children's Drawings and Poems from Terezin Concentration Camp 1942–1944.* New York: Schocken Books, 1993.

"Leaving You"

Written by Lily Brett

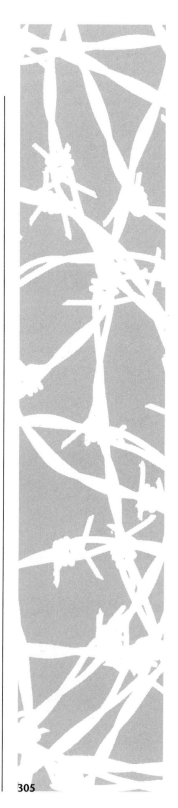

For survivors of the Holocaust, the suffering did not vanish at war's end. During World War II (1939–45), German dictator Adolf Hitler (1889–1945) and his Nazi troops had managed to systematically destroy two-thirds of Europe's Jewish population, killing nearly six million Jews and several million others. Many survivors endured ongoing grief over the loss of loved ones and feelings of guilt for having survived when so many perished. For many, the effects of the Holocaust continued into the next generation; the children of survivors grew up in households marked by the tragedy. While their experiences vary widely, many children of survivors have been strongly affected by their parents' trauma. Poet and novelist Lily Brett, born in Germany to Holocaust survivors, has written extensively about the Holocaust and about its effect on her life and her family. In her poem "Leaving You," published in her 1990 collection *After the War: Poems,* Brett explores her relationship with her mother. She expresses the difficulty she has had separating her own life from her mother's nightmarish experiences as a survivor of the Holocaust.

Lily Brett, author of the poem "Leaving You."
Reproduced by permission of Mr. Jerry Bauer.

Biography of Poet Lily Brett

Lily Brett was born in Germany in 1946, just a short time after the end of World War II. Her parents, Max and Rose, were refugees when Lily was born, living in a displaced persons camp. Such camps had been set up in Germany, Poland, and elsewhere in Europe to temporarily house Jews and other victims of Nazi persecution who could not return to their former homes. During the early years of the war, Brett's parents had lived in the Jewish ghetto in the city of Lodz, Poland. In most of the nations invaded by Nazi Germany, the Jews had been forced to live in prisonlike ghettos, small, walled-in neighborhoods where problems like disease, overcrowding, and hunger were widespread. Eventually, all residents of the ghettos were transported to concentration camps, large Nazi-run prisons where inmates were forced to perform slave labor, or to death camps, prisons that were built specifically to murder large numbers of people. Brett's parents were sent to Auschwitz-Birkenau, the infamous concentration and death camp complex. Brett's mother also spent some time imprisoned at Stutthof (sometimes spelled Stuthof), a concentration and death camp in what is now northern Poland.

Forced to be apart during the latter part of the war, Brett's parents found each other six months after the war ended. In 1948, two years after Lily was born, the family immigrated to Australia. Brett spent much of her life there. As a young adult, she worked as a music journalist, traveling to many distant countries and interviewing such prominent musicians as Jimi Hendrix, the Doors, and the Rolling Stones. After her first marriage ended, she met and married David Rankin, an Australian artist. Together they had two children, a son and a daughter; Rankin also has a daughter from a previous relationship. Rankin encouraged Brett to write about her feelings and experiences as the child of Holocaust sur-

January 27, 1945: Auschwitz-Birkenau is liberated by the army of the Soviet Union.

May 8, 1945: V-E Day; World War II ends in Europe.

May 9, 1945: Stutthof concentration camp is liberated by the Soviet army.

1946: Lily Brett is born in a displaced persons camp in Germany.

1948: Brett and her parents immigrate to Australia.

1986: Brett publishes her first volume of poetry, *The Auschwitz Poems.*

1990: Brett's collection of poems, *After the War: Poems,* which includes "Leaving You," is published.

vivors, and in 1986—the year her mother died—she published her first collection of poems, titled *The Auschwitz Poems*. This volume earned her an important Australian literary prize, the Victorian Premier's Award for poetry, in 1987.

Brett went on to publish other collections of poems, including *After the War: Poems* and *In Her Strapless Dresses* (1994) as well as novels and collections of short stories and essays. Her 1991 volume of short stories, *What God Wants,* features sixteen stories about adult children of Holocaust survivors. These stories, all set in Melbourne, Australia, can be read as individual stories or as loosely connected tales about a community of people bound together by their shared backgrounds. While Brett explores her characters' painful family histories, her stories are not without humor and optimism.

Brett's novels *Just Like That* (1994) and *Too Many Men* (1999) both contain details derived from her own life. *Just Like That* tells the story of Esther Zipler, a middle-aged woman whose parents are Holocaust survivors. Esther goes through life plagued by worries about her parents, her children, and her friends. Her outwardly ordinary, everyday life is colored by her internal turmoil over her parents' painful past. Reviewers have noted that Brett gracefully blends humor and sorrow, sketching a full and realistic portrait of Esther's life.

This novel earned Brett the 1995 New South Wales Premier's Award for fiction. *Too Many Men* also features a protagonist whose parents survived the Holocaust. In this work, Ruth Rothwax, a successful businesswoman living in New York, travels to Poland with her father to see firsthand the places where her parents lived and, during the war, suffered. (Brett took a similar trip with her father, visiting the sites of the Lodz ghetto and Auschwitz.)

Brett's collections of essays include *In Full View* (1997) and *New York* (2001). *In Full View* contains Brett's views on a variety of topics, including her lifelong concerns with weight and self-image and the connection these subjects have with her history as a child of Holocaust survivors. In *New York* Brett shares her observations on the many sides of life in her adopted city (she and her husband moved to Manhattan in the late 1980s or early 1990s). While she has lived in New York for many years, Brett continues to be best known in Australia, where all of her works have been originally published.

Historical Background of "Leaving You"

Adolf Hitler, head of the Nazi Party, became the leader of Germany in 1933. A magnetic public speaker, he rose to power in large part by promising to rebuild a wounded nation. Germany had suffered high unemployment, widespread poverty, and wounded pride in the years following its defeat in World War I (1914–18). Hitler made rousing speeches about the superiority of the German people and about his plans to reconstruct the nation. Part of that plan involved finding people to blame for Germany's problems, and Hitler's primary target was the Jewish people. While Jews made up only about 1 percent of Germany's population, Hitler claimed they were responsible for Germany's loss in World War I and the problems the country had suffered since then. Once he became Germany's dictator, Hitler immediately began translating his violent hatred of Jews into government policy; over a period of years, the German government passed numerous laws designed to separate the Jews from the rest of the population and to deprive them of many basic rights. Jews were only allowed to live in certain areas, they had to attend Jewish schools, they could not work in many professions, and

they could not own homes or businesses. Many Jews suffered random beatings on the street, and thousands were arrested for no reason other than their religion and sent to prisons known as concentration camps.

Throughout the mid-1930s, the goal of the Nazi policies toward Jews had been to encourage, and finally to force, Jews to leave Germany. By the beginning of the 1940s, however, as Germany had begun to conquer other European nations in its bid for world domination, the Nazi leadership devised a far more sinister plan. Hitler and the Nazi Party formulated what they called the Final Solution, a plan to systematically murder the Jews of Europe, in response to what was called the "Jewish problem."

Soon after Germany invaded Poland in September 1939—an invasion that sparked the beginning of World War II—the Jews of that conquered nation had been forced to relocate into ghettos, small neighborhoods surrounded by barbed-wire fences and concrete walls where the residents

Soon after Germany's invasion of Poland, all Polish Jews were forced to relocate into ghettos, small neighborhoods surrounded by barbed-wire fences and concrete walls. Whole families had to pack up and take with them only what they could carry.

Reproduced by permission of the Kobal Collection.

were kept like prisoners. Some two million Jews lived in the part of Poland controlled by Germany (the Soviet Union controlled the eastern regions), with a total of 600,000 crammed into the two largest ghettos, those located in Warsaw and Lodz. (The Lodz ghetto was home for many years to poet Lily Brett's parents.) Conditions in the ghettos included severe overcrowding, widespread disease, a lack of heating, and insufficient food, leading to the deaths of thousands of Jews. At first the Jews of Poland and other German-occupied nations were imprisoned in ghettos, and later in concentration camps, as a temporary measure while Hitler and the Nazi leadership decided what to do with them. One plan, known as the Madagascar Plan, involved deporting all the Jews of Europe to Madagascar, an island off the southeast coast of Africa. When it became clear that such plans could not work, the Final Solution came into being.

The Final Solution

Knowing that they could force the imprisoned Jews to work as slave laborers, the Nazis selected the stronger and healthier prisoners to work in concentration camps and labor camps. Those considered weakest—the elderly, small children, and the sick or disabled—were sent directly to death camps, called extermination centers. Death camps were built for the sole purpose of efficiently killing large numbers of prisoners on a daily basis. The largest and deadliest of the camps was Auschwitz, also known as Auschwitz-Birkenau, located in southern Poland. Auschwitz consisted of several camps; the main camp, Auschwitz I, was built as a concentration camp, while Auschwitz II, or Birkenau, was designed to be a killing center. The inmates of camps like Auschwitz were forced to work past the point of exhaustion. They were fed very little; their diets usually consisted of stale bread, a coffee-like beverage, and flavored water that vaguely resembled soup. Diseases raged through the camps, killing tens of thousands. And the slightest misstep could result in a brutal beating or torture by the camp guards. By the end of the war, more than 1.5 million people had been murdered at Auschwitz-Birkenau. The vast majority were Jews, but the Nazis also killed non-Jewish Poles, political prisoners, communists, homosexuals, members of the Roma tribes known as Gypsies, and others.

Brett's parents were sent from the Lodz ghetto to Auschwitz, where they were immediately separated. At one point, Brett's mother went to Stutthof, a smaller but no less brutal camp in northern Poland. In the final months of the war, Allied forces including the United States and the Soviet Union drove back the German army and liberated, or freed, the inmates of concentration camps. But the suffering of the prisoners was far from over. Half-starved and worn down from having been treated like animals by the Nazi guards, former concentration camp inmates also had to cope with the loss of family members who had not survived. Furthermore, most Jews did not have the option of going home and returning to the communities in which they had lived before the war. The Nazis' Final Solution had succeeded not only in murdering millions of people, but also in wiping out entire communities and all traces of Jewish culture. Anti-Semitism, or feelings of hatred toward Jews, was still very strong in many places in Eastern Europe. Even if they did still have homes to go back to, many Jews had no desire to return to the towns they had lived in, still feeling the shock of betrayal that their non-Jewish neighbors had turned against them or done little to help them avoid the Nazis' brutal treatment.

After the war

In countries formerly occupied by Germany, the British, American, and French armed forces established displaced persons (DP) camps for the thousands of refugees who had nowhere else to go and who needed assistance in rebuilding their lives. While the intentions behind such camps were positive, the conditions in some DP camps were little better than they had been in the concentration camps. In fact, some DP camps were even set up in former concentration camps, with refugees living in the same barracks where they had lived as prisoners and even wearing the same uniforms. Because the Allied forces had not accurately predicted the number of refugees that would need assistance, necessities like food, housing, and clothing were in short supply. A situation that was initially intended to be temporary stretched on for years as refugees struggled to gain admittance into nations that wished to limit the intake of immigrants, including the United States and British-controlled Palestine.

Displaced Persons Camps

The United Nations, recognizing that World War II would produce massive numbers of refugees, Jewish and otherwise, formed the United Nations Relief and Rehabilitation Administration (UNRRA) in 1943. Once the war ended, the UNRRA and the Allied armies would share responsibility for running the displaced person (DP) camps. The camps would provide food, shelter, assistance in finding new places for the refugees to live, and help in locating missing relatives. During the planning stages, the UNRRA and the Allied armies intended for the DP camps to be temporary homes for refugees. In reality, many DPs lived in the camps for years, with the last DP camp staying in operation until 1953.

The first problems of the DP camps arose soon after the war ended. The number of refugees that flooded the camps in the spring of 1945 far exceeded what the UNRRA had expected. Some 250,000 Jewish refugees were housed in DP camps as well as several hundred thousand non-Jews who had lost their homes during the war. The camps had too little money, too few workers, and insufficient space to accommodate the DPs. As a result, living conditions in the camps were poor, with some camps even using barracks of former concentration camps to house the DPs.

Harry S. Truman, the President of the United States, sent people to investi-

In spite of the poor conditions and rootlessness of their existence in the displaced persons camps, some refugees—eager to leave behind the horrors of the Holocaust and to begin new lives—had children during this time. Gradually, the refugees, like Brett and her parents, acquired the necessary papers and immigrated to other nations. In their adopted countries, they struggled to adapt to a new culture, a new language, and in many cases, a society that regarded them with suspicion and uncertainty. Survivors of the Holocaust rarely experienced a "happily-ever-after" feeling upon being freed from their Nazi captors; most tried for many years, often for the rest of their lives, to recover from the grief and humiliation they had suffered in the Nazi camps. For many survivors, rebuilding their lives involved having children, raising a Jewish family that would help compensate for the millions killed during the Holocaust. The children of survivors, growing up in households forever marked by the hor-

gate the living conditions in the DP camps during the summer of 1945. Led by Earl G. Harrison, the observers visited a number of camps in the American zone (the British- and French-operated camps in the zones that they controlled). Appalled by the conditions there, the Harrison commission strongly recommended a number of improvements in the way the camps were run. Conditions in the American-run camps soon improved, with special consideration given to the Jewish DPs because of the suffering they had endured during the war.

Even with the improvements, life in the camps continued to be difficult and frustrating. Many DPs still had trouble tracking down family members, and the immigration restrictions in most countries around the world complicated attempts to immigrate. In the United States and other countries, prejudices against Jews in particular and Eastern Europeans in general contributed to a reluctance to expand immigration quotas, or limits.

After the establishment of the state of Israel in 1948, the refugee crisis eased considerably because Israel allowed for unlimited Jewish immigration. Gradually, immigration restrictions loosened in the United States, Britain, and other nations, and by the early 1950s, most of Europe's DPs had found new homes.

rors of the Holocaust, dealt with a unique set of problems stemming from their parents' experiences.

Subject Matter of "Leaving You"

In Lily Brett's poem "Leaving You," the speaker addresses her mother, a survivor of the Holocaust. (As Brett's own mother experienced the events described in the poem and Brett often writes about her own life, the reader presumes the author is speaking in her own voice.) "Leaving You" expresses a child's difficulty in leading a life independent of her mother's harrowing experiences during the Holocaust. "It has taken me / a long time to know / that it was your war / not mine," begins the poem. Brett's experience as the child of Holocaust survivors seems similar in many ways to the experiences of others in the so-called second generation, the people who have grown up with survivor parents.

Displaced persons camp on the island of Cyprus where Holocaust survivors went after losing their homes during the war. At these camps they tried to locate lost family members and friends. *Reproduced by permission of AP/World Wide Photos.*

Many people who survived the daily cruelty and inhumanity of the Nazi guards in the ghettos and concentration camps struggled to regain a sense of their own value. Trying to rebuild their lives after the end of World War II, they experienced emotional difficulties: nightmares, depression, and severe anxiety. Children who grew up with survivor parents often felt the effects of their parents' emotional lives. Survivor parents were somehow "different" from other kids' parents: they seemed to always suffer from deep and painful emotional scars; they were frequently more protective of their children; and they were often more suspicious of other people, continually expecting to encounter anti-Semitism and mistreatment. Many children of survivors have written that as a result of such unique circumstances, they grew up feeling pressure to make up for their parents' horrific experiences. In her book *Children of the Holocaust,* Helen Epstein writes of her feelings as a child of survivors: "I was their first companion, a new leaf, and I knew this leaf had to be pure life. This leaf was as different from death as good was from evil and the present from the past."

As they were growing up, the children of survivors often felt a strong sense of identification with the lives their parents led during the Holocaust, a concept Brett explores in "Leaving You." Epstein writes of survivors' children as "a group of people who...were possessed by a history they had never lived." Judith S. Kestenberg writes, in *Generations of the Holocaust,* of the intense need among the second generation "to discover, to re-enact, or to live the parents' past.... These children feel they have a mission to live in the past and to change it so that their parents' humiliation, disgrace, and guilt can be converted into victory over the oppressors." Many children of survivors have expressed the notion that if they could have been with their parents in the camps or ghettos, they could have protected or comforted them. In "Leaving You," the poet details events of her mother's experience; these events seemed so real to the narrator that she thought at times that she could feel exactly like someone who had actually experienced them. As an adult, the narrator has come to terms with the fact that while she feels the impact of her mother's suffering, she was not actually at Auschwitz, she did not live in the Lodz ghetto, and she was not a prisoner at Stutthof.

In her poem, Brett lists several details that were central to the lives of Holocaust survivors: the windowless cattle cars used to transport Jews to the Nazi camps; the processes during which the Nazis would decide who was to be deported from the ghetto to the camps, or which concentration camp prisoners were to be sent to their deaths; and the ration cards and

From "Leaving You"

It has taken me
a long time to know
that it was your war
not mine

that I wasn't
in Auschwitz
myself

that I have never
seen
the Lodz Ghetto

or Stuthof
or a cattle wagon
or a selection

I thought
I knew
Nazis...

and what
it felt like
to fill your lungs

with
smoke
from flesh

to
live
with death

I have had
trouble
Mother
leaving you.

work permits that every ghetto inmate had to possess in order to live. The narrator explains that she spent much of her life thinking that she knew exactly what it had been like to live in the camps—to sleep on the straw mattresses, to see people around her dying every day, "to live with death." In the final stanza, however, she explains that she finally did, after some difficulty, separate her own life from that of her mother's.

Style and Themes in "Leaving You"

Lily Brett has written "Leaving You" in a spare, plain style. Each stanza is brief—the longest is four lines, sixteen words—and the language is clear and straightforward. Brett does not use elaborate metaphors or complicated symbols to convey her meaning; instead, her poem reads almost like conversational speech. Brett's seemingly simple language, however, suggests powerful emotions. The brief lines, many containing only one or two words, mimic the way people talk when they are having great difficulty expressing themselves because the words are painful to the speaker or perhaps to the listener. Such short lines also encourage readers to examine each word carefully. For example, the second-to-last stanza, consisting only of the words "to / live / with death," highlights the paradox (something contrary to common sense) of the concentration camps: because of their closeness to death inmates could hardly have been described as living in the fullest sense of the word.

Like many who have written about the Holocaust, Brett has chosen to describe overwhelming events in a plain-spoken way, perhaps in an attempt to help herself and others understand the incomprehensible. But while the poem's stanzas are brief and the language bare, the images of "Leaving You" are powerful, indicating that sometimes the slight suggestion of an image can be more affecting than a lengthy descriptive passage. In the poem, the image of "bodies gnawed by rats," for example, conveys in just a few words the fullness of the horrors experienced by concentration camp inmates. And Brett, imagining "what / it felt like / to fill your lungs / with / smoke / from flesh," chillingly summarizes life in a death camp: seeing the smoke and smelling the odors coming from the crematoria, the furnaces in which the bodies of prisoners were burned to ash.

The main theme of "Leaving You" is the difficulty Brett has had separating her own emotions and experiences from those of her mother. She admits in the final stanza, "I have had / trouble / Mother / leaving you." Brett exhibits a degree of empathy, or understanding of another's feelings, that may be unusual for most people but is quite common among the children of Holocaust survivors. With this poem, however, Brett suggests her desire to break free from the sense that she too experienced the nightmare of the Holocaust. At the same time she acknowledges that even the child of a survivor who has heard countless stories told in great detail cannot truly know what another person experienced. While she can recite the events of her mother's life during the Holocaust, and while she can imagine the misery her mother must have felt, Brett can never actually feel what it was like to live in a Nazi camp. Perhaps her difficulty in "leaving" her mother refers to a painful realization that she cannot erase her mother's painful memories by adopting them as her own.

The Lodz ghetto, where author Lily Brett's mother lived for a time, was a brutal and poverty-stricken place where deportations to concentration camps were frequent. *Reproduced by permission of the United States Holocaust Memorial Museum.*

Research and Activity Ideas

1) Examine the title of Lily Brett's poem "Leaving You." Do you think Brett meant it to be read literally, indicating an actual departure from her mother—perhaps referring to her mother's death in 1986? Or is the title meant to represent a symbolic departure as Brett recognizes her independence from her mother?

2) Read some examples of poetry or other writings by the children of Holocaust survivors. Do you see any common themes among them? If so, what are those themes? Does "Leaving You" express emotions that are found among other writings by the second generation?

3) Imagine that you are the child of parents who have undergone difficult and traumatic experiences, whether those of the Holocaust or another modern-day tragedy. Write a poem expressing how you might feel, what your relationship with your parents would be like, and how such a childhood would shape your personality.

Where to Learn More About ...

Lily Brett and "Leaving You"

Brett, Lily. *After the War: Poems*. Melbourne: Melbourne University Press, 1990.

"Field of Power: An Interview with Lily Brett." *Between the Lines*. http://www.thei.aust.com/books97/btlinlily.html (accessed on December 18, 2002).

Schiff, Hilda, ed. *Holocaust Poetry*. New York: St. Martin's Press, 1995.

Children of Holocaust Survivors

Bergmann, Martin S., and Milton E. Jucovy, eds. *Generations of the Holocaust*. New York: Basic Books, 1982.

Epstein, Helen. *Children of the Holocaust: Conversations with Sons and Daughters of Survivors*. New York: Penguin Books, 1979.

Florsheim, Stewart J. *Ghosts of the Holocaust: An Anthology of Poetry by the Second Generation*. Detroit, MI: Wayne State University Press, 1989.

Displaced Persons and the Postwar Refugee Crisis

"Jewish Displaced Persons." *Simon Wiesenthal Center Museum of Tolerance Online*. http://motlc.wiesenthal.org/pages/t018/t01826.html (accessed on November 25, 2002).

The Long Way Home [videorecording]. Moriah Films of the Simon Wiesenthal Center and Seventh Art Releasing, 1997.

"O the Chimneys"

Written by Nelly Sachs

From Adolf Hitler's (1889–1945) earliest days as a public figure, he made no secret of his violent hatred of the Jewish people and his belief that Jews were the enemies of Germany. After he became leader of Germany in 1933, Hitler instituted many laws that restricted Jews' rights, and he encouraged an atmosphere in which acts of hostility and brutality against the Jews became more and more common. Hitler and his followers in the Nazi Party initially intended to make conditions for the Jews so unacceptable that they would be compelled to leave Germany. At some point in the early 1940s, however, the official policy changed from intimidation to extermination. At that time, Hitler and the Nazi leadership devised the Final Solution, a plan to destroy the Jewish population of Europe. They built sophisticated, efficient killing facilities designed to murder large numbers of people each day, usually with the aid of poisonous gas. The bodies were often disposed of in large ovens called crematoria. Nelly Sachs, a German-born Jewish poet who fled Nazi Germany in 1940, wrote about the Final Solution in her poem "O the Chimneys." The poem is a lament for the dead and a pondering of the enormous inhumanity of Hitler's regime.

Nelly Sachs, author of the poem "O the Chimneys."
Reproduced by permission of Corbis Corporation.

Biography of Poet Nelly Sachs

Born December 10, 1891, and raised in Berlin, Germany, Nelly Sachs grew up in a privileged household, the only child of William and Margarethe Karger Sachs. She began writing poetry at age seventeen, but she did not publish her first work—a collection of tales and legends from the Middle Ages—until she was thirty years old, in 1921. Her pre-World War II writings, while more light-hearted than her postwar work, reflect an interest in religious mysticism, a quest for spiritual knowledge, that remained a significant aspect of her poetry throughout her entire life.

As a teenager Sachs began writing letters to Selma Lagerlöf, a Swedish novelist whose works she admired. Their correspondence lasted for many years, and as the circumstances for Jews in Germany worsened throughout the 1930s, Sachs's friendship with Lagerlöf proved invaluable. With the help of the Swedish writer, Sachs and her widowed mother obtained visas to move to Sweden in 1940, an impressive feat at a time when emigration from Germany was extremely difficult for Jews. By the time they arrived, the ailing Lagerlöf had died. But Sachs and her mother made Sweden their new home, both remaining there until their deaths. Sachs quickly learned the Swedish language and began earning a living translating Swedish works into German. She also continued to write her own poetry during this time. As World War II progressed, and as the facts about the Nazis' treatment of Jews in concentration camps and death camps became clear, Sachs became increasingly preoccupied by the suffering of her fellow Jews left behind in Germany. Her grief and horror over the events of the Holocaust affected her deeply, and writing poetry about the subject became a necessary emotional release for her.

While Sachs remained safe in Sweden throughout the Holocaust, her imagination—and a sense of guilt for escaping

Chronology of Events Relating to "O the Chimneys"

September 10, 1891: Nelly Sachs is born in Berlin, Germany.

January 30, 1933: Adolf Hitler becomes leader of Germany.

November 9–10, 1938: Widespread riots against Jews, in an event known as *Kristallnacht,* erupt throughout Germany and Austria.

September 1, 1939: Germany invades Poland, sparking the beginning of World War II.

Summer 1940: Sachs and her mother leave Germany, immigrating to Sweden.

Summer 1941: Hitler and his top aides begin to plan the Final Solution—the murder of all European Jews.

December 8, 1941: Chelmno, the first death camp, begins operations.

January 20, 1942: The Wannsee Conference takes place, at which the details of the Final Solution are formally laid out for government officials.

1966: Sachs wins the Nobel Prize in literature for her poetry and plays.

May 12, 1970: Sachs dies in Stockholm, Sweden.

what so many loved ones had to endure—made her feel as though she too had experienced a Nazi camp. Many of her poems, including one of her best known, "O the Chimneys," express anguish and remorse over the tragic loss of millions of lives. She also wrote several plays, including the acclaimed *Eli: A Mystery Play of the Sufferings of Israel,* a verse play that tells of the murder by Nazi troops of an eight-year-old Polish boy. Sachs's later works increasingly reflected her interest in Jewish mysticism, a field devoted to unlocking riddles about spirituality and the nature of reality. Many of her poems are rich with symbolism and metaphor; she wrote a number of works using the butterfly as a symbol for metamorphosis, or change, and flight. Her poems also frequently explore images of dust, ashes, and smoke.

By the late 1950s, after the publication of two important collections, *Und niemand weiss weiter* ("And No One Knows How to Go On," 1957) and *Flucht und Verwandlung* ("Flight and Metamorphosis," 1959), Sachs began to receive increased worldwide attention. She earned a number of important literary prizes, including the 1966 Nobel Prize in literature, which she shared with Israeli writer S. Y. Agnon. Two collections of her major works have been published in English: *O the Chimneys: Selected Poems, Including "Eli," a Verse Play* (1967) and *The Seeker and Other Poems* (1970). Sachs died of cancer in Stockholm, Sweden, on May 12, 1970.

Historical Background of "O the Chimneys"

Anti-Semitism, or prejudice toward Jews, had existed in Germany, and throughout Europe, for centuries, and Jews had been persecuted, harassed, and exiled before the rise of Adolf Hitler (1889–1945) and the Nazi Party in 1930s Germany. But the treatment of the Jewish people, and many other so-called enemies of the state, during Hitler's twelve years of leadership reached a horrifying new level of brutality and inhumanity. Hitler, and many of his followers, blamed the Jews for Germany's defeat in World War I (1914–18) and for its economic woes in the years after that war. Among the lies and misconceptions spread by Hitler was a claim that the Jewish people had devised an international conspiracy to control the world. In 1929 came the crushing poverty of the worldwide Great Depression. Many Germans who suffered the effects of widespread unemployment and the German currency's plummeting value sought a scapegoat, a person or group to bear the blame for their troubles. Many began to agree with Hitler's view that the Jewish people were at fault.

Hitler became leader of Germany in January 1933. Within months he had increased his powers enormously, becoming the dictator of Germany and assigning to himself the title of Führer, or leader, of the Third Reich (*reich* means "empire," a word that suggests Hitler's plan to conquer new territories and expand Germany's boundaries). To accomplish his vast goals of rebuilding German society, revitalizing the military, and seizing control of surrounding nations, Hitler felt the need to control every aspect of his citizens' lives. He controlled the media, including radio, books, and newspapers, as well as schools, clubs, private organizations, religious institutions, and businesses. Germans were bombarded with signs, posters, and literature describing the evils of Judaism and the ways in which Jews were poisoning German society. Encouraging neighbors to spy on neighbors and children to spy on parents and teachers, Hitler established an atmosphere in which support of the Nazi Party was the safest option. Those who dared to oppose or criticize Hitler were punished swiftly and severely.

The Jews of Germany received harsh treatment not because of political opposition or criminal activity, but simply because they were Jewish. Hitler sought to strengthen Germany by promoting the idea of a "master race" known as the Aryan race. Aryans, white Christians with German heritage, were said by Hitler to be superior to all other peoples of the world. Rather than view the Jewish people as a religious and cultural group, Hitler classified them as a race—and an inferior one at that. Within months of becoming Germany's leader, he began enacting laws to limit Jewish participation in German society and to separate Jews from their fellow Germans. Implemented over the next several years, these laws deprived Jews of their citizenship, made it illegal for them to marry non-Jews, forbade them from working in certain professions, and forced them to attend all-Jewish schools. The German government also seized the homes, businesses, and valuable property of Jews and required them to be identified as Jews in their passports. Throughout this period, Hitler intended to make life so unpleasant for Jews in Germany that they would leave the country, and never return. Many thousands did leave, but others could not afford to or chose to remain in their native land, hoping that the misery would soon end.

In November 1938 Jews throughout Germany and German-controlled Austria became the targets of violent, destructive riots that later came to be called *Kristallnacht,* or the "Night of Broken Glass". Thousands of homes, businesses, and synagogues were destroyed. Hundreds of Jews were beaten, dozens were murdered, and tens of thousands were arrested and sent to concentration camps. Less than a year later, on September 1, 1939, Germany invaded Poland. Two days later, Great Britain and France declared war on Germany, and World War II had begun. Upon invading Poland, Germany immediately established the same anti-Jewish decrees that had been put into place over the previous six years in Germany. In addition, Polish Jews were forced to live in ghettos,

The Final Solution

Although Adolf Hitler had long discussed a "final solution" to the question of how to rid Germany and other European nations of Jews, it was not until sometime in 1941 that the Final Solution took shape as a plan to systematically murder every Jew in Europe. Forcing Jews to leave German-controlled countries—and in the meantime imprisoning them in ghettos and concentration camps—proved increasingly impractical as Germany conquered more and more nations, bringing ever-growing populations of Jews under its control.

Hitler had previously approved the practice of getting rid of unwanted communities through government-sponsored murder. Beginning in 1939 Nazi Germany had conducted what is known as the Euthanasia program, an effort to "purify" the German "master race," white Christians that Hitler referred to as Aryans. Under this policy, tens of thousands of people—primarily those suffering from inherited diseases, or those with physical or mental disabilities—were killed by lethal injection or poisonous gas. In addition, when Hitler invaded Poland in September 1939, he planned to destroy Polish culture and patriotism in part by murdering prominent Polish citizens. Such policies paved the way for Hitler to devise a similar plan, although on a much larger scale, for the Jews of Europe.

As German troops progressed in the invasion of the Soviet Union in the summer of 1941, mobile killing squads, called *Einsatzgruppen,* followed behind, murdering many thousands of Jews and other "undesirables" by shooting them and small neighborhoods that were surrounded by walls and barbed-wire fences. From the ghettos, hundreds of thousands of Jews were gradually deported to concentration camps, large Nazi-run prisons where prisoners were treated like animals and forced to perform hard labor. In many nations invaded by Germany, particularly in central and eastern Europe, the treatment of Jews followed the same pattern: forcible relocation to ghettos followed by deportation to Nazi camps in Poland and elsewhere.

The leadership of the Nazi Party sought a solution to what they termed the "Jewish question": what to do with the Jews that came under German control as the Third Reich expanded to include one country after another. After various plans of relocating the entire Jewish population fell through,

burying the bodies in large pits. Meanwhile, plans were underway in Poland to construct killing centers, or death camps, that would employ factory-like technical precision to kill huge numbers of Jews on a daily basis. The primary method of killing at the death camps was poisonous gas. Prisoners were herded into buildings designed to look like public showers, and once the doors were sealed, gases such as Zyklon B were piped in, suffocating all inside in a matter of minutes.

In January 1942, at the Wannsee Conference, the Final Solution was explained to various German government officials, all of whom readily accepted the goal of murdering every Jewish man, woman, and child in Europe. From then on the mass murder of Jews was carried out with alarming efficiency. In addition to the construction of the death camps Belzec, Sobibor, Chelmno, and Treblinka, several existing concentration camps, such as Auschwitz and Majdanek, were expanded to include gas chambers, crematoria (large ovens used for burning dead bodies), and other such equipment. Before they were stopped by the advancing Allied troops toward the end of World War II (1939–45), the Nazis murdered approximately 3.5 million Jews and tens of thousands of non-Jews in the death camps. Several million additional civilians died from starvation, disease, execution by gunfire, and other means throughout the Holocaust, with a total of some 6 million Jews and approximately 5 million non-Jews being killed by the Nazis from the late 1930s through 1945.

Hitler and his advisors began thinking along different lines. The Final Solution, as it was known, began to be discussed as a plan for murdering millions of European Jews rather than relocating them. By the fall of 1941, a method of mass murder had been developed: the Nazis began constructing killing centers, called extermination camps, throughout Poland. In some cases, new facilities were constructed solely for the purpose of large-scale murder. In other cases, existing concentration camps were outfitted with the equipment to conduct mass exterminations. The most commonly used method to kill Jews and other victims in such camps was poisonous gas. The bodies were then burned, usually in large ovens called crematoria.

The Nazi death camps were run in an extremely efficient manner; several million Jews and numerous non-Jews were murdered at such camps between late 1941 and late 1944. Millions more, both Jewish and non-Jewish, died in other camps and of other means during the Holocaust. In all, approximately six million Jews were killed by the Nazis. In other words, two out of every three Jews in prewar Europe were murdered between 1939 and 1945.

Subject Matter of "O the Chimneys"

In "O the Chimneys," perhaps her most famous poem, Nelly Sachs addresses the devastation of European Jews in the Nazi death camps. The poem is preceded by an epigraph, a quote from the biblical Book of Job: "And though after my skin worms destroy this body, yet in my flesh shall I see God" (Job, 19:26). In the Book of Job, Job is a good, faithful man who endures many trials that test his devotion to God. The verse Sachs chose to precede her poem reveals that, in spite of what he feels are unfair punishments from God, Job remains steadfast in his belief that God does exist and will appear before him.

In the first stanza of "O the Chimneys," Sachs repeats the title of the poem, focusing on the chimneys of the crematoria where the Nazis burned their victims' bodies. She describes these ovens as "ingeniously devised," providing a chilling reminder of the scientific precision the Nazis used to design their killing machines. She further describes the ovens as "habitations [dwellings] of death," a seemingly contradictory phrase depicting the crematoria as places where death lives. Sachs envisions the smoke that rises from these chimneys as "Israel's body," indicating that the Nazis destroyed more than just individuals: they devastated the Jewish people. She imagines the chimney smoke rising through the atmosphere and being embraced by a star that then turns black, later questioning "Or was it a ray of sun?"

In the second stanza, Sachs reveals a new interpretation of the crematoria chimneys. She describes the chimneys as passageways to freedom, indicating a view of death as a release from suffering and as a pathway for the righteous to be united with God. Sachs again refers to figures from the Bible, depicting the smoke in the chimneys as "Jeremiah and Job's dust." Jeremiah, an Old Testament prophet, predicted a major

Overview of the dozens of chimneys at Auschwitz-Birkenau, the largest Nazi concentration and extermination camp in operation during World War II. *Reproduced by permission of Corbis Corporation.*

disaster for the Jewish people in biblical times; the mention of Jeremiah seems to serve as a reminder of the long history of suffering endured by the Jewish people. In this stanza Sachs again wonders about those who built the crematoria, asking "Who devised you and laid stone upon stone / The road for refugees of smoke?" In this passage, where the chimneys are depicted as "freedomways," Sachs suggests a transformation: despite the evil intentions of those who constructed them, the machines of death can also be viewed as a trail to a higher level of existence.

The third stanza returns to a description of the ovens as "habitations of death" rather than as passages to freedom. Sachs depicts these habitations as "invitingly appointed," or constructed in a welcoming way, "For the host who used to be a guest." The ovens are clearly not welcoming to the victims; the only entity that would find such constructions inviting is death itself. In referring to death as the "host," Sachs gives it a human form and personal qualities, a technique known as

Ovens like this one from the Bergen-Belsen concentration camp were used by the Nazis to dispose of the bodies of millions of Jews. *Reproduced by permission of the United States Holocaust Memorial Museum.*

personification. In this stanza Sachs first refers to the people who committed the atrocities in the death camps, but rather than use the word "Nazi," she reduces the perpetrators to a small body part: "O you fingers." The mention of fingers recalls the fact that the ovens were built by human hands; while the Nazis discussed the Final Solution as an impersonal government policy, the killing facilities were constructed—and the murders themselves were carried out—by individuals. Sachs compares the crematoria's threshold, or entranceway, to "a knife between life and death."

The final stanza serves as a brief summary of the ideas explored in the poem: "O you chimneys, / O you fingers / And Israel's body as smoke through the air!" In these three lines, Sachs recalls the machinery of death, the people who committed the murders, and the remnants of the victims rising through the air. The poet does not attempt to find the words to express the fullness of her grief; instead she simply cries out, helpless against an overwhelming anguish.

Style and Themes in "O the Chimneys"

Like many of Nelly Sachs's poems, "O the Chimneys" bears a resemblance to a biblical psalm (a song or poem recited during worship), particularly in the rhythmical repetition of certain phrases, such as the poem's title. The mournful tone of the poem gives it the feeling of a lamentation, an outpouring of intense grief and sorrow. Each stanza begins with a cry of inexpressible anguish—"O the chimneys," "O the habitations of death." Sachs's language is minimal and restrained, but it conveys powerful emotions. In keeping with the psalmic style of the poem—and with her intense interest in religion and spirituality—Sachs makes references to biblical figures and ancient Judaism. Job, whose name appears in the opening quotation and in the poem's second stanza, represents a faith in God that undergoes numerous tests. Many of those imprisoned in Nazi camps wondered how a just and fair God could allow the Germans to commit such terrible crimes against humanity. A number of them rejected God; others, like Job, refused to let go of their faith in spite of tremendous suffering. Sachs's reference to the prophet Jeremiah, as well as her description of the Jewish victims as "Israel's body," connects modern-day Jews with their ancestors, and with the entire history of the Jewish people.

In the introduction to the collection *O the Chimneys*, Hans Magnus Enzensberger describes Sachs's work as "great and mysterious." She wrote complicated poetry, rich with symbolism. In her poetry, Sachs often uses the word "dust," recalling the biblical quote: "Dust thou art and unto dust thou shalt return" (Genesis 3:19). In "O the Chimneys," she speaks of "Jeremiah and Job's dust" rising through the crematoria chimneys. The dust, or ash, is all that remains of those killed in Nazi death camps. Sachs also represents the remains

From "O the Chimneys"

O the chimneys
On the ingeniously devised habitations of
    death
When Israel's body drifted as smoke
Through the air—
Was welcomed by a star, a chimney sweep,
A star that turned black
Or was it a ray of sun?

O the chimneys!
Freedomway for Jeremiah and Job's dust—
Who devised you and laid stone upon stone
The road for refugees of smoke?

O the habitations of death,
Invitingly appointed
For the host who used to be a guest—
O you fingers
Laying the threshold
Like a knife between life and death—

O you chimneys,
O you fingers
And Israel's body as smoke through the air!

A man lights a candle in the crematorium at the former Nazi concentration camp of Buchenwald to remember all of those who died in these ovens. *Reproduced by permission of AP/World Wide Photos.*

of these victims as smoke, which drifts through the air to be "welcomed by a star," or embraced by a heavenly body. The star that embraces the smoke of "Israel's body" gives it comfort and a resting place. But the star itself does not remain unaffected by the smoke: it turns black, colored by the soot. Black can also be interpreted as a symbol representing grief and destruction. Sachs alternatively suggests that the smoke is welcomed not by a star but by "a ray of sun," a symbol of hope and life.

The ovens and the attached chimneys referred to in the title are described in two contrasting ways within the poem: as "habitations of death" and as "freedomways." In the former view, the crematoria embody a contradiction: the word "habitations" implies that they are homes, but only death exists in these structures. Describing the chimneys as "freedomways" suggests that, while the Nazis murdered millions of Jews, they could not destroy the Jewish people or the Jewish spirit. Millions of bodies were defeated, but their souls rose up and found immortality in heaven. The image of the smoke rising up to be welcomed by a star is somewhat hopeful, but even as the poet describes the spiritual afterlife of the Nazis' victims, she mourns the tragic loss of their physical selves.

Research and Activity Ideas

1) Write a poem in the style of Nelly Sachs's lamentation "O the Chimneys." Choose as a subject either the Holocaust or another modern-day, large-scale tragedy.

2) Research the Nazi death camps and the Final Solution. Write an essay about the atrocious crimes committed in the name of the Final Solution, exploring the question of blame and responsibility. Can the guards who worked in such camps be blamed as much as, or even more than, the high-ranking officers who devised the plan and ordered them to carry it out? How much blame should be assigned to the Polish citizens who lived near the camps and did nothing to protest their existence?

Where to Learn More About ...

Nelly Sachs and Her Poetry

"Nelly Sachs." *Encyclopedia of World Biography,* 2d ed. Detroit, MI: Gale, 1998.

"Nelly Sachs—Autobiography." *Nobel e-Museum.* www.nobel.se/literature/laureates/1966/sachs-autobio.html (accessed on December 11, 2002).

Sachs, Nelly. *O the Chimneys: Selected Poems, Including "Eli," a Verse Play.* New York: Farrar, Straus and Giroux, 1967.

The Nazi Death Camps and the Final Solution

"Extermination Camps" and "Final Solution." *Learning about the Holocaust: A Student's Guide,* Vols. 1 and 2. New York: Macmillan, 2001.

Rice, Earle. *The Final Solution.* San Diego, CA: Lucent Books, 1998.

"Shema"

Written by Primo Levi

In 1944, Primo Levi, a Jewish Italian chemist, was deported to the infamous Nazi concentration camp Auschwitz, also known as Auschwitz-Birkenau. He spent nearly a year there, enduring inhumane conditions and brutal treatment. Throughout his imprisonment, Levi felt a driving need to communicate to the rest of the world the atrocities committed by the Nazis and his own traumatic experience at their hands. That desire to communicate led Levi to write some of the most compelling works of literature—memoirs, poems, novels, short stories, and essays—about the Holocaust. "Shema," perhaps his most famous poem, deals with the horrors of the Holocaust as well as Levi's feelings about the importance of informing the world, and future generations, about the events perpetrated by Adolf Hitler (1889–1945) and the Nazis.

Biography of Poet Primo Levi

Primo Levi was born on July 31, 1919, in Turin, Italy. His parents, Cesare and Ester, raised him and his sister in a comfortable home and encouraged a love of learning. As upper-middle-class Jews who were highly assimilated, or blended, into the larger Italian society, the Levis did not consider themselves as culturally distinct from their non-Jewish friends and neighbors. With the rise of anti-Jewish laws in the late 1930s, however, the Levis and other Italian Jews were forced to view themselves in a different light: their Jewishness became something that divided them from their fellow Italians.

Levi was a good student, excelling at many subjects. During his high school years, he discovered a love and talent for the sciences. In 1937 he enrolled at the University of Turin, studying chemistry. In spite of the racial laws adopted by the Italian government the following year—laws that stated, among other things, that Jews could not enroll in universities or work in certain professions—Levi completed his studies, graduating in 1941. His Jewishness made it difficult for him to find work, but he acquired false papers that hid his religion and obtained a job as a chemist. In September 1943, Italy surrendered to the military forces from Great Britain, the United States, and the Soviet Union, known as the Allies or Allied forces. Southern Italy fell under Allied control, while Nazi Germany held northern and central Italy. Levi joined with Italian partisans, loosely organized bands of fighters who attacked the occupying German army, but he was soon captured by Italian soldiers collaborating with the Nazis.

Levi admitted to his captors that he was a Jew, in part out of a youthful defiance and in part because Italy had pledged that it would not allow its Jews to be deported. He was sent to Fossoli, a concentration camp in northern Italy, where he was held prisoner for several weeks. On February 22, 1944, in spite of Italy's promises to the Jews, Levi and some 650 others were sent in cattle cars to the infamous concentration and death camp known as Auschwitz-Birkenau. Levi was sent to Buna-Monowitz, a forced-labor camp within the

Primo Levi, author of the poem "Shema." *Reproduced by permission of Mr. Jerry Bauer.*

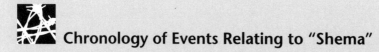

Chronology of Events Relating to "Shema"

July 31, 1919: Primo Levi is born in Turin, Italy.

September 1943: Italy surrenders to the Allies; Germany takes control of the northern and central regions of Italy.

December 13, 1943: Levi is arrested by the Italian militia.

February 22, 1944: Levi is sent to Auschwitz.

January 27, 1945: Auschwitz-Birkenau is liberated by the army of the Soviet Union.

1946: Levi writes the poem "Shema."

April 11, 1987: Levi dies from a fall down a stairwell in a possible suicide, in Turin, Italy.

Auschwitz complex. The prisoners there became slave laborers for German corporations, including the massive group of chemical manufacturers known as I.G. Farben. Because of his training as a chemist, Levi was able to prove his usefulness to the Nazis at Buna-Monowitz, a fact that contributed significantly to his survival. He spent nearly a year in the camp before being liberated by soldiers from the Soviet Union on January 27, 1945.

Levi spent the next several months slowly making his way back to Turin. He later discovered that, of the 650 Jews taken to Auschwitz from Fossoli that day in February 1944, less than two dozen survived to return to Italy. Levi worked as a chemist, and in his free time he wrote of his months in the German *Lager,* or concentration camp. The resulting book, a memoir initially published in 1947 as *Se questo è un uomo (If This Is a Man),* was later published as *Survival in Auschwitz: The Nazi Assault on Humanity.* Also in 1947, Levi married Lucia Morpurgo. The couple had two children, a daughter named Lisa Lorenza, born in 1948, and a son named Renzo, born in 1957.

Survival in Auschwitz begins with one of Levi's best-known poems, "Shema," which is based on a principle Jewish prayer. Levi wrote this book and his other Holocaust-related works out of an intense need to communicate the horror of what he had experienced at Auschwitz. He explains in the preface that this memoir resulted from "an immediate and violent impulse," and it was written to help him achieve "an interior liberation." He also felt driven to warn the world that what the Nazis did in Europe during World War II could happen anywhere, anytime, as long as fear and hatred of those who are different can be allowed to flourish. "The story of the death camps," he wrote in the preface to *Survival in Auschwitz,* "should be understood by everyone as a sinister alarm-signal."

Although it took a decade for his book to find a large audience, *Survival in Auschwitz* came to be viewed as a masterpiece among memoirs of the Holocaust. Levi's moving account details acts of unthinkable brutality and instances of extraordinary compassion. He describes the camp system that was designed to strip prisoners of their dignity and humanity, but he writes without self-pity or bitterness. Levi followed *Survival in Auschwitz* with *The Reawakening,* an account of his journey home to Turin in the months after Auschwitz was liberated. For many years, Levi divided his professional life into the dual pursuits of chemistry and literature, often incorporating scientific principles into his writing. One of his better known examples of such writing is the book *The Periodic Table,* an autobiographical collection of essays and stories. Each chapter of the book takes as its title the name of an element from the periodic table such as carbon, oxygen, or iron, with Levi gracefully drawing comparisons between the defining traits of the elements and the events of his life.

In addition to his memoirs, Levi wrote novels, short stories, poems, and essays. While his prose works are written in a restrained, calm manner, his poetry reveals a much darker, angrier side. The bitterness and despair that would be expected from a former concentration camp inmate are openly expressed in such poems as "Shema," which was written in 1946, just one year after Levi's liberation. When Levi died in 1987 after toppling over a stair railing in the apartment building where he lived, many concluded that he had succumbed to those feelings of despair and taken his own life. Those close to the author, however, insisted that while he was continually troubled by the events of the Holocaust—and by the lack of interest in those events on the part of many young people—he was not suicidal; they have asserted that Levi's death was accidental. Whatever the cause of his death, Levi's

Auschwitz

For many people, the infamous concentration and death camp complex known as Auschwitz-Birkenau represents all Nazi camps and even symbolizes the Holocaust itself. Auschwitz was the largest of about two thousand Nazi camps in Europe. It was divided into three main parts: Auschwitz I was a large concentration camp, a prison where inmates experienced brutality and torture and lived amidst terrible filth; Auschwitz II, or Birkenau, included several sub-camps and contained the gas chambers and crematoria, or ovens used for burning bodies; Auschwitz III comprised numerous sub-camps, including Buna-Monowitz, most of which were forced-labor camps where prisoners worked as slaves for various German industries.

Located near the Polish city of Oświęcim, Auschwitz was established in the summer of 1940. The Germans forced thousands of Poles to move out of their homes so a large area could be cleared for the camp's construction. The first inmates were Polish political prisoners, people who were considered threatening to the Nazi regime in Poland, but eventually Auschwitz contained primarily Jews, with large numbers of Roma (sometimes called Gypsies), Poles, homosexuals, Soviet prisoners of war, and others.

Prisoners arrived at Auschwitz by the trainload, greeted by the deceptive words over the main gate: *Arbeit macht frei,* meaning "work makes you free." The new prisoners immediately endured the *selektion,* the process that divided the elderly and sick from the young and strong. The former went directly to their deaths in the gas chambers; the latter were sent on

voice can still be heard through numerous literary works that reveal his sharp mind and generous spirit.

Historical Background of "Shema"

On January 30, 1933, Adolf Hitler became the leader of Germany. He quickly gained extraordinary power, crushing all political opposition and seizing total control of the government. His position as dictator was made possible partly through his use of force and partly because he had persuaded a large percentage of German citizens that a strong leader was necessary to return Germany to its former glory. Before its defeat in World War I (1914–18) and subsequent economic troubles, Germany had been a strong and influential nation. Hitler

to another part of the camp to be "processed": their clothes were taken, their heads shaven, and numbers were tattoed on their arms. They were later assigned to forced-labor detail. This procedure was designed to humiliate and torture the prisoners, stripping them of their dignity and individuality. They were forced to give up all personal belongings, including shoes and clothing. Their heads were shaved, they received uniforms, and they were assigned numbers that were tattooed onto their arms to take the place of their names.

The daily routine for the prisoners at Auschwitz involved back-breaking physical labor, inadequate food, constant humiliation, brutal beatings, and even random executions by the guards—all of which took place against the backdrop of the gas chambers and crematoria, where thousands of their fellow prisoners met their deaths each day. In all, according to many estimates, 1.5 million Jews—approximately one-quarter of all the Jews killed during the Holocaust—and tens of thousands of others were murdered at Auschwitz.

As the army of the Soviet Union approached Auschwitz in January 1945, the Germans began to retreat, taking all able-bodied prisoners with them on what came to be known as a death march. Forced to walk for miles, enduring bitter-cold temperatures and prevented from resting or eating along the way, thousands of prisoners died during the death march. The prisoners left behind at Auschwitz—mainly those too ill or injured to go on the death march—were liberated by the Soviet army on January 27, 1945.

promised to rebuild Germany's military and revitalize the economy, and he called upon the Aryan citizens of Germany—those who were white, Christian, and of Germanic ancestry—to unite in that effort. A significant part of his plan for renewal involved ridding Germany of what the Nazis considered undesirable elements: Jews, Roma (sometimes referred to as Gypsies), those of African descent, homosexuals, the physically and mentally disabled, and others. These elements, Hitler claimed, were destroying the fabric of German society and clouding the purity of the naturally superior Aryan race.

Almost immediately upon assuming control of Germany, Hitler began passing laws intended to make life so unpleasant for Jews that they would have little choice but to leave the country. They were prevented from working in numerous professions or owning most businesses, barred from living where they chose, and forced to attend all-Jewish schools. In a nation where anti-Semitism, or hatred toward Jews, was already significant, the Nazis created an atmosphere that encouraged German citizens to humiliate, intimidate, and even physically attack their Jewish neighbors. Several hundred thousand Jews did flee Germany, but many stayed behind either because they could not afford to leave or because they believed the situation would improve. As the 1930s progressed, however, the situation worsened considerably. Riots and other instances of spontaneous violence toward Jews became more frequent, reaching a peak with the event known as *Kristallnacht*, or the "Night of Broken Glass." These riots, taking place throughout Germany and the territories it controlled on November 9 and 10, 1939, were so named because of the smashing of thousands of windows in Jewish homes and businesses. In addition to the destruction of property, nearly a hundred Jews were murdered and tens of thousands were arrested and sent to concentration camps. *Kristallnacht* signaled to the German Jews, and to the world, that more violence lay ahead.

By the end of the 1930s, it became clear that Hitler's ambitions stretched well beyond the borders of Germany. In 1938, backed by his newly rebuilt and extremely powerful army, Hitler began conquering other European nations. He started by taking control of Austria in March, followed by seizure of the Sudetenland, a region in Czechoslovakia, in October. In March 1939 Germany invaded the remaining regions of Czechoslovakia, and in September Hitler's troops brutally conquered Poland, an act that triggered the beginning of World War II. Nation after nation in Europe succumbed to Hitler's army, and in nearly every case, the Jews of those nations were immediately subjected to the same horrors faced by German Jews. They were denied basic rights, segregated from the rest of the population, and eventually deported to concentration camps, where they were forced to perform hard labor, or death camps, where millions were systematically murdered.

Hitler's alliance with Mussolini

In his quest for world domination, Hitler had an important ally in Benito Mussolini (1883–1945), the dictator of Italy. Mussolini and his Fascist Party had ruled Italy since 1922.

Inmates at the Mauthausen concentration camp in Russia. In his writings author Primo Levi vividly describes how the prisoners who worked incessantly for the Nazis were treated like animals by their captors.
Reproduced by permission of the United States Holocaust Memorial Museum.

Fascism is a system of government that places all importance on the nation rather than on the rights or significance of individuals. Fascist governments, like that in Italy, are led by a dictator, a leader with complete and total power over the people. Such authoritarian leaders seek to control all aspects of their citizens' lives, dominating such areas as education, business, and the media. In many ways, Hitler modeled his Nazi Party on Mussolini's Fascism. In Italy, however, anti-Semitism was

Benito Mussolini and Adolf Hitler. In his quest for world domination, Hitler had an important ally in Mussolini, the dictator of Italy.
Reproduced by permission of the National Archives and Records Administration.

not widespread and the government did not initially seek to enact anti-Jewish laws or policies. Wishing to cement his alliance with Hitler, Mussolini did institute anti-Jewish laws in 1938. These laws prevented Jews from marrying non-Jews, restricted their access to education, and barred them from working in numerous professions. But Italy's Jews, at least during the early years of World War II, were protected by the government from arrest and deportation to concentration camps.

During the summer of 1943, Mussolini's government collapsed, and in early September, his nation surrendered to the Allied armies, which controlled southern Italy. Germany maintained its hold on northern and central Italy. Once Mussolini lost control of his country, the Italian Jews lost all protection from the Nazis, who began arresting them by the hundreds. While many Italian citizens and religious leaders sought to protect Jews or help them escape to the Allied-controlled regions, the Nazis succeeded in deporting some 8,000 Jews to Auschwitz and other death camps. Only about 400 of them survived the war.

Subject Matter of "Shema"

Primo Levi's poem "Shema" is based on an important Jewish prayer of the same name. The prayer, recited by devout Jews twice daily, declares the central Jewish belief in one God. Jews are commanded to take the words of the Shema to heart and to teach them to their children; the words should be spoken "when you sit in your house, and when you walk by the way, and when you lie down, and when you rise." In his poem, Levi issues similar commandments, although his "Shema" urges readers to speak not of God but of the Holocaust. Levi wrote often of his own need to share details of his experience as a concentration camp prisoner. In "Shema," he writes of the crucial importance for all of humanity to discuss the Holocaust and teach it to future generations. Such discussion offers a testament to the suffering of the victims as well as a condemnation of the murderous cruelty of the perpetrators, and it offers some hope that events like the Holocaust will not happen again.

Levi begins his poem by addressing all of those who live with a sense of comfort and safety. He speaks to people who live in "warm houses" and eat "hot food." All but the least fortunate of his readers can claim such luxuries and, furthermore, consider such things not luxuries at all but basic necessities. With these opening lines Levi alerts his readers that he aims to disrupt their safe and comfortable lives with disturbing images of those who were far less fortunate.

Levi then invites readers to "consider if this is a man," words that echo the title of his memoir, *If This Is a Man* (later known as *Survival in Auschwitz*), in which this poem appears as an epigraph, a poem or quotation placed at the beginning of a book in order to shed light on that book's message. "Shema" goes on to describe the conditions endured by this man, who represents the experience of all men in a Nazi concentration camp. Levi depicts a man "who labours in the mud / Who knows no peace / Who fights for a crust of bread / Who dies at a yes or a no." He then describes the suffering of a woman prisoner, asking readers to "consider if this is a woman": "Without hair or name / With no more strength to remember / Eyes empty and womb cold / As a frog in winter." In a few lines, Levi has captured the essence of life in the *Lager*. The Jewish prisoners were treated worse than animals:

humiliated, beaten, stripped of their individuality, and repeatedly reminded that their lives were worthless in the eyes of the guards.

After describing the conditions of life in the concentration camp, Levi urges readers to always remember what happened during the Holocaust. Just as Jews are commanded to make the words of the Shema part of their lives, Levi urges all readers to hold on to the words of his poem: "Engrave them on your hearts / When you are in your house, when you walk on your way, / When you go to bed, when you rise. / Repeat them to your children." Levi believes that the way to honor those who suffered and died—to give meaning to lives that the Nazis tried to make meaningless—is for future generations to learn about and remember the Holocaust. His passion on this subject, and his anger and bitterness over the desire of the world to ignore the painful events of the Holocaust, become clear in the final lines of his poem, when he issues a kind of curse on those who fail to remember: "[M]ay your house crumble, / Disease render you powerless, / Your offspring avert [turn] their faces from you."

Style and Themes in "Shema"

Across many genres—poems, memoirs, essays—critics have noted Primo Levi's simple, straightforward style and his ability to communicate his ideas clearly. "Shema" is no exception. While some poets fill their verse with extended metaphors and complicated symbols, Levi wrote "Shema" and many other poems in plain, everyday language. In Levi's view, the best way to convey his message was to write simply and clearly, and with "Shema," the result is a poem of tremendous power.

In his memoirs, Levi detailed the Nazis' horrific treatment of Jews in a remarkably restrained, even-handed tone. As he wrote in the Afterword of *The Reawakening,* "I have deliberately assumed the calm, sober language of the witness, neither the lamenting tones of the victim nor the irate voice of someone who seeks revenge." He wrote that as a witness, he felt it was his duty to present his experience in an objective manner so that it would be more believable. Levi was aware that his memoirs would be read as historical documents, and he recognized the need for them to be accurate

Liberation of Auschwitz concentration camp, 1945. *Reproduced by permission of the United States Holocaust Memorial Museum.*

and as objective as possible. Levi considered his poetry further opportunity to share his experiences with the world, but in that form of writing, restraint and objectivity were far less important to him. Through his poems, Levi unleashed the full intensity of his emotions. In "Shema," his despair and bitterness are plain in his descriptions of what prisoners in the Nazi camps endured. The complete impact of his anger, however, is reserved for the final lines of the poem, when he wishes ill to those who refuse to consider the suffering of the Nazis' victims.

One of the primary themes of "Shema" is the importance of remembering the Holocaust. In Levi's view, this act goes beyond simply remembering that the Holocaust happened; it involves learning about the Holocaust, discussing it with others, and teaching it to future generations. The prayer on which Levi's poem is based contains a central idea of the Jewish religion: having faith in, and love for, one God. In referring to this important prayer and by making the subject of his "Shema" the remembrance of the Holocaust rather than the love of God, Levi communicates his feelings about the crucial act of remembering.

Another important theme of "Shema" is the loss of identity and humanity among prisoners of Nazi concentration camps. The trauma of life in the *Lager* lay not in the details of the prisoners' difficult daily lives—the physical labor, the scarcity of food, the lack of warmth—but in their treatment at the hands of the Nazi guards. The Nazis took away more than just the prisoners' freedom and comfort; they took their dignity and sense of humanity. They treated inmates like beasts, addressing them by number instead of by name, casually beating or even murdering whomever they chose. While enduring such treatment, Levi asks, how can prisoners hold on to the things that make them human? In *Survival in Auschwitz,* Levi describes the process undergone by prisoners in the camps as "the demolition of a man." After listing the many things the prisoners have been deprived of, Levi reminds readers that "he who loses all often easily loses himself."

In "Shema," Levi asks readers to consider whether the prisoners can be thought of as men and women when such basic rights and privileges have been denied them. Levi wonders whether people who fight each other for scraps of food, who have been deprived of the things that define them as individuals, who have lost the ability to bear children, can still be human. Beneath the anger and bitterness of the poem's concluding lines can be found a glimmer of hope regarding those prisoners' humanity. On the one hand, for those who turn away from the reality of the Holocaust, Levi wishes terrible things: the destruction of their homes, the weakening of their bodies, the severing of their relationships with their children. On the other hand, Levi suggests that if future generations do remember the Holocaust, that remembrance can help restore the dignity, individuality, and humanity of the victims of Nazi concentration camps.

Research and Activity Ideas

1) Read Primo Levi's memoir *Survival in Auschwitz,* at the beginning of which appears the poem "Shema." The

poem and the memoir address the same subject, but they are written in different forms and in different styles, with the poem revealing far more anger and bitterness than the memoir. Compare the two works, explaining the ways in which they are alike and different.

2) Research an aspect of the Holocaust that you find especially compelling. Write a brief essay about the subject, and then write a poem on the same topic. Examine the different ways in which you've communicated information and emotions in the two forms of writing.

Where to Learn More About ...

Primo Levi and "Shema"

Belpoliti, Marco, and Robert Gordon, eds. *The Voice of Memory, Primo Levi: Interviews 1961–1987*. New York: New Press, 2001.

Hirsch, Edward. "Poet's Choice." *Washington Post* (March 24, 2002): p. BW12.

Klein, Ilona. "Primo Levi: The Drowned, the Saved, and the 'Grey Zone.'" *Simon Wiesenthal Center, Multimedia Learning Center Online*. http://motlc.wiesenthal.com/resources/books/annual7/chap05.html (accessed December 18, 2002).

Levi, Primo. *Collected Poems*. Translated by Ruth Feldman and Brian Swann. New York: Faber and Faber, 1992.

Levi, Primo. *Survival in Auschwitz: The Nazi Assault on Humanity*. New York: Collier Books, 1993.

Auschwitz

"Auschwitz." *Learning about the Holocaust: A Student's Guide,* Vol. 1. New York: Macmillan, 2001.

"Auschwitz." *Simon Wiesenthal Center: Multimedia Learning Center Online*. http://motlc.wiesenthal.com/text/x02/xm0207.html (accessed on December 18, 2002).

Holocaust Plays

Drama, with its combination of the written word and live performance, can present stories in a uniquely powerful style, involving and engaging audience members in a way that can't be done with books or movies. Perhaps because of the intimate, immediate nature of theater, relatively few plays have been written about the Holocaust. Playwrights have grappled with the difficulty of addressing the broad scope of the Holocaust, of staging scenes of terrible, graphic violence, and of capturing the horror and trauma on stage without overwhelming the audience. Some experts who study Holocaust literature believe that the realities of the Holocaust are just too graphic to portray accurately within the structure and limitations of a live stage play. Another point of view, however, is that live drama provides a personal way for playwrights, actors, and audience members to remember and learn from the painful events of the Holocaust.

Among all the plays that have been written about the Holocaust, most fall into two basic categories. One category includes the type of play that focuses on the experience of an individual or a family. This format personalizes the overwhelming horrors of the Holocaust, allowing audiences to see those affected by the tragedy as individuals rather than statistics. The second category includes plays that focus on an event or an aspect of the Holocaust that reflects a wider point of view and explores broad themes of social, historical, or political significance. Holocaust plays of particular interest to young adults generally belong to the first category.

A number of plays about the Holocaust are based on books written by victims or survivors. Based on the famous diary, the stage production *The Diary of Anne Frank* is one of the best-known plays about the Holocaust. Acclaimed American playwright Arthur Miller based *Playing for Time,* which has also been produced as a film, on a book written by survivor Fania Fenelon. *I Never Saw Another Butterfly* is a play based on the experiences of a woman who was one of the few children to survive the concentration camp Terezin. While the play is not strictly based on a book, it takes its title from a line in the famous poem that appears in a book by the same name. That book collects artwork, stories, and poems written by numerous children at Terezin, many of whom did not survive.

Holocaust-related plays appropriate for young audiences cover a broad spectrum, portraying a wide variety of people and situations. Alina Kentof's *Dr. Yanush Korczak* tells the story of a respected man who ran an orphanage in the Warsaw ghetto, refusing to abandon the children under his care even when his own life was at stake. Anatoly Aleksin's *The Young Guard* recalls the activities of a youth organization in the former Soviet Union that secretly fought against the Nazis. *Angel in the Night,* a play by Joanna H. Kraus, tells the story of a woman who courageously provided shelter for four Jews, hiding them from the Nazis for more than a year. Niklas Radstrom's play *Hitler's Childhood* examines the early years of the man who conceived of and presided over the Holocaust.

Two plays are featured in *Experiencing the Holocaust,* both of which relate stories from the point of view of Holocaust survivors. *Dear Esther,* by Richard Rashke, is a play based on the true experiences of Esther Raab, a woman who survived a dramatic escape from the Sobibor death camp. Raab had received many invitations to speak at schools about her Holocaust experiences; she initially refused, partly because of the painful memories she had to relive in doing so, and partly because she did not believe that American audiences, young people in particular, would be interested in hearing about them. She eventually agreed to share her life stories with students and was amazed at their highly emotional and supportive responses, which were often communicated in heartfelt letters sent to thank her for sharing her difficult memories. Incorporating parts from several of these letters, *Dear Esther* recounts Raab's harrowing ordeal and the ways in which the outpouring of love and compassion from young people helped her cope with her grief.

A Shayna Maidel, written by Barbara Lebow, focuses on a fictional Polish Jewish family that was divided several years before World War II (1939–1945) began and partially reunited after the war's end. A series of circumstances led to the Weiss family being split up, with the father and one daughter moving to the United States in 1928 and the mother and another daughter staying behind in Poland. Stuck in Poland with no way out, the mother and elder daughter suffered through the persecutions of the Holocaust, while the father and younger daughter lived through the war years in relative comfort in the United States. The play takes place in 1946, when the father learns that his daughter Lusia, the lone survivor of the family left behind in Poland, is coming to New York to live. The story focuses on the difficulties that arise for the two sisters who have spent so many years apart and led such different lives—one a successful, modern, American career woman, the other a traumatized survivor from war-torn Poland. Throughout the play, they struggle to understand each other and overcome the differences separating them. Although not based on an actual family, the story offers audiences an American view of the post-Holocaust experience that reflects the real-life circumstances of many Jewish refugees.

Representative Plays about the Holocaust

Aleksin, Anatoly. *The Young Guard.* New Plays, 1977. *This play tells the story of a youth resistance organization in the Soviet Union, called the Young Guard, that fights back against Nazi occupation, freeing prisoners of war and sabotaging German efforts in any way possible.*

Bennett, Cherie, and Jeff Gottesfeld. *Anne Frank and Me.* Dramatic Publishing, 1997. *An American Christian girl travels back in time to Paris in 1940, becoming a young French Jew who must go into hiding with her family to escape Nazi persecution.*

Goodrich, Frances, and Albert Hackett. *The Diary of Anne Frank*. Random House, 1956. *This classic play—possibly the most-performed of all Holocaust dramas—is based on the famous diary written by Anne Frank during her years of hiding from the Nazis in Amsterdam.*

Kentof, Alina. *Dr. Yanush Korczak*. Published online by *A Teacher's Guide to the Holocaust*, http://fcit.coedu.usf.edu/holocaust/resource/plays/Korczak.htm (accessed on January 15, 2003). *Dr. Korczak, an author and educator, directed the Jewish Orphanage in the Warsaw ghetto. Refusing to accept offers to help him escape the ghetto, he insisted on staying with the children, eventually accompanying them to—and dying alongside them in—the death camp Treblinka.*

Kraus, Joanna H. *Angel in the Night*. Dramatic Publishing Company, 1996. *This play relates the true story of Marysia Pawlina Szul, a young Catholic Polish woman who hid four Jews from the Nazis in her family's barn, without her family's knowledge.*

Lebow, Barbara. *A Shayna Maidel*. Dramatist's Play Service, 1998. *Two Jewish sisters—one who grew up in the United States and the other who endured the Holocaust in Poland—struggle to reconnect with each other and to come to terms with their difficult father.*

Miller, Arthur. *Playing for Time*. Dramatic Publishing Company, 1985. *This play is based on the experiences of Fania Fenelon, a Jewish survivor who spent part of the Holocaust as a member of a concentration camp orchestra.*

Radstrom, Niklas. *Hitler's Childhood*. Alan Brodie Representation, 1983; English translation by Frank Gabriel Perry, 1995. *Without trying to excuse his actions as an adult or seek answers for his behavior in his childhood experiences, this play examines what is known about the first ten years of the life of Adolf Hitler (1889–1945).*

Rashke, Richard. *Dear Esther*. Dear Esther Productions, 2000. *This play relates the true story of Esther Raab, who survived the Holocaust after taking part in an escape from the death camp Sobibor. The play details Raab's traumatic experience during the war and her struggle to come to terms with her painful memories in the years following.*

Raspanti, Celeste. *I Never Saw Another Butterfly*. Dramatic Publishing Company, 1971. *This stage drama, which is available as a full-length play as well as a one-act version, relates the true story of Raja Englanderova, a Holocaust survivor who spent part of her youth imprisoned at the concentration camp Terezin. Of 15,000 young people confined at Terezin, only about 100, including Englanderova, survived the war.*

Samuels, Diane. *Kindertransport*. Penguin Putnam, 1995. *This play addresses the long-ranging consequences for one participant in the Kindertransports, a rescue effort that sent thousands of Jewish children from their homes in Germany and elsewhere to the homes of strangers in England. The play examines the life of a woman who painstakingly covered up her painful past as a Kindertransport child, only to have her adult daughter force her to confront it.*

Still, James. *And Then They Came for Me*. Dramatic Publishing Company, 1997. *A multimedia stage production, this play incorporates filmed interviews with Holocaust survivors Ed Silverberg and Eva Schloss, who were childhood friends of Anne Frank. Live actors portray scenes from their experiences in hiding from the Nazis.*

Dear Esther

Written by Richard Rashke

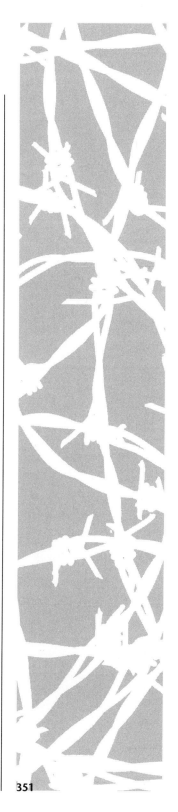

While researching his book *Escape from Sobibor* (1982), which chronicles the dramatic attempt at escape made by hundreds of prisoners from the Sobibor death camp, author and playwright Richard Rashke met Esther Raab, one of the survivors of that escape. As he got to know Esther better, Rashke learned of Esther's reluctance to speak publicly about her experiences in spite of many invitations from schools and organizations; the horrors of the Holocaust and of her experience in Sobibor still haunted her, and speaking of it only made her painful memories more vivid. In addition, Esther wondered if young audiences would understand and appreciate her recollections of decades-old events. To American kids, living far away in time and space from the events of the Holocaust, Esther believed that her experiences would seem like ancient and irrelevant history.

In spite of her doubts, Esther agreed to speak to school audiences in her home state of New Jersey. The audiences' responses overwhelmed her. Obviously touched by her retelling of painful memories, students approached Esther after her talks; as Rashke explains in the introduction to *Dear*

Esther, "They wanted to shake her hand and hug her. They wanted to exchange photos and be pen pals." Unable to forget Esther, many students wrote her letters to say that her stories had changed their lives. In the late 1990s, Rashke and Esther Raab agreed that the playwright would make Esther's Holocaust experiences, and her later encounters with students, the basis for a play. The resulting work, *Dear Esther,* weaves letters children have written into Esther's recounting of her imprisonment in and escape from Sobibor. Described by Rashke as "a chorus of hope," the students' letters speak of the lingering effects of the tragedy of the Holocaust and emphasize the importance of remembering such catastrophic events for future generations.

Biography of Playwright Richard Rashke

Born in Milwaukee, Wisconsin, in 1936, Richard Rashke grew up in a working-class neighborhood, far more interested in sports than schoolwork. Neither of his parents received much education; as adults, his mother worked in a paper factory and his father worked in road construction. While attending a Catholic grade school, Rashke showed little interest in academic subjects, but that attitude changed when he completed grade school and was enrolled in a boarding school for boys. There he studied Latin and Greek and discovered the joys of reading. After graduating from high school, Rashke became the first member of his family to go to college. He moved to a town outside Rochester, New York, to attend a small school called Divine Word College.

While he loved reading, Rashke struggled to develop his writing skills during his college years. Through those struggles, however, he learned that writing can bring tremendous emotional rewards. As a young man in his early twenties, Rashke sold his first essay, deciding from that point forward that he would be a professional writer. After he graduated from college, Rashke took a job teaching English and drama at a high school in Pennsylvania. In addition to teaching, he directed plays, coached the debate team, and even spent some time as band leader and director of the school glee club.

Rashke's aspirations to become a writer soon led him to seek other avenues, and he left teaching to accept a jour-

Chronology of Events Relating to *Dear Esther*

1922: Esther Terner (later Raab) is born in Chelm, Poland.

January 30, 1933: Adolf Hitler becomes chancellor of Germany.

1936: Playwright and author Richard Rashke is born.

September 1, 1939: Germany invades Poland; World War II begins days later.

Summer 1941: The Final Solution is devised by the Nazi leadership to rid Europe of Jews.

Spring 1942: Sobibor, a death camp in eastern Poland, begins operating.

October 14, 1943: Hundreds of prisoners attempt escape from Sobibor; most are killed during the attempt, but dozens, including Esther Raab, successfully flee.

1981: Rashke meets Raab for the first time while researching his book, *Escape from Sobibor.*

1982: Rashke's *Escape from Sobibor* is published.

January 1998: The play *Dear Esther* is performed for the first time.

nalism fellowship and to pursue a master's degree in communications at American University in Washington, D.C. During the journalism fellowship, Rashke founded the American News Service, an organization that helped student journalists get their stories published in local newspapers. While earning his master's degree, Rashke worked as an intern for the United Press International (UPI) wire service. He later worked as the Washington correspondent and photographer for the *National Catholic Reporter,* a weekly paper. His journalism jobs did not satisfy him, however, and he began working on his own as a freelance writer and photographer.

While working in Washington in the mid-1970s, Rashke learned of the story of Karen Silkwood, a woman who had died under mysterious circumstances after she began investigating unsafe conditions at the Oklahoma nuclear plant where she worked. Fascinated by her story, Rashke began researching the details surrounding her life and death. He wrote articles and a pamphlet about Silkwood, attempting for years to find a publisher interested in a book-length work about her. *The Killing of Karen Silkwood* was published in 1981, earning praise from readers and reviewers alike.

While researching another project, Rashke came across the story of the daring and deadly escape from the Nazi death camp Sobibor. Enthralled and inspired by the story of the Jewish captives breaking out of the tightly guarded camp, Rashke delved deeper and found a number of survivors to interview for the book he planned to write. He traveled around the world talking to survivors of the Sobibor escape, and in 1982 he published *Escape from Sobibor*. This book, which was later made into a movie with the same title, received international acclaim and was translated into seven languages. One of the survivors Rashke met while researching *Escape from Sobibor*, Esther Raab, particularly touched him. As he got to know Esther better—and as he read the hundreds of letters students wrote to her after she began speaking at schools about her nightmarish experiences—Rashke began to feel that her story could reach even more people if it were translated into a play. *Dear Esther* was first performed in January 1998 at the United States Holocaust Memorial Museum and the Jewish Community Center of Northern Virginia.

Rashke has written several other stage plays, including the children's plays *David's Big Secret* and *Crane Wife*. His play *Bang!* takes a satirical, or humorous, look at guns and violence, and *Season to Season* examines the struggles and conflicts of two artists living together. Rashke has also written several nonfiction books exploring the same issues of social justice that informed *The Killing of Karen Silkwood* and *Escape from Sobibor*. *Runaway Father* tells the story of a family's search for the husband and father who had left them years earlier. In *Trust Me*, Rashke relates the struggle of an undercover police officer to shut down a Washington drug ring. *Capitol Hill in Black and White*, written with Robert B. Parker, details Parker's life as an African American waiter working in the U.S. Senate dining room during the civil rights era.

Rashke lives in Washington, D.C., with his wife, Paula Kaufmann, an editor and artist. In addition to his many publications, Rashke has taught writing at American University, the University of Maryland, and the Maui Writers School. At the age of sixty he pursued his longheld passion for music by enrolling at the Levine School of Music to study alto saxophone.

Occasionally his twin loves of music and writing intersect, as when he composed original music for some of his plays.

Historical Background of *Dear Esther*

Long before coming to power in Germany, Adolf Hitler and the Nazi Party had made it clear that anti-Semitism, or hatred of Jews, was a fundamental part of their ideology, or system of beliefs. When Hitler did become leader of Germany, in 1933, he wasted no time in putting those beliefs into practice. His government established numerous laws intended to restrict the rights of Germany's Jewish citizens, including one of the 1935 Nuremberg Laws that took German citizenship away from Jews. Such laws, which separated Jews from the larger society in areas of business, education, and social life, were initially meant to intimidate Jews into leaving Germany. Further intimidation came in the form of harassment and brutality by non-Jewish citizens; Jews were beaten and humil-

A monument at the Sobibor Nazi death camp in Poland. The play *Dear Esther* tells the story of a dramatic escape attempt by hundreds of prisoners from this camp. *Reproduced by permission of Corbis Corporation.*

iated simply because they were Jewish. The Nazis' goal was to make the entire nation *Judenfrei,* or free of Jews. Many thousands of Jews did leave Germany, but hundreds of thousands stayed behind, unable to leave or unwilling to believe the Nazi terrorization would last.

It soon became clear that Hitler's ambitions went far beyond rebuilding Germany's economic and military strength and forcing the emigration of the nation's Jews. In a bid for world domination, Hitler began conquering other European nations in 1938. In that year Germany annexed, or took over, Austria and parts of Czechoslovakia. In early 1939, Germany invaded the remainder of Czechoslovakia. In September Hitler's armies brutally invaded Poland, prompting England and France to declare war on Germany and starting the conflict that became known as World War II (1939–45). Later that month the armies of the Soviet Union invaded eastern Poland, leaving no part of that nation to be independently governed. In the following year Germany invaded Denmark, Norway, the Netherlands, and other western and central European nations. And in 1941 Hitler invaded the Soviet Union, including the eastern regions of Poland that had been controlled by the Soviets since the autumn of 1939. In each nation Germany invaded, the Nazis faced a new dilemma: how to manage that country's Jewish population and make the newly conquered territory *Judenfrei*. This dilemma was particularly problematic in Poland, which had a prewar population of nearly three million Jews.

The Nazis' vicious anti-Semitic policies took hold in each country they controlled, particularly in Eastern Europe. The Jews in these nations were first subject to the same humiliating and restricting laws that had been inflicted on the Jews of Germany. Then, beginning as early as the autumn of 1939 in Poland, Jews were forced to relocate into ghettos, small and usually poor neighborhoods in major cities. These ghettos, usually surrounded by concrete walls and barbed wire, acted as prisons for the Jews. Conditions inside the ghettos were appalling: starvation, disease, and extreme poverty affected most of the population, and many thousands died. In the spring of 1940, the Germans began deporting Jews to concentration camps, large prisons designed to house huge numbers of so-called "enemies of the state," including prisoners of war, political opponents of Nazism, Poles, Jews, homosexuals, Roma

(Gypsies), and others. Both the ghettos and the concentration camps were intended as temporary measures that would hold and control the Jewish population until a better plan could be devised to solve what Nazis called the "Jewish question": how to rid Europe of all Jews. One idea, known as the Madagascar Plan, proposed sending the Jews of Europe to Madagascar, an island off the southeast coast of Africa. When it became clear that the expulsion of millions of people was impractical, the Nazis began formulating a new plan.

The Final Solution

In the summer of 1941, coinciding with the German invasion of the Soviet Union, Hitler and other leaders of the Nazi Party devised what came to be known as the Final Solution to the Jewish question. The Final Solution dispensed with any plans to expel the Jews from Europe, focusing instead on the mass murder of the entire Jewish population. This campaign of genocide (the destruction of an entire racial, religious, or ethnic group)

Train station at Sobibor where prisoners arrived by the train load, with most being immediately sent to their deaths. *Photograph by Richard Rashke. Reproduced by permission of KR Associates, Inc.*

began with the *Einsatzgruppen,* or Operational Squads. These mobile killing squads followed behind the invading troops in the Soviet Union, herding hundreds or even thousands of Jews into a remote, wooded area, forcing the prisoners to dig a mass grave, and then shooting them. When the Nazi leadership realized that the methods of the Operational Squads were both inefficient and psychologically difficult for the soldiers in the squads, new methods of mass killings were devised. The Nazis had already instituted a program of mass murder using poisonous gas to kill mentally and physically handicapped Germans. With some changes made to accommodate larger numbers of victims, and using the existing concentration camps as model facilities, the Nazis created extermination centers, or death camps.

Under the plan known as Operation Reinhard (named for Reinhard Heydrich, a high-ranking Nazi officer who had been instrumental in devising the Final Solution), four new camps were built in Poland to be highly efficient, systematic killing factories: Chelmno, Belzec, Treblinka, and Sobibor. In some existing concentration camps, including Auschwitz and Majdanek, new facilities were added on to act as killing centers. At the death camps, trainloads of newly arriving prisoners were immediately "processed," their clothing and valuables handed over to the Nazis and their heads shaved. They were then sent to gas chambers. (In Chelmno, the first death camp to open, the prisoners were packed into large vans, into which carbon monoxide gas was piped in until all the inhabitants were dead.) The gas chambers at death camps were designed to look like public showers; hundreds of prisoners were forced into these rooms, the doors were sealed, and poisonous gas filled the room, suffocating all inside. The bodies were usually buried in pits; later, in an attempt to get rid of evidence of what they had done, the Nazis ordered that the bodies be dug up and burned over large, open fires or in huge ovens called crematoria. The prisoners most physically able to perform hard labor were spared the gas chambers so they could help process incoming trainloads. These so-called "permanent" prisoners or *SonderKommando*, also called forced-labor prisoners, sorted the clothing and shoes of new arrivals, shaved their heads, cleaned out the train cars and gas chambers, and disposed of the dead bodies. When forced-labor prisoners became too sick or weak to work, they too were sent to the gas chambers.

The combined figure of those murdered at the four death camps totals nearly two million people, mostly Jews. Between 150,000 and 300,000 were killed at Chelmno; some 600,000 were killed at Belzec; more than 250,000 were killed at Sobibor; and between 700,000 and 850,000 were killed at Treblinka. In some cases, documentation of the number of prisoners killed is incomplete, and some accounts from survivors and other witnesses estimate much higher figures. For example, in *Dear Esther,* Esther recalls the day the guards in Sobibor celebrated the millionth murdered Jew, yet historical estimates of those killed there fall far short of that number. In addition to those killed at the camps built exclusively for murdering prisoners, well over one million people were gassed at Auschwitz-Birkenau and nearly 200,000 were killed at Majdanek.

Resistance and escape

Tight security at the camps, including armed guards, dogs, barbed wire, and landmines planted just outside the camp gates, discouraged escape attempts. Any instances of resistance or rebellion within the camp were difficult to arrange and punished severely if caught. Prisoners caught trying to escape or planning a rebellion were often killed in front of the other prisoners, and, to discourage further attempts, innocent prisoners were sometimes chosen for execution at random. The physical and mental condition of the forced-labor prisoners also made resistance attempts unlikely. Weakened by lack of food and illness, they were also emotionally devastated by their brutal treatment at the guards' hands and by their knowledge of the daily murders of thousands of innocent people. In spite of such conditions, prisoners at several camps did stage uprisings and attempt escapes. Several hundred prisoners at Treblinka obtained weapons as part of a planned revolt in the summer of 1943. They stormed the gates, set the camp buildings on fire, and engaged in gun battles with the Nazi guards. Hundreds of Jews were killed, but several hundred managed to escape. Of those who made it out of the camp, most were soon captured and killed, but some did survive.

On October 14, 1943, most of the six hundred forced-labor prisoners at Sobibor staged a revolt and attempted an escape. They understood that the camp would soon be shut down, and they knew that death for the remaining prisoners

was inevitable. Led by Leon Feldhendler, a Polish Jew and a cousin of Esther Raab, and Aleksandr (Sasha) Pechersky, a Jewish Russian prisoner of war, the prisoners attacked the guards, killing eleven Germans and several Ukrainian guards. Approximately three hundred prisoners escaped Sobibor. Many of them were killed soon after by Nazi soldiers who had pursued the escapees. The prisoners who had remained in the camp were killed the following day. Of those who escaped, only about fifty survived the duration of the war, including Esther Raab. In the years following the end of World War II, Raab got married and immigrated to the United States, settling in New Jersey.

Plot and Characters in *Dear Esther*

In *Dear Esther,* which is written about real-life Holocaust survivor Esther Raab, playwright Richard Rashke has created two characters to portray the title role: the present-day Esther and a younger version of herself, Esther 2. In his introduction to *Dear Esther,* Rashke writes that Esther 2 "...is more than Esther's memory. More than her alter-ego [a different part of her personality]. More than her conscience." When Esther is visited by a memory of her past, it is Esther 2 who acts out the flashback. When Esther has doubts about speaking publicly of her experiences, or about telling the whole story to an audience, Esther 2 encourages her to continue. Existing in Esther's imagination and memory, the youthful Esther 2 can be seen and heard only by her older counterpart.

The primary setting of the play is a school auditorium. Esther has agreed to speak to an audience of schoolchildren about her experiences during the Holocaust. Throughout the play, as Esther struggles to confront her painful memories, she has arguments and conversations with Esther 2. Esther is reluctant to speak about the Holocaust because talking about her past makes her painful memories even more vivid. She wonders if enduring the pain of speaking about such things will be worthwhile; will the students believe her, will they care about what happened to her? Esther 2 feels sure that the students will understand, and pushes the older Esther to continue. As Esther speaks, Esther 2 periodically interrupts her, urging her to tell her story more completely, more honestly.

Esther's story

Esther begins by describing to the students the early years of the war in her hometown of Chelm, a city in eastern Poland near the border with the Soviet Union. First the Germans came, and for a short time, life continued on almost as it had before the war. At this point, the German soldiers in Chelm had not yet begun their violent and murderous cam-

Hannah Senesh: Resistance Fighter

Opposition to the Nazis, among both Jews and non-Jews, took many forms. A small but significant number of Christians in Nazi-occupied Europe fought against the Nazis simply by hiding Jews, helping them escape to safety, or giving them jobs or money. Some Jews imprisoned in ghettos and in concentration and death camps staged uprisings and attempted escapes. In numerous countries, members of underground, or secret, organizations resisted the Nazis by publishing newspapers, smuggling goods into—and people out of—closed ghettos, and sabotaging, or destroying, German military equipment.

A young Jewish Hungarian woman named Hannah Senesh (sometimes spelled Szenes) became famous worldwide for her courageous dedication to the causes of de-feating the Nazis, helping the Jews of Europe, and creating a Jewish homeland in Palestine, later known as Israel. Born in 1921, Senesh grew up in Budapest, Hungary, raised by loving parents in a comfortable home. As she approached adulthood, she was deeply disturbed by the increasing anti-Semitism in her native land, and she became a determined Zionist—a person dedicated to the establishment of an independent Jewish nation in Palestine. In September 1939, at the very beginning of World War II, Senesh left her mother to enroll as an agricultural student in Nahalal, in Palestine.

Senesh led a peaceful and satisfying life in Palestine for several years, farming the land and honing her skills as a poet and playwright. News of the war in Europe

paign against the Jews. Soon the Germans left and were replaced by Russian soldiers from the army of the Soviet Union, which invaded eastern Poland just weeks after Germany had invaded from the west. The Russian soldiers treated the townspeople decently. A kind Russian soldier who lived with Esther's family warned them one day that the Russians were leaving and the Germans were returning. He urged Esther's mother to take the family to the Soviet Union, to flee from the Germans. Esther's mother refused, declaring her unwillingness to be chased from her own home. At this point, Esther 2 interrupts to express her anger and frustration that her family—and in fact the millions of Jews captured by the Nazis—didn't anticipate what the Nazis would do to them. And once captured, Esther 2 continues, why didn't more Jews fight back? Esther replies that many, including herself and

and the Nazis' systematic murder of Jews there soon became impossible to ignore, however, and Senesh decided to return to Budapest to help her mother and other Jews escape. Soon after, she learned of a joint mission involving Jewish volunteers and the British army. With the help of the British, the volunteers would parachute into German-held territory with the goal of spying on German troops and providing escape routes for Allied soldiers (the Allies included the United States, Great Britain, and the Soviet Union). The volunteers also understood that this mission, while extremely dangerous, might enable them to help their own people escape the Nazis' brutal and murderous treatment.

In March 1944, Senesh and three others parachuted into Yugoslavia. They managed to convey important information about German troop activity to her British allies, but Senesh was anxious to cross into Hungary and find her mother. In June 1944, she crossed the border, only to be captured almost immediately by German soldiers. Their discovery of her radio transmitter convinced them that Senesh was a spy. She was thrown into prison; guards beat and tortured her for days, trying to force her to tell them what she knew. She refused, even when the authorities arrested her mother and threatened to kill her if Senesh did not talk. After a brief trial, Senesh was executed by a firing squad. Her body, along with the remains of six of her fellow parachutists, was later buried in Israel's National Military Cemetery.

---

her fellow escapees from Sobibor, did fight, and that many died trying. "Those who fought back are dead," she tells Esther 2. "All memory is buried with them."

Esther continues her talk to the students, describing the return of the Germans and the sudden realization the people of Chelm had that this time it would be different. The Nazis rounded up the prominent citizens of the town, including Esther's father and brother, Yidel, marched them out of town, and shot them, leaving the bodies in a ditch. Yidel, shot in the foot, remained hidden among the bodies until he could sneak out after nightfall; he then returned to his home and told his family what had happened. Esther's mother, devastated by the loss of her husband, lost her will to live. Soon after, a ghetto was established in Chelm, and Esther and her family had to leave their home and march to the ghetto. They soon escaped, traveling to a nearby town. But the Nazis established a ghetto there, too, and Esther and her brother began working in a nearby labor camp. They hid their mother in the woods each day before going to work; her depression sapped her of all strength, and Esther and Yidel knew that if their mother could not work, she would be killed. Later, when they were told they would be marched to a labor camp and that no older Jews would be allowed to go, they urged their mother to hide in the woods and sneak to her sister's house after dark. But Esther's mother, who "refused to hide in cellars like a rat," who "was tired of being humiliated," gave herself up to the Gestapo, the Nazi police, who promptly killed her.

From heated discussions with Esther 2, it becomes clear that Esther has never made peace with her mother's death. She can't fully understand why her mother gave up, and part of her has never quite forgiven her mother for yielding to the pressure of life under the Nazis. At this point in the play, several letters from students who heard Esther's talk are read aloud. In their letters, the children tell Esther that they were touched by what she told them, and they admired the courage it took to speak of such painful events. One student confesses that she hadn't understood what had happened during the Holocaust until Esther told her. "I promise," the girl writes, "to tell my kids and make them tell theirs."

From work camp to death camp

Esther describes to the students the humiliating and inhumane conditions in the work camp, explaining that sometimes it is the small deprivations—like not having soap—that make an experience intolerable. "Eight hundred stinking bodies crammed into a building the size of an old schoolhouse," she describes. Esther traded pillowcases that her mother had embroidered for a bar of soap. "To survive," she explains, "you need self-respect. Without self-respect, there can be no hope." Soon after arriving at the work camp, Esther heard rumors that all the inmates there would eventually be taken to Sobibor, where every prisoner was murdered. Her brother Yidel, not wishing to take his chances at Sobibor, escaped one night. When Esther heard the gunshots soon

after his escape, she believed her brother was dead; she mourned his passing, but could not cry. "None of us could cry any more," Esther says, and Esther 2 adds: "We lost touch with our souls." Esther decided to postpone her own attempt at escape until arriving at Sobibor.

A few days later, Esther tells the students, on December 22, 1942, the inmates of the work camp were transferred to the death camp Sobibor. Esther was one of six women chosen to work, knitting socks for German soldiers and sorting the clothes of murdered prisoners instead of being sent to die. Esther describes the daily routine of life at Sobibor. She and the other workers tried to remain numb, but the regular sound of train whistles, signaling the arrival of a new load of prisoners who would be murdered, reminded them of what really went on at Sobibor. Esther continues to be haunted by a song, "Eli," that the prisoners often sang as they were marched to the gas chambers. While admiring them for being able to sing even as they walked toward certain death, Esther also felt frustrated that they did not make any attempt to resist their fate. While life at Sobibor was run according to a strict schedule, Esther explains that it was also quite random and unpredictable. Sometimes the camp laborers were shot by the guards for tripping or walking too slowly. Esther describes the thwarted escape attempt by a group of Dutch prisoners. The Nazi guards forced each of those who had tried to escape to select one of the other prisoners to die along with them. The guards then shot those who had attempted escape as well as the innocent bystanders who had been chosen at random.

Escape

Esther tells the students about the arrival of two men at Sobibor who changed everything. Leon Feldhendler, Esther's cousin, was a young rabbi who persuaded the Sobibor inmates that they could and should fight back and try to escape. In September 1943, a group of Jewish Russian prisoners of war arrived at the camp. Among them was Sasha Pechersky (also spelled Pershersky), a lieutenant who became the military leader of the prisoners planning the uprising. A few weeks later, after cutting the camp's phone lines, putting sand in the gas tanks of the guards' vehicles, and killing as many of the guards as possible, hundreds of prisoners stormed the camp gates. Many were killed by land mines planted outside the camp; others were shot by the remaining guards. Esther was shot in the head, but the bullet simply tore through flesh and did not enter her skull. She finally made it to the woods. The surviving prisoners divided up into small groups to better their chance at survival. Esther and eight men decided to try to find a barn owned by a Catholic baker who had helped Esther's family when they lived in the ghetto; Esther had had a dream in which her mother had guided her to safety in that barn. After a night of walking through the woods, Esther and the others realized that they had been walking in circles and were right back at Sobibor.

Soon Esther and the others reached a farmhouse. It was not the baker's house, but Esther was desperate for food and treatment for her wound, so she decided to approach the house and ask for help. Fortunately, the homeowner was a sympathetic Pole who gave Esther fresh food and cleaned her wound. She soon left, still searching for the farm of the

Catholic baker. She walked for three weeks, encountering numerous obstacles and dangers along the way. The men she traveled with were all killed by Polish Nationals, resistance fighters who lived in the woods and conducted raids on the German army. (Many Poles, while despising the Nazis, hated Jews even more.) She finally reached the baker's farm and, sneaking into the barn, she climbed to the top of a haystack to rest. A man crept up behind her and covered her mouth with his hand. Fearing she would be killed, Esther instead discovered that the man was her brother Yidel. He had actually survived his escape from Sobibor and made his way to the same barn as his sister.

At war's end

Yidel created small rooms within the haystack, and for nine months, Esther and Yidel lived there. The baker regularly brought them food, and they left the barn only at night to get water. When the Red Army of the Soviet Union entered Poland in July 1944, Esther and Yidel left their hiding place, hoping that the end of the war would bring them freedom. But even as the German soldiers retreated, the Jews were still not safe from the violent hatred of many Poles. Esther and Yidel followed the Russian army for several months, hoping to gain some protection from the violence in Poland. When the war in Europe ended in May 1945, they were finally free.

After the war, Esther fell in love with Izzy, a man she had known before the war. After several years of hardship in postwar Europe, they immigrated to the United States, settling in New Jersey. Esther's brother Yidel moved to New York. To the students listening to her in the late 1990s, Esther explains that, while more than fifty years have passed since the Holocaust, her experiences still exist vividly for her. Remembering the words of Leon Feldhendler as the Jews began their escape from Sobibor, "If anyone survives, tell the world what went on here," Esther vows that she will "tell our story for as long as God gives me strength."

Style and Themes in *Dear Esther*

In the introduction to *Dear Esther*, playwright Richard Rashke describes an obstacle he encountered while writing

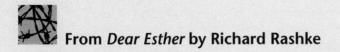

From *Dear Esther* by Richard Rashke

ESTHER 2: We let our guard down.

ESTHER: There was no reason to keep it up. There was peace. We got along with our neighbors. The German soldiers weren't so bad the first time.

ESTHER 2: We were asleep.

ESTHER: We were living our lives.

ESTHER 2: We still should have known.

ESTHER: How? Tell me!

ESTHER 2: We should have seen it coming.

ESTHER: How? Tell me how! We couldn't smell it. We couldn't hear it. We couldn't taste it. We couldn't feel it.

ESTHER 2: We trusted too much. No more.

ESTHER: That's your anger talking.

ESTHER 2: That's my humiliation talking.

ESTHER: Your humiliation, then. It was 1940, not 1990.

ESTHER 2: We should have fought back.

ESTHER: Pardon me! How do you think I got here?

ESTHER 2: I'm not talking about you. I'm talking about them.

ESTHER: Them! You mean the millions you didn't see. How do you know they didn't fight back? You were behind a barbed wire fence in Sobibor, remember?

ESTHER 2: I saw enough to know.

ESTHER: Those who fought back are dead. All memory is buried with them.

the play. Within the structure of the play, which has Esther speaking to a group of schoolchildren about her experiences during the Holocaust, how could he depict Esther's "inner conflicts and contradictions"? To resolve this problem, Rashke created the character Esther 2. Appearing in the play as a figment of Esther's imagination—unseen by anyone besides Esther—Esther 2 represents a younger, angrier, more forthright version of the woman who survived the Holocaust more than fifty years earlier. Esther's struggle to come to terms with her painful past is played out in discussions and arguments she has with Esther 2, and through these conversations, many of the play's themes are presented.

One of the play's most significant themes is the tension between past and present. For Esther, the past is very much a part of her daily life; it haunts her dreams and invades her waking thoughts. She feels that even those who physically survived Sobibor cannot escape the emotional and psychological effects of having lived in a Nazi camp. Esther acknowledges that part of her struggle to deal with the past is a reluctance to let go of the painful feelings that remain her only tie to her dead parents and her own lost youth. "To feel pain," she explains to Esther 2, "is to be with mama and papa. To feel pain is to give meaning to their death." Esther feels that if she somehow could escape her own suffering, it would dishonor the memory of her parents and of the millions of others who died. She does not know how to cling to memories without also clinging to grief.

The presence of Esther 2 symbolizes the events in Esther's past that she has not yet made peace with, particularly her mother's death. While the older Esther claims to understand why her mother gave herself up to the Nazis, the younger Esther believes she has never forgiven her mother for not having the strength to continue living. At the end of the play, a letter from a student helps Esther view her mother's death in a new light. The student writes that she admires Esther's mother for being so brave and for loving her children so unselfishly: "She knew that if you kept hiding her and bringing her food, the Germans would catch you. So she gave up her life to save yours." That letter brings a new understanding to Esther and Esther 2, and as they reflect on this new perspective on the past, Esther 2 exits the stage and, presumably, Esther's life.

Dear Esther also explores the theme of holding on to faith in the midst of terrible tragedy. The events of Esther's life, and the horrible things she has witnessed, have complicated her religious beliefs. On the one hand, religion helped her endure life in the camps; she prayed during the most trying times, and she relied on a faith in God when her faith in humankind wavered. Esther 2 recalls, "God was all I had. He carried half my misery." Even after the war ended, Esther continued to rely on God to give her a better understanding of why the Holocaust happened. On the other hand, she can't help but wonder how a just and fair God could allow the murder of millions of innocent people. The answers she sought from God did not come. When asked in a letter from a student how she can still believe in God, Esther replies that she knows her faith doesn't necessarily make sense, "[b]ut then, faith means believing when it makes no sense."

Another issue raised in *Dear Esther* is the question of luck. Esther repeatedly points out in her speech to the students that there were many points at which she could have died, but luck helped her survive. Esther 2 strongly disagrees, claiming that "[l]uck is the ultimate insult." She feels that Esther's survival was the result of determination, skill, and strategy. She wants Esther to take credit for her survival rather than attributing it to chance. Perhaps Esther, however, cannot bear the thought that she engineered her own survival. If she were responsible for her survival, then those who didn't survive could be said to have chosen death over life. Esther compromises in the end, agreeing that survival required "hope, determination, and instinct. But without some luck, there was no survival."

While the character Esther 2 symbolizes the past in *Dear Esther,* the letters from the students represent the future. Esther's initial reluctance to revisit her past is due in part to a suspicion that the students she is speaking to will not understand or care about her suffering. The responses she receives from the students reveal how touched the children were by her story. Many of the students write of a new understanding about the dangers of prejudice and hate. They are filled with a desire to spread the word to their peers, their families, and, someday, to their children about what happened during the Holocaust and how important it is to guard against such a tragedy ever happening again. The students' letters give Esther a sense of hope that future generations will not forget the Holocaust and that those who died at the hands of the Nazis will be remembered. In addition, the letters give Esther new insight into her own feelings about her mother's death, her faith in God, and her struggle to survive and find contentment in the decades after the war. This insight, and the outpouring of love and support from so many young people, helped Esther reach a new level of acceptance and understanding about her past.

Research and Activity Ideas

1) Examine the scene in *Dear Esther* where Esther and Esther 2 argue about the role of luck in Esther's survival. Why do you think Esther 2 feels so strongly that luck had nothing to do with it, and why does Esther feel just as strongly that luck was a vital part of her survival?

2) Research the historic escape from Sobibor or a similar uprising at a death camp or a concentration camp. Write an essay or short play about the rebellion, highlighting the major figures and the details involved in the plan.

3) Write your own letter to Esther Raab, explaining the way it made you feel to read her story in *Dear Esther*. Did you learn new things about the Holocaust from Esther's remembrances? Did Esther's story change the way you feel about the harmful effects of prejudice?

Where to Learn More About …

Dear Esther

Rashke, Richard. "Introduction." *Dear Esther*. Washington, DC: Dear Esther Productions, 2000.

Hannah Senesh

Ransom, Candice F. *So Young to Die: The Story of Hannah Senesh*. New York: Scholastic, 1993.

Senesh, Hannah. *Hannah Senesh: Her Life and Diary*. New York: Schocken Books, 1983.

Sobibor and the Final Solution

Blatt, Thomas Toivi. *Sobibor: The Forgotten Revolt—A Survivor's Report*. Evanston, IL: Northwestern University Press, 1997.

Escape from Sobibor [made-for-television movie]. Zenith Productions, 1987.

Rashke, Richard. *Escape from Sobibor: The Heroic Story of the Jews Who Escaped from a Nazi Death Camp*. Boston, MA: Houghton Mifflin, 1982.

Rice, Earle. *The Final Solution*. San Diego, CA: Lucent Books, 1998.

A Shayna Maidel

Written by Barbara Lebow

During the Holocaust, perpetrated by Adolf Hitler (1889–1945) and the Nazi Party of Germany, six million Jews and some five million other victims were murdered. In addition to those lives that were ended, many millions more were forever changed by the tragedy. Haunted by the memory of lost loved ones and of their harrowing experiences, survivors sought out living relatives and new homelands where they could begin to reconstruct their lives. In *A Shayna Maidel,* Yiddish for "a pretty girl," playwright Barbara Lebow depicts the tentative rebuilding of a relationship between two sisters: Rose, who spent the years of World War II in the United States, and Lusia, who stayed behind in Poland and endured the trauma of the Holocaust. In dramatizing the bruised lives of those in the Weiss family, Lebow brings a large-scale tragedy to a personal, intimate level, allowing audiences a glimpse of the complicated, painful emotions experienced in the aftermath of the Holocaust.

Biography of Playwright Barbara Lebow

Lebow has loved the process of creating dramas since she was a child, when she and her friends would make up plays and then perform them for neighborhood audiences. Her mother supported her interest in the theater and provided her with opportunities to experience the joys of the stage. After moving as an adult with her own two children to Atlanta in 1962, Lebow began taking her children to performances of children's plays at the Academy Theatre. She became increasingly involved with the theater, attending shows regularly and volunteering to paint sets. She decided to try writing plays for children. After showing part of a script to the theater's artistic director, she was invited to work with a group of actors to further develop her script. Her work with the actors resulted in the play *I Can't Help It,* which was later produced on the Academy Theatre's main stage. After the birth of her third child, late-night hours became the only time she could work on her writing.

Barbara Lebow, author of the play *A Shayna Maidel*. *Reproduced by permission of AP/World Wide Photos.*

Her early success and her love of writing plays prompted her to continue as a playwright. She has tackled a diverse array of subjects over the years, writing plays that take place in a variety of time periods and locations. Her works include *Little Joe Monaghan,* which depicts the real-life story of Josephine Monaghan, a woman who passed as a man and worked as a cowboy in the late-nineteenth-century American West. *The Keepers* tells the tale of a married couple, Nathaniel and Octavia, and a young black woman whom they have raised as their daughter. While living in a lighthouse in Maine in 1854, the three struggle with Octavia's increasing madness and with long-hidden secrets about the past. *The Left Hand Singing* takes place in the 1960s and depicts events of the civil rights movement. *Cobb County Stories* presents conflicts and controversies that arose in the 1990s in the Georgia community of Cobb County. *A Shayna Maidel,* which debuted at Atlanta's Academy Theatre in 1985, is perhaps her best-known work. The play has been

Chronology of Events Relating to *A Shayna Maidel*

January 30, 1933: Adolf Hitler becomes leader of Germany.

July 1938: Evian Conference is attended by representatives from thirty-two countries to discuss Germany's refugee crisis; thirty-one countries refuse to allow in more refugees.

September 1, 1939: Germany invades Poland; World War II begins two days later.

October 8, 1939: The first Jewish ghetto is established in Poland.

May 20, 1940: The infamous Auschwitz concentration camp begins operating.

Summer 1941: The Final Solution is mapped out by Nazi leaders.

April–May 1945: Numerous concentration camps are liberated, or freed, by Allied troops; many thousands of survivors stay in displaced persons camps while awaiting immigration papers.

May 8, 1945: World War II ends in Europe.

April 18, 1985: *A Shayna Maidel* is performed for the first time, at the Academy Theatre in Atlanta, Georgia.

performed in numerous regional productions as well as Off-Broadway from 1987 to 1989, and it has earned praise from theatergoers and critics alike across the United States.

Lebow has conducted several workshop projects with groups that traditionally don't find expression through the theater. She developed the play *I Want to Be* working with adults who are developmentally disabled; *On the Edge* was created with a group of people who were on parole for drug-related crimes; and *Windows* came about through collaboration with prisoners at the Georgia Women's Correctional Institution. Lebow conducted a similar project with the Tutwiler Women's Prison in Alabama. In each case, the playwright worked with the groups to translate their personal experiences and insights into a play; her collaborators served as fellow playwrights and, in some cases, actors in the finished product. In all, Lebow has had about thirty plays produced, including ten for children. She has also taught playwriting at the Academy Theatre.

Historical Background of *A Shayna Maidel*

When Adolf Hitler came to power in Germany in 1933, few could have ignored the signs that his rule would pose problems for German Jews. Hitler made no attempt to hide his hatred for Jews; in fact, his Nazi Party's anti-Semitic, or anti-Jewish, policies were a fundamental part of the campaign. Even though his negative attitude toward Jews was widely known, few could have predicted the devastation the Nazis would spread throughout Europe; few could have comprehended the lengths Hitler would go to in order to get rid of the Jews in the nations he controlled.

After years of persecuting German Jews and restoring the nation's military might, Hitler began conquering other European territories. In March 1938 Germany annexed, or took over, Austria. In September of that year he successfully seized control of the Sudetenland, a part of Czechoslovakia; in March 1939 Germany invaded and occupied the rest of Czechoslovakia. The most aggressive move came on September 1, 1939: Germany invaded Poland, prompting Britain and France to declare war, sparking the beginning of World War II (1939–45). Germany's invasion of Poland was swift and brutal and within the month, Poland was conquered. More than 65,000 Polish troops had been killed in battle and more than 15,000 civilians, Jews, and non-Jews were executed in those weeks. Regarding Poles and the entire Slavic ethnic group as an inferior "race" of people, Hitler planned to enslave the Polish population, depriving them of most of their basic rights and property. Polish government, religious, and community leaders, as well as artists and intellectuals, were massacred in the hopes that the population would be easier to control without leadership.

The Jews of Poland were treated far worse than the non-Jews. Within a month of the invasion, the Nazis had begun to force Polish Jews to live in ghettos, small neighborhoods, usually surrounded by walls or barbed-wire fences, from which residents could not leave without permission. Overcrowding, lack of heat and food, and inadequate, or sometimes nonexistent, medical care led to widespread disease and starvation in the ghettos. Regular deportations took thousands of Jews at a time from the ghettos to concentration camps, large prisons where those who were strong enough were forced to perform back-breaking labor for long hours each day. The weak, sick, very young, and injured were immediately executed. Troops of the SS, the elite Nazi guard unit that ran the concentration camps, treated the concentration camp prisoners worse than animals, seizing every opportunity to punish, humiliate, or beat them. Such minor offenses as stumbling during a forced march could result in a prisoner being shot by a guard. Inmates slept on hard, wooden cots, and meals consisted of stale bread and thin, watery soup.

By the summer of 1941, Hitler and other Nazi leaders had begun to devise an answer to the "Jewish question": how to rid Nazi-occupied Europe of its Jewish population. Plans to deport the millions of Jews living in Nazi-controlled nations to another region of the world were deemed impractical. Jews in the ghettos and camps were dying at a rapid rate, but Hitler felt the pace was too slow. As Germany prepared to invade the Soviet Union, the Nazi leadership came up with what they called the Final Solution: a plan to murder every Jewish man, woman, and child in Europe. At first, mass murder was to be carried out by *Einsatzgruppen,* mobile killing squads that followed behind regular army units as Germany invaded the Soviet Union and Soviet-occupied eastern Poland. The *Einsatzgruppen* went from village to village, rounding up so-called enemies of Nazi Germany—Jews, communists, Roma (Gypsies). The victims were marched to remote, wooded areas and shot, sometimes thousands at a time. The Nazi leadership soon determined, however, that such methods were too costly, inefficient, and psychologically difficult for the soldiers in the killing squads.

Building on the concept of the existing concentration camps, Hitler and his top advisors developed the idea of extermination centers, or death camps. These camps would use methods such as poisonous gas to systematically murder Jews and other prisoners. Such camps as Treblinka, Sobibor, Chelmno, and Belzec were built solely for this purpose. In other instances, extermination facilities were added to existing concentration camps. The infamous Auschwitz complex, for example, was expanded to include the death camp Birkenau. As many as 1.5 million Jews were murdered in the gas chambers of Auschwitz-Birkenau, with millions more killed at the other death camps.

In the last months of World War II, as the German troops began losing territory and retreated back to Germany,

German soldiers watch Jews dig ditches in an empty lot in Krakow, Poland. German soldiers used to make Jewish men work long hours with little food and no rest. *Reproduced by permission of the United States Holocaust Memorial Museum.*

Allied troops (including British, American, and Soviet soldiers) liberated one Nazi camp after another. The few thousands who survived were near death, sick and weakened from their harrowing experiences. Their physical recovery was slow and painful, but the emotional scars proved even more difficult to overcome. Most survivors immediately set out to find relatives and friends from whom they had become separated during the war. Some returned to their hometowns, looking everywhere for a trace of the past that survived the devastation. Particularly in Poland, survivors generally discovered that entire Jewish communities had been wiped out: synagogues had been destroyed, homes had been taken over by non-Jewish people in the town, and strong currents of anti-Semitism made for an unwelcome atmosphere.

Unable to return to their former homes, many refugees lived in displaced persons camps that had been set up by the United Nations, in some cases suffering through conditions that were not much better than those in the concentra-

The United States's Response to the Holocaust

The United States's level of involvement in the rescue of Jews from the Holocaust has been a subject of much debate in the decades since World War II. A powerful and influential nation, the United States could have done a great deal to save Jewish lives. A complex set of circumstances influenced the role the United States played before and during the war. Many critics feel that the United States should have done more to help the Jews.

In the years leading up to World War II, and after the United States entered the war in December 1941, American Jews lobbied the government to change its immigration policies to allow more Jewish refugees to enter the United States. But the State Department, responsible for issuing visas and negotiating with foreign powers, refused to ease the situation for European Jews. This refusal was due in part to a high degree of anti-Semitism and xenophobia, or mistrust of foreigners, among members of the State Department and in the country at large. While anti-Semitism was not part of government policy as it was in Germany, many people—private citizens and government workers alike—exhibited prejudice. In addition, the devastating effects of the Great Depression during the 1930s contributed to the desire to severely restrict the number of immigrants allowed into the country; there weren't enough jobs for the people already in the United States, let alone for new immigrants.

tion camps. Various organizations were set up to help survivors find missing relatives and begin their lives anew. Survivors desperately checked lists of those killed in the camps, too often finding scores of familiar names on such lists. Feeling shut out of their home countries, many survivors sought to leave Europe, immigrating to Palestine, the United States, or elsewhere. But tight immigration restrictions all over the world made it difficult to enter a foreign country unless a resident of that country would declare financial responsibility for the immigrant. Wherever the survivors made their new homes, they struggled with day-to-day living—learning a new language and culture, finding a job and a home, and starting a new family. Mourning the deaths of loved ones and coping with lingering nightmares and fears, survivors faced the nearly insurmountable obstacle of getting on with life after having lived so close to cruelty, barbarism, and death.

After the United States entered the war, American Jewish organizations begged the nation's leaders to intervene militarily to help the Jews in Europe, suggesting the American army bomb the railroad lines leading to the death camps as well as destroying the gas chambers within the camps. No such bombings ever took place, even when the U.S. military spent several days in the summer of 1944 bombing the camp known as Buna-Monowitz, a forced-labor camp within the Auschwitz-Birkenau complex located just a few miles from the gas chambers at Birkenau. American military officials, possibly not realizing the horrible devastation that the death camps were actually causing, claimed they needed every resource to win the war against Germany and could not spare soldiers, planes, or ammunition to help the Jews. The administration of Franklin D. Roosevelt (1882–1945) believed that popular support for the war would diminish if Americans thought the war was being fought on the Jews' behalf.

In 1944, under pressure from Jewish American activists, Roosevelt established the War Refugee Board (WRB) to assist in rescue operations in Europe. While the WRB provided some assistance in Europe—helping Jewish underground groups devise escape routes for Jews in Hungary, for example—it was too little, too late for the millions of Jews suffering and dying in the Nazi labor, concentration, and death camps.

Plot and Characters in *A Shayna Maidel*

The play opens with a brief scene that takes place in 1876, in a Polish *shtetl,* or village. In a small home, a baby boy, Mordechai Weiss, is born. As the birth takes place inside, a terrifying pogrom—a violent riot directed at Jews—takes place in the village outside. This scene fades into the next, which takes place many decades later and thousands of miles away from nineteenth-century Poland: the setting is an apartment on New York's West Side in 1946. Mordechai, now an older man, knocks on the door of his daughter's apartment late one night. His daughter calls herself by the Americanized name of Rose, but Mordechai calls her by her birth name, Rayzel. He explains to Rose that he has just discovered that her sister, Lusia, who was left behind in Poland when Rose and Mordechai emigrated in 1928, has survived the Holocaust and is coming to New York. In spite of Rose's protests that her apartment is too small and her sister a complete stranger, Mordechai insists that Lusia stay with Rose when she arrives.

Less than three weeks later, a few days ahead of schedule, Lusia arrives in New York and calls her sister. Flustered by the change of plans and nervous about the reunion, Rose agrees to pick Lusia up and take her back to the apartment. They return to the apartment, Rose rushing nervously about, talking nonstop, and Lusia quietly taking in the furnishings, modern conveniences, and small luxuries. Rose tries to remain cheerful but is clearly struck by her sister's pale, thin, and subdued appearance. In a fantasy sequence, Lusia talks to her husband, Duvid, for whom she has been searching since the war's end. She tells him, "Rayzel is afraid of me. She tries to hide it, avoids looking at me as one avoids a cripple." During their first night together, Rose hears Lusia moaning and crying in her sleep. Deciding not to wake her, Rose turns up the radio and covers her ears to avoid hearing her sister's nightmare.

The sisters attempt to get to know each other, but the gulf between them is wide. Having left Poland eighteen years earlier at age four, Rose remembers little about her sister and mother, and about her life in Poland. She has spent most of her life as an American, while Lusia grew up in a vastly different culture, speaking Yiddish (a language combining German dialects with Hebrew and other tongues spoken by most Jews in Eastern Europe) rather than English. The entire family had planned to leave Poland in 1928, but at the last minute Lusia became ill and had to stay behind with her mother. The expense of and restrictions on immigration during the Great Depression, and later World War II, prevented the family from reuniting—and left Lusia and her mother caught in the Nazi trap during the Holocaust.

Lusia spends a great deal of time thinking about the past. She reminisces about life with her mother, and about her best childhood friend, Hanna. She remembers her father as a well-dressed but strict and temperamental man. Lusia is determined to find her husband with the help of immigrant aid organizations in New York. Rose, feeling that Duvid may not even be alive, let alone in the United States, tries to discourage Lusia from hoping for too much. When Lusia and her father first see each other, they are awkward and tentative. Mordechai begins reading from a list of his relatives that had stayed be-

hind in Poland; as he reads the names, Lusia checks a list of her own and mechanically reads aloud the fate of each relative. Most are dead or missing, including Rose and Lusia's mother and Lusia's young daughter, Sprinze, who died at Auschwitz. In an imaginary conversation with her mother, Lusia expresses frustration with Mordechai's calm acceptance of the murdered relatives and his belief that it all happened according to God's will. Part of her wants Mordechai to feel some of the pain experienced by those who lived through the Nazi occupation.

From *A Shayna Maidel* by Barbara Lebow

LUSIA: (*Thrusting envelope out to* ROSE.) You open, please. Is your letter.

(ROSE *opens the envelope carefully.*)

ROSE: It's very fresh. Like it was just written.

LUSIA: Mama keeps the paper, I think, for long time before she sends this letter. Was all ready for when someone comes like the countess. I never seen her write nothing.

(ROSE *hands the open letter to* LUSIA, *who hesitates, then smells the scent of the letter.* LUSIA *can hardly speak.*)

Is Mama. Before…

(*She tries to give the letter back to* ROSE.)

Ich ken nit…Ken nit!

(ROSE *keeps looking at her, waiting.* LUSIA *breathes deeply, composes herself, then slowly sits apart from* ROSE, *begins shakily, relaxes more as she feels and enjoys her recognition of* MAMA *in the words. As she continues* ROSE *stiffens, reacting almost politely, as someone at a tea party. There are no tears.*)

Mayn tyereh tuchter, Rayzel…

Mine dearest daughter, Rayzel,

I'm not a learned woman. I wish I could be so I could say everything to you the right way. For a long time I have written and I know it could happen you don't get the letters. This one is meant by God's will to reach you. Maybe it is the last one for a time so I want to tell you how I feel.

If I could really be with you and put around you mine arms, it would be

Devastated by what she has seen and heard in the news about the Holocaust, Rose longs to have Lusia tell her what it was like and how their mother died. Lusia tells her it's too painful to talk about, but she does describe their mother during happier times. As the days pass, the sisters begin to feel more comfortable with each other. Lusia tells Rose about her dear friend Hanna; after spending their childhoods together, Lusia and Hanna also endured the Nazi camps together, both surviving. Hanna, however, was too ill with typhus, a deadly disease common in the unsanitary conditions of the camps, and did not live long after the liberation. Lusia is deeply troubled by the deaths of her loved ones, but she is also able to remember the laughter and good times from before the war.

One afternoon, Mordechai arrives at Rose's apartment with a box of family photos and a package that he received several months earlier from a woman who had known Rose and Lusia's mother in Poland. The woman, a countess, had carried the package with her to the United States and kept it safe

much better, but that is impossible. It cannot be.....

I want you should have your baby spoon. Your favorite, just your size and you could first feed yourself with it. Everyday since you and Papa went away, I keep it in a pocket with me, to touch what you touch. I knew I would give it back to you before you were five years old and now look what happened! Well, who are we to question the plan from God? Now when you have this baby spoon, you must get a feeling from your mother. Sometime you will have a child to use it, too, and she will feel from her grandmother. Or, who knows, maybe the family will be together by then.

You would think I would have more to tell you besides this baby spoon; advice and so forth, but I can't think of any more important right now. You can't put life on a piece of paper. Or love. I am not a smart person with writing down words, but I wish you understand how I am feeling for you, mine pretty little girl.

Your only mother,

Liba Eisenman Weiss

Chernov, Poland, June four, nineteen hundred and forty-two.

(LUSIA and ROSE *sit silently for awhile, then* LUSIA *puts the letter back in the envelope, kisses it, and gives it to* ROSE.)

ROSE: Thank you, Lusia.

until she found Mordechai. Inside the package are letters to Mordechai and Rose as well as keepsakes from Rose's childhood. Lusia retreats from the room, lost in a memory of a conversation with her mother from 1942, just before they are to be deported to a concentration camp. The countess had offered to take the mother with her in an attempt to escape from Poland, but the mother refused to go without Lusia and her baby. Lusia, her thoughts back in the present, begins to speak angrily to her father. She explains to Rose that, in the years after the Great Depression began but before the war, Mordechai had an opportunity to borrow enough money to bring Lusia and her mother to the United States. But in his determination not to owe money to anyone, Mordechai refused the loan. He claims he could not have known that Hitler would invade Poland and imprison Jews, but Lusia and Rose feel betrayed that he did not do all he could to save his daughter and wife.

Rose asks Lusia to read to her the letter their mother had written. Mordechai begins to leave the apartment, but before he goes he shows his daughters a picture of their mother when she was sixteen years old. "A shayna maidel," he says. In the glossary of Yiddish terms that accompanies the script, the playwright explains that the expression means more than just physical attractiveness: "It describes inner beauty and is an expression of love and of yearning hope." Deeply moved by the sight of their mother's handwriting, Lusia reads the letter to Rose, translating from Yiddish to English. The letter is a heartfelt expression of the mother's love for Rose and her longing to be reunited with her younger daughter. After reading the letter, Lusia leaves to go with Mordechai to look for her husband. Overcome by sadness for the mother she doesn't remember, Rose cries out for her mother and, as if in a trance, draws a number on her arm to match the tattooed prisoner number that Lusia was branded with in the Nazi camp. When Lusia returns to the apartment and sees what Rose has done with the pen, she is horrified. To Lusia, the number on her arm is a symbol of all her suffering, and she can't understand why Rose would elect to imitate that symbol. But Rose cries out for her, and Lusia embraces her sister.

In the final scene of the play, Lusia nervously paces the apartment. She hears a knock at the door; it is her husband, Duvid. Having been apart for six years, and spending every day of those years thinking of being together again, Lusia and Duvid are unsure how to behave with each other. Both have endured so much, but at first they don't know how to share their painful memories or their joy at being reunited. Lusia loses herself in a fantasy of a family gathering, including their mother and her friend Hanna, to celebrate their reunion and a baby that will soon be born to Lusia and Duvid. Returning to reality, Lusia tells Duvid that their daughter, who was born after Duvid had been arrested, resembled him. The doorbell rings; Rose has arrived at the apartment with Mordechai. Lusia introduces them, proud and nervous. Mordechai approaches his son-in-law and embraces him, reaching behind him to hold Lusia's hand in a gesture of unity and family togetherness.

Style and Themes in *A Shayna Maidel*

In *A Shayna Maidel*, Lebow has chosen to approach the Holocaust indirectly, showing the effects of the tragic events on one family in 1946, the year after World War II

Cover of the program for the play *A Shayna Maidel.* *Reproduced by permission of Playbill, Inc.*

ended. By focusing on one family's separations, losses, and deep emotional scars, Lebow makes it easier to comprehend the atrocities of the Holocaust. Grasping the suffering of millions of Jews and other victims can be a nearly impossible task. Through acquaintance with the Weiss family's pain, however, the audience can begin to understand the lives that were devastated by the Nazis' deeds. Lebow uses such techniques as flashback and fantasy sequences to reveal details about Lusia's life and to demonstrate the impact of the Holocaust on her mental and emotional state.

While the action of the play takes place far from Europe and a year after the war's end, the Holocaust plays a powerful role in the drama. Lusia represents the Holocaust itself, bringing with her painful reminders of grief, sorrow, and unspeakable suffering. She spends nearly as much time lost in thoughts and memories of the past as she does living in the present, and through those memories the audience catches a glimpse of the traumas she endured. Rose's reaction to her sister blends sorrow and sympathy with discomfort and even resentment that Lusia has arrived and disrupted her life. Rose is deeply troubled by thoughts of her mother and sister suffering, but, like millions of people who observed the events of World War II from afar, she perhaps would rather not be confronted by the overwhelming grief caused by the Holocaust.

Before Lusia's arrival, Rose's life was pleasant and comfortable. Lusia's presence unleashes a torrent of emotions for Rose: guilt that she did not have to endure life in Nazi-occupied Poland, sadness for having never really known her mother, and confusion about her identity—a confusion that serves as a major theme of *A Shayna Maidel*. Rose has spent most of her life in the United States, and, like many immigrants, she is determined to be thoroughly American. She changes her first name from the Polish "Rayzel" to the more American-sounding "Rose," and, without her father's knowledge, she has changed her last name, "Weiss," to "White." She longs to shed her ties to the "old country," avoiding the Yiddish accent that colors her father's speech and making a career out of observing American fashion trends. Closely tied to her desire to blend in as an American is her reluctance to be seen as Jewish. While her father proudly maintains his ties to Judaism, Rose has abandoned some of the customs. For example, she keeps kosher, Jewish dietary laws, only to please her father. Lusia's arrival in New York, however, alters Rose's perspective. Lusia has come to America because everything she had in Poland was destroyed; she finds American ways strange and forbidding and thinks longingly of her old life in Poland. As someone whose existence was threatened simply because she was Jewish, Lusia could not so easily abandon her religious identity.

Lebow also explores the theme of responsibility toward others. Mordechai had the opportunity to bring his wife and daughter to America, but he failed to act on it. His reluctance to borrow money for their overseas passage led to terrible and unforeseen consequences. On the one hand, he could not have known when he refused the loan that the Great Depression would be so widespread and long-lasting, and he could never have anticipated Hitler's rise to power and his brutal and murderous campaign against the Jews. On the other hand, he never told Rose that he had turned down a chance to bring the rest of the family to the United States; keeping that circumstance a secret indicates that he does blame himself and deeply regrets turning down the loan. His daughters blame him as well: Lusia harbors resentment toward him for not rescuing her and her mother from their terrible situation in Poland; Rose cannot believe that her old-fashioned father let pride prevent him from reuniting the family. Mordechai's actions, in all their complexity, can be seen to represent the actions of millions of people who did not do enough to save those whose lives were threatened by the Nazi regime.

While it explores the magnitude of the Holocaust and many other themes, *A Shayna Maidel* is basically a play about family ties and the complicated emotions that bind one family member to another. Rose and Lusia, having grown up apart and out of touch with each other, are virtual strangers when they meet in 1946. But, as their father points out, they are each other's flesh and blood, and they share a strong connection regardless of their dramatically different upbringings. Both daughters have a strained relationship with their father, whose strict and overbearing approach rarely allows them to voice their opposition. Rose belongs to a new generation that embraces the New World; Mordechai represents an old-fashioned, Old World lifestyle. Lusia's feelings toward her father are colored by the sense that he should have done more to bring her and her mother to the United States; she assigns him partial blame for her mother's death. In spite of the resentment and bitterness they occasionally feel toward each other, however, Rose, Lusia, and Mordechai realize that family relationships are precious. Especially in consideration of all they have lost, they understand that they must treasure the family they have.

Research and Activity Ideas

1) Research your own family's immigration history. When did your relatives arrive in the country you call home? What were their experiences—the obstacles, the adventures—upon arrival? In what ways did your family members assimilate, or blend in, to the dominant culture, and in what ways did they retain traditions from their former home?

2) In *A Shayna Maidel,* Lusia leaves Poland after the war with nothing. But when Mordechai and Rose left years earlier, they had the opportunity to bring many belongings with them. If you were to move to a new country, what personal items would you take with you to help you build a new life and to help you remember your old life? Assume that you have limited space—perhaps one suitcase—and you'll only be able to take truly cherished items.

3) Research the immigration laws in the United States in the years during and after World War II. Why do you think the government continued to restrict immigration even after it became clear that the actions of Nazi Germany were creating a severe refugee crisis? What more could have been done to save Jews and other victims of Nazi tyranny during the war, and what could have been done to ease the refugee situation after the war?

4) When Rose first shows Lusia around at the beginning of *A Shayna Maidel,* she points out several features of her apartment that seem to symbolize the good fortune of her life in America. If you were welcoming someone from another country, what objects would you choose to represent your lifestyle and culture? Choose three objects and write about what each one means in your life and what it says about your country's culture.

Where to Learn More About ...

Barbara Lebow and *A Shayna Maidel*

"Barbara Lebow." *Contemporary Theatre and Drama in the U.S.* http://www.fb10.uni-bremen.de/anglistik/kerkhoff/ContempDrama/Lebow.htm (accessed on December 18, 2002).

Miss Rose White [videorecording]. Republic Pictures/Hallmark Hall of Fame, 1991.

"Vanguard Theatre Ensemble Presents *A Shayna Maidel.*" *Vanguard Theatre Ensemble.* http://www.vte.org/shows/shayna.htm (accessed on December 18, 2002).

Holocaust Survivors in the United States

Diner, Hasia R. *Jewish Americans: The Immigrant Experience.* Westport, CT: Hugh Lauter Levin Associates, 2002.

Gruber, Ruth. *Haven: The Dramatic Story of 1,000 World War II Refugees and How They Came to America.* New York: Random House, 2000.

Wolman, Ruth, ed. *Crossing Over: An Oral History of Refugees from Hitler's Third Reich.* New York: Twayne Publishers, 1996.

Holocaust Films

6

Generations of filmmakers have attempted to portray the Holocaust on film, struggling to depict the significance, complexity, and tragedy of the event while remaining respectful to the memory of the millions who died at the Nazis' hands. Films made about the Holocaust include documentaries (factual, nonfiction films designed to educate and inform) and feature films that are based on real-life events but also make use of fictional stories and characters. Today's students of World War II (1939–45) can also learn about the time period from newsreels, factual films made during the war to be shown to the public as a source of information and inspiration. Regardless of the type of film, whether grounded in fact or intended as fiction, filmmakers present their own perspectives on history, shaping what the audience sees and influencing what the audience believes.

From the time of the first Holocaust-related films, some scholars have voiced their opposition to any fictional films addressing that subject. They have questioned filmmakers' ability to show, in a two-hour timeframe, enough information to give audiences a fair understanding of the complexity of the era and the inhumanity of the crime. Critics have also pointed out numerous issues filmmakers must cope with, including the movie's level of violence; directors must strike a fine balance between showing enough horror to be accurate but not so much that audiences become desensitized to the disaster. They must impose structure and order on complex events so brutal and horrifying that they defy simple understanding and ready explanation.

In his foreword to Annette Insdorf's book *Indelible Shadows: Film and the Holocaust,* Holocaust survivor and scholar Elie Wiesel points out some of the many difficulties associated with making a Holocaust-related feature film: "To direct the massacre of Babi Yar [at which tens of thousands of Ukrainian Jews and others were murdered by the Nazis in 1941] smells of blasphemy. To make up extras as corpses is obscene…. [T]he Holocaust as filmed romantic adventure seems to me an outrage to the memory of the dead, and to sensitivity." Many scholars have expressed concerns about the Holocaust being addressed in feature films because such movies are often made according to a Hollywood formula. These films tend to oversimplify ideas, reducing complex and serious issues to a straightforward battle between good and evil, for example. The Hollywood formula also dictates that all plot elements be neatly tied up by the film's end, with redemption for the "good guys" and punishment for the "bad guys." But the nature of the Holocaust—during which millions of innocent people were tortured and murdered, and the perpetrators often went unpunished—defies such tidy, familiar methods of storytelling.

Even documentary films, which avoid many of the pitfalls of feature films because they are factual in nature, have potential problems. Documentaries often use film footage—of ghettos and concentration camps, among other things—made by the Nazis, footage that was shot with a specific purpose. In his foreword to *Indelible Shadows,* Wiesel wonders, "Will the viewer continue to remember that these films [included in documentaries] were made by the killers to show the downfall and the baseness of their so-called subhuman victims?" In other words, can the archival footage shot by the Nazis show an accurate, "true" portrayal of life for the Jews during that era? Viewers tend to accept documentary films as authoritative, historically accurate representations, but even the most objective film reflects the views of the filmmaker, showing one person's version of the truth.

Despite many possible problems, Holocaust-related films possess some distinct benefits. Feature films, and even some documentaries, can reach millions of people all over the world. People who might otherwise never study the Holocaust can watch a movie about the subject and learn a great deal in a short time. The moving image can bring to life major elements of the era—the vitality of the Jewish community in the pre-Hitler years, the poverty and desperation of the ghetto, the terror and brutality of the concentration camp—in ways that cannot be done on the printed page. Movies can also effectively explore smaller, more intimate stories—such as a tale of the devastated life of a survivor in the war's aftermath—that help audiences grasp the impact of the Holocaust on individuals. Films can make historical events and faraway places seem immediate and vital, improving viewers' ability to broaden their understanding and remember what they've learned.

Filmmakers have addressed a variety of subjects related to the Holocaust, from broad overviews to specialized topics. Some films, such as *A New Germany, 1933–1939,* explore the social and political culture in Germany in the years after Hitler took power. Others, including *Image Before My Eyes,* examine the history of the Jewish community in Eastern Europe, a history that took a decisive turn under Hitler's rule. Many films, including *Lodz Ghetto* and *Kitty: Return to Auschwitz,* address the ghettos and the Nazi camps. Some films emphasize rescue and resistance (*The Courage to Care* and *Escape from Sobibor*), while others attempt to illustrate the tragedies suffered by the victims (*Survivors of the Holocaust*). A number of films cover the war's aftermath, exploring survivors' attempts to piece their lives back together (*The Long Way Home*) as well as the efforts to bring the Nazi perpetrators to justice in international courts (*Judgment at Nuremberg*).

Experiencing the Holocaust includes discussions of three films. *Au Revoir Les Enfants* ("Goodbye, Children") is a feature film based on events from the childhood of director Louis Malle. During World War II, Malle attended a Catholic boys' boarding school in German-occupied France. As depicted in the film, the priests and headmaster of the school risk their own safety to shelter several Jewish boys by allowing them to blend in with the other students. The film focuses on two boys at the school—one Jewish, one Catholic—who are first rivals and then friends. One boy must keep his identity a secret in order to survive; the other boy discovers that secret and must bear the burden of protecting his friend. Both boys learn hard truths about cruelty and hatred when the Jewish boy's identity is uncovered at the film's end. While Malle's film is based on actual events, some details of the story were altered in the making of the film.

Into the Arms of Strangers: Stories of the Kindertransport is a documentary film about an extraordinary program that saved the lives of thousands of Jewish children who otherwise probably would have perished during the Holocaust. In 1939 some 10,000 Jewish children from Poland, Germany, and elsewhere were sent by train, and then by boat, to England, where they lived in group homes or with the families of strangers. The film was produced by Deborah Oppenheimer, whose mother, Sylvia Avramovici, was one of the children saved by the Kindertransports. Many of the children in this program, including Oppenheimer's mother, never saw their parents again. Two years after her mother's death in 1993, Oppenheimer met a man who had also survived the Holocaust as a Kindertransport child. After researching the program and meeting other Kindertransport survivors, Oppenheimer decided to create this award-winning documentary.

Schindler's List is an Academy Award-winning feature film based on a novel by the same name that was written by Thomas Keneally. While both the book and the film were based on historical events and real people, some elements were changed in order to effectively tell the story. *Schindler's List* depicts several years in the life of Oskar Schindler, an Austrian-German factory owner and member of the Nazi Party. A complicated man, Schindler initially considers only his business's profitability, arranging for Jews to work as virtual slaves in his factory to avoid paying wages. Eventually he begins to sympathize with his workers, realizing that the jobs he provides them could save them from deportation to a death camp. Through his ever-growing list of "essential" workers (required, he says, for the German war effort), Schindler manages to keep more than 1,100 Jews from being sent to their deaths in a Nazi camp.

Representative Films about the Holocaust

The Attic: The Hiding of Anne Frank. Directed by John Erman. Telecom Entertainment, 1988. *This feature film is based on* Anne Frank Remembered, *a book written by Miep Gies. A Dutchwoman, Gies took care of Anne Frank and her family during their years in hiding.*

Au Revoir Les Enfants. Written and directed by Louis Malle. Orion Classics, 1987. *Set at a Catholic boys' school in German-occupied France, this film depicts two boys' loss of innocence as they are forced to confront the horrors of the Holocaust.*

Children Remember the Holocaust. Directed by D. Shone Kirkpatrick. Schoolbreak Special, 1995. *This documentary includes excerpts from diaries kept by children during the Holocaust. Photographs and archival film footage complement the diary entries.*

The Courage to Care. Produced and directed by Robert Gardner. United Way Productions, 1986. *This documentary examines the actions of several caring citizens who risked their own safety to help those being persecuted by the Nazis.*

The Devil's Arithmetic. Directed by Donna Deitch. Showtime, 1999. *Based on a novel of the same name by Jane Yolen, this feature film tells the story of a modern American Jewish teenager who is mysteriously transported back in time to a German-occupied Polish village in 1941.*

The Diary of Anne Frank. Directed by George Stevens. Twentieth Century Fox, 1959. *One of the first movies to focus on Holocaust experiences, this classic feature film is based on the play that is itself based on Anne Frank's diary.*

Escape from Sobibor. Directed by Jack Gold. Zenith Productions, 1987. *Based on a nonfiction book with the same title, this feature film depicts the courageous and deadly escape attempt made by several hundred prisoners from the death camp Sobibor.*

Heil Hitler: Confessions of a Hitler Youth. HBO, 1991. *In this documentary, former Hitler Youth member Alfons Heck, who went on to become a Holocaust educator in the United States, examines his participation in the Nazi youth group. The film explores the effectiveness of the Hitler Youth in converting a nation of young people into enthusiastic supporters of Germany's violently anti-Semitic policies.*

Image before My Eyes. Directed by Joshua Waletzky. YIVO Institute, 1980. *Incorporating interviews, photographs, and home movies, this documentary traces the rich history of the Jewish community in Poland from the nineteenth century until the destruction of that community during the Holocaust.*

Into the Arms of Strangers. Written and directed by Mark Jonathan Harris, produced by Deborah Oppenheimer. Warner Bros., 2000. *This powerful documentary examines the impact of the Kindertransport program, which sent thousands of Jewish children away from German-occupied countries to live with families in England and escape the Nazis' slaughter of the Jewish people.*

The Journey of Butterfly. Directed by Robert Frye. American Program Service, 1995. *Incorporating the poetry, music, and art of the children at Terezin, this film provides a history of this unusual concentration camp between 1941 and 1945.*

Judgment at Nuremberg. Directed by Stanley Kramer. United Artists, 1961. *This feature film explores the complexities of some of the postwar trials in Nuremberg, Germany, that attempted to bring Nazi perpetrators to justice.*

Kitty: Return to Auschwitz. Produced and directed by Peter Marley. Social Studies School Service, 1979. *Kitty Felix Hart was a prisoner at Auschwitz as a teenager. In this documentary, she visits Auschwitz decades later in an attempt to understand and cope with her haunting memories.*

The Last Seven Months of Anne Frank. Directed by Willy Lindwer. Moriah Films, 1988. *This documentary, filmed in the Netherlands, is based on interviews with eight women, all Holocaust survivors who lived with Anne Frank and her sister Margot in the concentration camps of Westerbork, Auschwitz-Birkenau, and Bergen-Belsen.*

Life Is Beautiful. Directed by Roberto Benigni. Miramax Films, 1997. *This Academy Award-winning Italian feature film focuses on a fictional Jewish man and his young family who are captured and sent to a concentration camp. Arousing controversy for including elements of comedy and fantasy, the movie deals with themes of good versus evil and hope in the face of hopelessness.*

Lodz Ghetto. Directed by Alan Adelson and Kathryn Taverna. Jewish Heritage Project/National Endowment for the Humanities, 1989. *Using photographs, archival film footage, and the secret diaries left behind by residents who were sent to their deaths by the Nazis, this documentary film recounts the lives and struggles of 200,000 Jews in the Lodz ghetto.*

The Long Way Home. Written and directed by Mark Jonathan Harris. Moriah Films/Simon Wiesenthal Center, 1997. *Often overlooked in Holocaust literature and film are the years following World War II, when Jewish refugees struggled to find a place for themselves. This documentary film focuses on the years 1945 through 1948, when lingering anti-Semitism prevented Holocaust survivors from returning to their prewar homes, and tight immigration restrictions kept them out of other countries around the world.*

A New Germany, 1933–1939. Written and directed by Michael Darlow. Thames Television, 1975. *Part of the World at War series, this documentary explores the social and political culture in Germany during Hitler's first six years as leader.*

Schindler's List. Directed by Steven Spielberg. Amblin Entertainment/Universal Pictures, 1993. *This Academy Award-winning film is based on the true story of businessman Oskar Schindler, who saved the lives of over one thousand Jews by designating them as essential workers in his World War II factory.*

Survivors of the Holocaust. Directed by Allan Holzman. Survivors of the Shoah Visual History Foundation/Turner Original Productions, 1996. *This documentary, initiated by film director Steven Spielberg, collects testimonies of survivors as well as photographs, artifacts, and film footage from the World War II era.*

Terezin Diary. Directed by Dan Weissman and written by Zuzana Justman. First Run/Icarus Films, 1989. *In this documentary, men and women who spent unforgettable childhood years imprisoned at Terezin recall their experiences and talk about the lives they've led since the end of the war.*

Weapons of the Spirit. Written, produced, and directed by Pierre Sauvage. Pierre Sauvage Productions, 1989. *This film relates the story of the French village Le Chambon-sur-Lignon, whose residents saved five thousand Jews from death during World War II.*

Witness to the Holocaust. Produced and directed by C. J. Pressma. Holocaust Education Project, 1984. *A seven-part overview of the Holocaust using survivor testimony and photographs from the period, this documentary covers topics from the rise of the Nazis to the Final Solution to liberation and its aftermath.*

Au Revoir Les Enfants

Directed by Louis Malle

Au *Revoir Les Enfants,* which translates to "Goodbye, Children," was written, directed, and produced by the late French filmmaker Louis Malle (1932–1995). The film is based on events from Malle's childhood, events that haunted him for decades. This award-winning film tells a story of a Catholic boys' boarding school in German-occupied France during World War II (1939–45). A tale of friendship and the loss of innocence, *Au Revoir Les Enfants* depicts the developing bond between two boys, Julien and Jean, one of whom is hiding a life-threatening secret. The school's headmaster, Father Jean, has agreed to hide three Jewish boys, including young Jean, at his school, disguising them as Christians so they will be protected from the Nazis. In a nation tightly controlled by Nazi Germany, a dictatorial regime bent on imperial domination and the destruction of European Jews, the priests at the school risk their lives to shelter the three young boys.

Awards: Academy Award nominations, 1988, for Best Foreign Language Film, Best Writing (screenplay written directly for the screen). British Academy of Film and Television Arts (BAFTA) Award, 1989, for Best Direction. César Awards (France), 1988,

Chronology of Events Relating to *Au Revoir Les Enfants*

October 30, 1932: Filmmaker Louis Malle is born in Thumeries, France.

September 3, 1939: World War II begins as Great Britain and France declare war on Germany, two days after Hitler's invasion of Poland.

May 10, 1940: Northern France is invaded by Germany.

June 1940: France is divided into the German-occupied zone in the North and the unoccupied zone, run by the collaborating Vichy government, in the South.

June 6, 1944: D-Day; Allied troops land in Normandy, France; France is liberated from Nazi control a few months later.

May 8, 1945: World War II ends in Europe.

1987: Malle releases his semi-autobiographical film, *Au Revoir Les Enfants.*

November 23, 1995: Malle dies of cancer in Beverly Hills, California.

for several categories, including Best Director, Best Film, Best Writing (original or adaptation). Los Angeles Film Critics Association Award, 1987, for Best Foreign Film.

Rating: PG; contains disturbing material.

Biography of Director Louis Malle

Louis Malle was born on October 30, 1932, in Thumeries, a city in northern France. The son of Pierre and Françoise Malle, Louis grew up in a large, wealthy family. He was descended from a nobleman who had made a fortune in refined sugar, and his family's wealth enabled him to spend summers in Ireland and attend expensive schools. When Malle was a young boy, northern France was invaded by Germany. As the war progressed, Malle's parents sent him to a Catholic boarding school in the quiet northern town of Fontainebleu. While there, he experienced the traumatic event that would later inspire the film *Au Revoir Les Enfants*: some Jewish children being hidden at the school by the priests were discovered by Nazi troops and taken, along with the headmaster, to concentration camps.

In the early 1950s, Malle began studying political science, but film was his true love, and, against his family's wishes, he transferred to film school in 1953. After graduating, he worked with undersea explorer Jacques Cousteau to direct the 1956 film *Le Monde du Silence,* or *The Silent World.* The film earned Malle widespread acclaim and some important awards, including the 1956 Palme d'Or at the Cannes Film Festival in France and the 1957 Academy Award for best documentary. This documentary marked the beginning of a forty-year career filled with a wide variety of movies—some controversial, some groundbreaking, many highly praised. In the 1950s and 1960s, Malle was associated with the French New Wave, an important cinematic movement. But many film scholars have pointed out that his insistence on embracing a variety of styles and subjects rather than fully exploring just a few separated him from his somewhat more celebrated peers, including François Truffaut (1932–1984) and Jean-Luc Godard (1930–).

Several of Malle's films sparked controversy, particularly in the United States, due to what was considered at the time to be bold sexual content. His 1958 film *Les Amants,* or *The Lovers,* resulted in the owners of a movie theater in Ohio being convicted of obscenity charges (the conviction was later overturned by the U.S. Supreme Court). While shocking to some moviegoers, the film earned critical praise and several awards. *La Vie Privée* (*A Very Private Affair,* 1962), a film starring French sex symbol Brigitte Bardot, and *Le Souffle au Coeur* (*Murmer of the Heart,* 1971), a movie depicting an incestuous relationship between mother and son, also caused a stir with American audiences but won the admiration of critics. In the late 1960s, Malle spent time in India and created two well-reviewed documentaries, *Calcutta* and *Phantom India.*

Malle also made a number of films in the United States, beginning in 1978 with *Pretty Baby,* the film that launched the career of model and actress Brooke Shields, who plays a twelve-year-old prostitute in the film. *Atlantic City,* released in 1980, starred Burt Lancaster and Susan Sarandon. The film won several international awards and is considered to be among Malle's best American films. The unusual *My Dinner with André* (1981), starring playwright and actor Wallace Shawn and playwright André Gregory as themselves, consists entirely of the two men having a lively conversation over dinner in a restaurant. Around this time Malle married American actress Candice Bergen. Together they had one child, a daughter named Chloe, born in 1985. (Malle had been married previously and had fathered two children, a son named Cuote and a daughter named Justine, in prior relationships.) Malle and Bergen divided their time between the United States, where Bergen starred in the long-running television show *Murphy Brown,* and France.

In 1987 Malle released his most personal—and, to many reviewers, his most accomplished—film, *Au Revoir Les Enfants.* This semi-autobiographical movie represents a crucial turning point in Malle's own childhood. While several details of the story were changed for the film, the central plot elements—the sheltering of Jewish boys at Malle's Catholic boarding school, and their eventual discovery and arrest by Nazi soldiers—did take place. As quoted in *Indelible Shadows: Film and the Holocaust,* Malle describes the moments when the boys were taken away by the Nazi police as "the most important event of my childhood: it really changed my life." Malle had long wanted to make a film about this haunting childhood event, but he delayed doing so for decades until he was satisfied he could handle the sensitive subject matter with the proper respect. He had tackled the subject of World War II-era France in an earlier film, *Lacombe, Lucien* (1974), but *Au Revoir Les Enfants* was less about the French response to Nazi Germany than it was about friendship and the moment when a boy leaves his childhood behind.

In 1992 Malle again earned notoriety for his sexually frank film *Damage,* starring Jeremy Irons and Juliette Binoche. His 1994 film, the experimental *Vanya on 42nd Street,* reunited him with the stars of *My Dinner with André* in an exploration of the play *Uncle Vanya,* written by acclaimed Russian playwright Anton Chekhov. Hailed by critics as bold and original, *Vanya on 42nd Street* stands as Malle's final achievement in film. After a long struggle with lymphoma, a kind of cancer, Malle died on November 23, 1995, at his home in Beverly Hills, California.

Historical Background of *Au Revoir Les Enfants*
When Adolf Hitler (1889–1945) sought to become the leader of Germany, he was motivated by the fanatical pursuit

of two different—but in his mind, closely related—goals. First, he wished to rebuild Germany's economy and its military forces, both of which had been devastated by the nation's humiliating defeat in World War I (1914–18). A second and equally important goal to Hitler was ridding Germany of all Jewish people. Hitler mistakenly considered the Jews a separate race, rather than a religious or ethnic group. He felt that Germany's future depended on the protection of a pure, strong master race he called the Aryan race from what he considered poisonous, diseased elements, such as Jews, mentally and physically disabled people, people of color, Roma (Gypsies), and others. As he rose through the ranks of the National Socialist, or Nazi, Party and began to attract national attention, Hitler persuaded many Germans to feel the same way he did. Anti-Semitism, or hatred of Jews, had existed throughout Europe for centuries, and in the mid-twentieth century, it was still widespread in Germany. Through an extremely effective campaign of propaganda (the spreading of information, and sometimes misinformation, to persuade people to adopt a certain viewpoint), Hitler capitalized on existing anti-Semitism and convinced a large number of German citizens that Jews were a plague capable of destroying German society. He also convinced Germans that he was the man to take care of this "problem" and to create a new and even more powerful German empire, which he called the Third Reich (*reich* means "empire").

From persecution to the Final Solution

Hitler became the chancellor (prime minister) of Germany in January 1933. Within two months, he had persuaded the German public and lawmakers that Germany faced a dangerous enemy, the Jews, that could only be dealt with by a strong leader. He declared himself the Führer—the dictator, or sole leader—of Germany, and he possessed tremendous power. From the beginning, he encouraged German citizens to humiliate and harass Jews. He immediately began enacting laws that separated Jews from the larger society, limiting their participation in certain professions and their enrollment in schools and universities. Over the next several years, the government of the Third Reich implemented ever more severe laws that resulted in depriving Jews of most of their rights. The Nuremberg Laws of 1935, for example, declared Jews a separate race, no longer entitled to the protections of German citizenship. Other laws forced Jews to hand over their businesses for a minimal fee to Aryans, a process called Aryanization, and to give up their valuables and their homes. By the late 1930s, many Jews were impoverished, unable to earn a living. But the worst was yet to come.

On November 9, 1938, widespread riots took place throughout Germany and Austria (which Germany had taken over in March), during which Nazis and their supporters destroyed many Jewish homes, businesses, and synagogues. Known as *Kristallnacht,* or the "Night of Broken Glass," because of the thousands of smashed windows, these riots resulted in the deaths and beatings of numerous Jews, and the arrest of tens of thousands of Jews, who were sent to concentration camps. The Nazis' determination to rid Germany—and all nations conquered

by Germany—of Jews had taken on a new urgency. In the first months of World War II, which began with Germany's invasion of Poland on September 1, 1939, high-ranking Nazi officers puzzled over what they termed the "Jewish question." As more and more nations came under Germany's control, the number of Jews to be dealt with increased. Various plans emerged, including deporting all Jews to be imprisoned in a region of Poland or forcing Jews to immigrate to Madagascar, an island off the coast of southeast Africa. Both plans were dismissed as impractical.

Many thousands of Jews and other so-called enemies of the Third Reich were forced to perform slave labor in labor camps and concentration camps. The conditions in such camps were brutal and inhumane, and many prisoners died of disease, starvation, and exhaustion. Many others who developed an illness or injury that prevented them from working, or who happened to be nearby when a guard became possessed with a murderous impulse, were executed by Nazi

Through an extremely effective campaign of propaganda, Adolf Hitler convinced a large number of German citizens that Jews were a plague capable of destroying German society. *Reproduced by permission of Corbis Corporation.*

guards. While the rate of death in the camps was extremely high, Hitler and his associates searched for a faster and more effective way to eliminate the Jews. By the middle of 1941, the Nazi leadership had determined that the most effective way of answering the Jewish question was to murder every last Jew in Europe, a plan known as the Final Solution.

Germany invades France

Hitler's territorial ambitions knew no bounds. In 1938 he took over Austria and the Sudetenland, part of Czechoslovakia. In 1939 Germany invaded the remaining regions of Czechoslovakia and then Poland. In April 1940 German troops invaded Denmark and Norway, and May brought an invasion of the Netherlands, Belgium, Luxembourg, and northern France. In spite of its powerful army and the support of several hundred thousand British troops, France suffered great losses under the onslaught of the German army. French troops were further taxed when the dictator of Italy, Benito Mussolini (1883–1945), sent troops into southern France and declared war on that nation and on Britain. To spare Paris the complete destruction that was bound to come from the bombs of German planes, the government fled, along with millions of citizens, declaring the French capital an open city. In mid-June 1940, the German army marched into Paris, unopposed by the French.

The French government took up residence in the city of Vichy, naming Marshal Philippe Pétain (1856–1951) the nation's new prime minister. (A Marshal is a high-ranking military officer.) Pétain immediately called for an armistice, or truce, between France and Germany. On June 22, 1940, the armistice agreement was signed, dividing France into several parts. The complex arrangement divided most of France into two zones: the occupied zone in the north, run by the German military, and the unoccupied zone in the south, run by Pétain's Vichy government. Vichy France, as it was known, was allowed to maintain sovereignty, or independent rule, although in reality it was strongly influenced by the policies of Nazi Germany. In late 1942, even the appearance of independence was abolished when Germany invaded the southern portion of France, effectively controlling the entire nation.

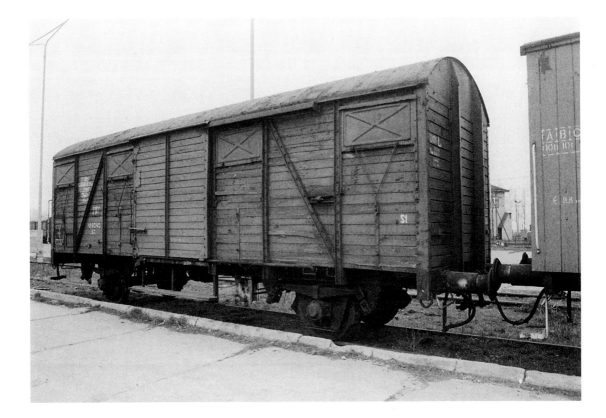

France: A divided nation

French society was deeply divided during this period. Some citizens, desiring peace, supported the Vichy government. At the time of the German invasion of France, it appeared that Hitler would win World War II, and some in France felt that it was in the nation's best interest to become an ally of Germany rather than an enemy. They further believed that France had little choice but to cooperate with the powerful German forces. In addition, anti-Semitism was fairly widespread in France; some French people even blamed the Jews for causing World War II, and some citizens were sympathetic with Nazi Germany's aim to rid Europe of Jews. Many French citizens, however, despised the Vichy government and its supporters, known as collaborators for their cooperation with the Nazis. The Vichy government seemed to embrace Germany (although some Vichy leaders said they were going along with Hitler to protect France), cooperating far more than was necessary, and far more than the governments of other occupied nations.

Freight car used for transporting Jews to concentration camps.
Reproduced by permission of Corbis Corporation.

Rescue in a French Village

While many French citizens cooperated with the Nazis occupying their country, a significant number worked actively to oppose the Nazi policy of genocide, or mass murder, toward the Jews. Religious figures, local leaders, and ordinary citizens throughout the country helped to hide Jews or transport them to safer places. In one case of extraordinary heroism and courage, an entire village banded together to provide a safe haven for thousands of Jews.

In Le Chambon-sur-Lignon, a small village in south central France—the part of the country ruled by the Nazi-influenced Vichy government—a pastor named André Trocmé preached nonviolence and encouraged acts of kindness and decency. In this village of Protestants, a tiny minority with a history of religious persecution in a largely Catholic country, his message of tolerance carried a great deal of weight with the citizens. When the Vichy government began actively cooperating with the Nazis in the deportation of French Jews to concentration camps, the people of Le Chambon felt a sense of moral outrage and vowed to defy their government and to protect as many Jews as possible.

The Vichy government volunteered to work with Germany in the area of policy toward Jews; the French leaders thought that such cooperation would not outrage French citizens as much as other types of cooperation. By the fall of 1940, anti-Jewish laws—similar to those passed in Germany and other German-occupied nations—were passed in France. Foreign-born Jews, many thousands of whom had come to France in the 1930s to escape Hitler's wrath, were especially targeted. When the Nazis began deporting Jews from France to concentration camps and death camps in Poland, the Vichy government, with the help of the French police force, agreed to conduct roundups of foreign-born Jews. Vichy leaders refused to cooperate in rounding up French-born Jews, but in spite of the government's stand, tens of thousands of native French Jews were deported and killed during Germany's occupation of France, particularly in the period after Germany occupied the Vichy region.

French resistance

Throughout France, numerous citizens—including a large percentage of Jews—offered resistance to the Nazis in

Pastor Trocmé, his wife, Magda, and another pastor, Edouard Theis, worked tirelessly with the residents of Le Chambon to protect every Jew that came to them for help. Jews were hidden in village homes, farmhouses, and other places in the surrounding countryside. Group homes were established for Jewish children whose parents had been deported to Nazi concentration and death camps. Jewish refugees were smuggled out of France and taken to countries where they would be safe from the Nazis. Every act of kindness and aid toward Jews carried with it a tremendous risk of arrest and deportation, but the people of Le Chambon felt they could not turn away people in dire need of assistance.

In 1943 Trocmé was arrested, although someone in a position of power obtained his release a short time later. His cousin Daniel, devoted director of a house of refugee children, was far less fortunate. Arrested in the summer of 1943, Daniel was sent to the Majdanek death camp, where he was later murdered. In all, the people of Le Chambon managed to save the lives of somewhere between 3,000 and 5,000 Jews, many of them children and all of them targeted for destruction by the Nazis.

various forms. Some participated in military sabotage, bombing railroad lines and destroying German military equipment. Others helped with the secret spread of information to British troops about the movements of the German army. Some provided shelter for Allied troops (including those from Great Britain and the United States) whose planes had been shot down over France. Many people offered resistance to the Nazis—and support for the Jews—by hiding Jews, especially children, or by providing false documents that allowed Jews to pass as Christians. While the Catholic church and other Christian religions failed to strongly protest the Nazis' treatment of Jews, many individual clergy members felt it was their duty to help Jews. Particularly after the widespread deportation of Jews began and after hearing the rumors that these Jews were taken to camps and killed, many religious leaders offered to hide Jews or help them escape to safe countries. All of those who participated in the resistance did so at great personal risk; those found to be involved in such activities were arrested and frequently sent to concentration camps.

As the war progressed and Germany's position began to weaken, the resistance grew more powerful and French collaborators were more openly despised. Particularly hated were those who volunteered for the French militia, a citizens' military-style organization that worked closely with the Nazis. When the British and American troops landed on the beaches of Normandy on June 6, 1944, an event known as D-Day, many resistance groups actively assisted the Allies in driving the Germans out of France. Desperately trying to complete their mission of destroying all French Jews, the Nazis continued deporting Jewish prisoners to death camps even at the expense of military operations. By the end of August, Paris had been liberated from the Nazis, and by the winter, German troops had been completely forced out of France. In spite of the efforts of resistance workers, nearly eighty thousand Jews living in France perished in the Holocaust. That figure makes up nearly a quarter of the overall Jewish population of France.

Plot and Characters in *Au Revoir Les Enfants*

Au Revoir Les Enfants opens with a farewell scene in a train station between Julien Quentin and his mother. Julien, who represents filmmaker Louis Malle as a child in this semi-autobiographical film, is returning from vacation to a Catholic boarding school some distance from his family's home in Paris. Julien boards the train slowly, resentful that he is being sent away and reluctant to leave his mother. At the school, Julien and the other boys unpack their things in the large dormitory room they share. One of the monks brings a new boy, one of three new students, into the dormitory and assigns him the bed next to Julien. The other students tease and harass the new student, Jean Bonnet, as a way of evaluating whether he is worthy of their friendship. In his first weeks at the school, Bonnet keeps to himself as much as possible, responding to the teasing with a pride and toughness that, over time, earns grudging respect from Julien. Julien observes that he and Bonnet share an appreciation for literature, especially adventure stories. A bright and accomplished student, Julien also sees Bonnet as a rival; Bonnet performs well in classes and receives praise from the teachers.

While the students' days are filled with classes, church services, and schoolyard games—just as they would be

under ordinary circumstances at a Catholic school—the presence of the war is felt by all. Food and heat are rationed, and classes are occasionally interrupted by sirens announcing a bombing raid. At such times the staff and children take refuge in an air-raid shelter, trying to continue with classes but occasionally resorting to prayer when the bombs get too close. Several of the students, including Julien and his older brother, François, trade black-market goods (items forbidden under the wartime regulations) with Joseph, the young kitchen worker who walks with a limp and clearly comes from a different social class than the wealthy students. The boys trade food brought from home and other valuables for hard-to-find items like stamps or cigarettes.

Observing the new student, Julien senses that Bonnet is different from the other boys. He notices certain things that set Bonnet apart, yet he doesn't initially understand the significance. He sees, for example, that Bonnet does not say the "Hail, Mary" prayer with the other students during a bombing

The character Julien leaving his mother at the beginning of *Au Revoir Les Enfants*. *Reproduced by permission of the Kobal Collection.*

raid (Bonnet has told the others that he is a Protestant). In the middle of one night, Julien wakes up to see Bonnet quietly saying prayers over lighted candles. And when French militia members arrive at the school to conduct a surprise search one day, Julien sees one of the teachers whisking Bonnet away from the playground. Eager to learn more about the mysterious student, Julien looks through Bonnet's things while alone in the dormitory one afternoon. He discovers that Bonnet's real name is Jean Kippelstein, a name that suggests his Jewish heritage. Julien finally pieces together the fact that Bonnet is being hidden from the Nazis by the monks at the school.

Julien, a smart boy who is nonetheless somewhat ignorant about the world outside his own social circle, asks his brother what it means to be a Jew. François responds that Jews don't eat pork and that they crucified Jesus. Julien points out that the Romans crucified Jesus, and then asks why the Jews are forced to wear yellow stars. François does not answer, concerned primarily with getting a love note to the attractive young woman who gives Julien and other students piano lessons. Later, Julien questions Bonnet about his background and the whereabouts of his parents. Bonnet simply says that his father is a prisoner-of-war, which means nothing to Julien but can be assumed by the audience to mean that his father is in a concentration camp because he is a Jew. He also acknowledges that he doesn't know where his mother is because he hasn't heard from her in several months, a fact that clearly upsets him. Julien, who is extremely attached to his own mother, feels a surge of sympathy for Bonnet.

One day, the students play a game in the forest involving warring sides, the taking of prisoners, and the search for the other team's hidden treasure. Julien and Bonnet become separated from the rest of the kids, and while Julien is elated to find the other team's treasure, the boys soon realize they are lost and darkness is approaching. They are found by two German soldiers, and Bonnet, in a panic, tries to run from them. The soldiers quickly catch him, but they suspect nothing unusual and return the boys to the school. Considered heroes for their adventure and for their encounter with the Germans, Julien and Bonnet do not reveal that they were terrified during the incident. While still unsure whether they can trust each other, the boys have begun to develop a bond. Afterwards, while resting in the infirmary, Julien reveals that

he knows Bonnet's secret. Bonnet reacts angrily, lashing out at Julien for uncovering his Jewish identity.

During parents' day, when Julien's mother has come to the school for a visit, Julien and Bonnet get into a fight in the playground. This fight somehow allows the boys to set their hostilities aside and align themselves as friends. Julien invites Bonnet to join his family for lunch in a fancy restaurant in town. While there, French militia men enter the restaurant and begin harassing a well-dressed elderly Jewish man, questioning why he is in a restaurant that does not allow Jews. When they order the man to leave, many of the diners object, feeling more furious with the French collaborators than offended by the presence of a Jew where he is legally forbidden. A German officer, in part to impress Julien's attractive mother, tells the militia members to leave the restaurant.

One day, Joseph the kitchen worker is accused of stealing food supplies from the school to sell on the black

A scene from *Au Revoir Les Enfants,* **a movie in which Jewish boys are disguised as Christians to avoid Nazi persecution.** *Reproduced by permission of the Kobal Collection.*

market. He admits that he has occasionally traded with students, and he gives the names of those students to the headmaster, Father Jean. Joseph, who is poor and has few options outside his job with the school, is fired, while the wealthy students are merely scolded. Not long after, members of the Gestapo, the powerful Nazi police force, show up at the school. They interrupt a math class, asking which of the students is named Jean Kippelstein. No one replies—only Julien and some of the teachers know Bonnet's real name. When the Gestapo agent doing the questioning turns his back on the class for a moment, Julien steals a glance at Bonnet. The Gestapo agent notices the glance and immediately knows that Bonnet is the boy he is looking for. Bonnet is then removed from the classroom. The Nazis find the other Jewish boys hidden at the school and arrest Father Jean for his role in hiding the children. One of the Jewish students manages to run away from the troops, but his hiding place is betrayed by a nun working in the school infirmary.

The Gestapo orders the school to be closed and tells all of the students to pack their things. Julien is in the dormitory when Bonnet is brought in to gather his belongings, and Bonnet comforts his friend by saying that Julien's glance did not seal his fate; Bonnet assures him that the Nazis would have found him regardless. Stepping outside, Julien encounters Joseph and learns that he, in an act of revenge against Father Jean for firing him, had notified the Gestapo that Jewish children were being hidden at the school.

In the film's final scene, the students have gathered in the courtyard to be questioned by one of the Gestapo officers. They stand helplessly by as Father Jean and the three Jewish boys are taken away by the Nazis. A chorus of voices calls out, "Au revoir, mon père" ("goodbye, father"). Father Jean turns to the students and replies, "Au revoir, les enfants" ("goodbye, children"). Audiences then hear the voice of the filmmaker describing what actually happened to the Jewish boys and the school headmaster after they were taken from his school. The three boys died at the infamous concentration camp and death camp known as Auschwitz, while Father Jean died at a concentration camp called Mauthausen. Malle states that in spite of the passage of many decades since that incident in his childhood, he cannot forget what happened: "I will remember every second of that January morning until I die."

Style and Themes in *Au Revoir Les Enfants*

Louis Malle, after deliberating for many years over addressing a traumatic childhood event in a movie, chose to present the personal story of *Au Revoir Les Enfants* in a straightforward, low-key style. The story is told as a series of everyday events—tests of skill and bravery on the playground, competitions in the classroom, a trip to a public bathhouse—rather than a highly dramatic buildup to an earth-shattering climax. When the crucial scene does arrive and the three Jewish boys are led away by the Gestapo, the audience feels the same sense of shock that the other students, including Malle himself, must have felt when the event actually took place in 1944. The style of the actors is natural and understated. The actors portraying Julien and Bonnet strike audiences as ordinary boys, never giving the impression that they are acting in a role or trying to convey serious emotions.

While the film's style may be described as spare and simple, the characters in the story are quite complex. Julien is the film's main character, and we see events unfold through his point of view. He is not, however, a hero. Malle has created a character based on himself who is not immediately likable. In *Indelible Shadows,* Malle explains: "It was important to show Julien as arrogant, a little spoiled, with moments of anguish and solitude." Malle wished to explore themes of guilt and innocence, good and evil, without providing easy answers about who falls into which category. Julien behaves unkindly to Bonnet in the first part of the film, doing little to make the new student feel more comfortable. But he does possess kindness and sensitivity, and he eventually displays these qualities with Bonnet. In addition, when Julien turns in the final scene to look at Bonnet in the presence of the Gestapo, the audience knows he is simply a child who behaves without thinking rather than a cruel person intending another's destruction.

Other characters in the film further illustrate the complexity of the time period and of Malle's recollection of his childhood. The teachers at the school are heroic, risking their lives and the school's future by harboring Jewish children. Not all French citizens are portrayed in such a positive light, however. In fact, the most vicious and hateful characters in the film are not the Nazi troops but the French collaborators. Several German characters, in fact, are presented in an almost positive light. The German officer in the restaurant, for example, ridicules the French militia members and allows the elderly Jewish man to stay at his table. And the soldiers who find Julien and Bonnet after their adventure in the forest treat them with kindness and respect (not suspecting, of course, that Bonnet is a Jew). Malle had no intention of portraying all Germans in a favorable way, however: the Gestapo agent who comes to the school at the end is quietly menacing and frighteningly businesslike as he roots out the Jewish children at the school and sends them off to certain death. The very fact that the Nazis put such effort into uncovering the hiding place of three young boys conveys the depths of their murderous hatred of the Jewish people.

Malle explores many themes in *Au Revoir Les Enfants*, addressing primarily the complexities of friendship and the loss of innocence. The bond between Julien and Bonnet develops gradually and far from smoothly. The boys do not initially trust each other, and Julien sees Bonnet as more of a rival, or competitor, than a friend. (The actual relationship between the boys in Malle's own childhood, in fact, was that of rivals; Malle and the new boy were not friends, and Malle did not suspect he was Jewish until he was led away by the Gestapo.) Eventually, however, they realize that they like and admire each other. Through their common interest in books, their adventure together in the forest, and the secret they share about Bonnet's true identity, the boys forge a friendship.

The theme perhaps most touchingly explored in *Au Revoir Les Enfants* is the loss of innocence and the end of childhood. As the audience learns that Bonnet is a Jew desperately trying to protect his life, and that he has lost contact with his parents, it becomes clear that his childhood has abruptly ended. He admits to Julien that he is afraid "all the time," and the gravity of his situation has made it difficult for him to experience the pleasures of youth. Julien, through his contact with Bonnet and his dawning understanding of what it means that his friend is a Jew in Nazi-occupied France, also experiences an end to innocence. Julien reaches a new level of maturity and understanding by the end of the movie. He had never really known a Jew before, and he also had not been acquainted with the terrible power of hate and prejudice. Malle is quoted in *Indelible Shadows* as saying that the arrest of the Jewish boys at his boarding school confirmed his suspicion that "the world of adults was one of injustice, deception, false explanations, hypocrisy and lies." The character in the film, as well as the person he is based on, could no longer view the world with a child's innocence after that day.

With the loss of innocence comes the acknowledgment of guilt, another major theme of *Au Revoir Les Enfants*. In the film, Julien accidentally reveals his friend's identity to the Gestapo agent. In spite of Bonnet's assurances that he would have been discovered anyway, it is clear that Julien will struggle with the regret of that moment for the rest of his life. In reality, that fateful glance never took place; Malle has acknowledged that he added that incident to the movie as an obvious representation of the guilt he felt when the boys were arrested by the Gestapo. His guilt, and that of many bystanders who witnessed the events of the Holocaust, involves a failure to grasp the enormity of the situation and to speak out against it. While a twelve-year-old boy could do little to change the actions of the Nazis and to protect his friend, Malle clearly struggled for years with a sense of failed responsibility toward fellow human beings.

Research and Activity Ideas

1) Examine the issues of guilt and innocence as explored in *Au Revoir Les Enfants*. What do you think were Louis Malle's feelings about the level of guilt of uninvolved bystanders and of those who actively sought out Jews to punish? Compare the actions of bystanders to the Nazis and the French collaborators; then compare the bystanders' actions to the heroic behavior of Father Jean and the other teachers who risked so much to protect the Jewish boys.

2) Either in an individual essay or in group discussion, explore the definition of prejudice and the ways in which this concept is addressed in *Au Revoir Les Enfants*. Prejudice can be expressed in horrible, hateful ways—as in the Nazis' attempts to eliminate Jews during the Holocaust—or in milder forms. Discuss the various levels of prejudice seen in the film. Examine in particular the

scene in the restaurant when the French militia members humiliate the Jewish customer and tell him to leave. In a conversation after the incident is over, Julien's mother is alarmed at her son's suggestion that some of their relatives are Jewish, but she then claims that she has nothing against Jews. Do you think the mother is prejudiced?

3) *Au Revoir Les Enfants* deals with the developing friendship between Julien and Bonnet. Make a list of qualities that you think are important in a friend. Think about your closest friend, and write an essay about your friendship with that person. How did the friendship form? Was it gradual, or did it happen quickly?

Where to Learn More About …

Louis Malle and *Au Revoir Les Enfants*

"*Au Revoir Les Enfants.*" *IMDb: Internet Movie Database.* http://us.imdb.com/Title?0092593 (accessed on December 18, 2002).

Insdorf, Annette. *Indelible Shadows: Film and the Holocaust.* Cambridge: Cambridge University Press, 1989.

LaSalle, Mick. "The Compassionate Observer: Louis Malle's Films Shed Light on Humanity." *SF Gate: The San Francisco Chronicle.* http://www.sfgate.com/ea/lasalle/1125.html (accessed on December 18, 2002).

Malle, Louis. *Malle on Malle.* London: Faber and Faber, 1993.

Occupation, Cooperation, and Resistance in World War II-Era France

Cretzmeyer, Stacy. *Your Name Is Renee: Ruth Kapp Hartz's Story As a Hidden Child in Occupied France.* New York: Oxford University Press, 1999.

Meltzer, Milton. *Rescue: The Story of How Gentiles Saved Jews in the Holocaust.* New York: Harper & Row, 1988.

Weapons of the Spirit [videorecording]. Pierre Sauvage Productions and Friends of Le Chambon, 1989.

Zuccotti, Susan. *The Holocaust, the French, and the Jews.* Lincoln: University of Nebraska Press, 1999.

Into the Arms of Strangers: Stories of the Kindertransport

Written and directed by Mark Jonathan Harris
Produced by Deborah Oppenheimer

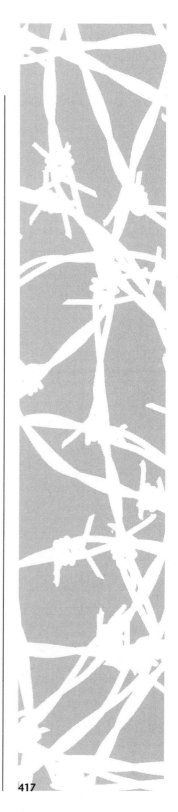

In November 1938, the situation for Jews in Nazi Germany and German-controlled Austria took a decisive turn for the worse. The riots and attacks directed at Jews during the event known as *Kristallnacht,* or the "Night of Broken Glass," indicated that the Nazi regime would not be content with stripping Jews of their rights, depriving them of homes and jobs, and treating them as outcasts. The brutality and destruction of *Kristallnacht,* during which hundreds of Jews were beaten, dozens murdered, and tens of thousands arrested, marked the first organized, large-scale act of violence toward the Jewish population under Nazi control. As news of *Kristallnacht* spread to other countries, citizens around the world reacted with horror and outrage. Few governments, however, were willing to allow large numbers of immigrants across their borders. Due to the efforts of a few activists and lawmakers, the British government decided to allow thousands of children from Germany, Austria, Czechoslovakia, and Poland to take refuge in England. That program came to be known as the Kindertransport (*kinder,* pronounced "kihn-der," is the German word for "children"), and it saved the lives of more than 10,000 Jewish children who might otherwise have died.

Producer Deborah Oppenheimer, whose mother was one of the *Kinder* saved by this program, felt inspired to research the Kindertransport and learn the stories of its participants. Along with writer/director Mark Jonathan Harris, Oppenheimer created *Into the Arms of Strangers: Stories of the Kindertransport,* a feature-length documentary film. The film brought this little-known event to the attention of millions, recounting both the tragedy of the Holocaust and the generosity and humanity of the Kindertransport rescue. Reviewers and audiences praised the film's sensitive depiction of its subject, and in 2001 the director and producer won the Academy Award for best feature documentary.

Awards: Academy Award, 2001, for Best Feature Documentary.

Rating: PG; contains disturbing themes.

Biographies of Writer/Director Mark Jonathan Harris and Producer Deborah Oppenheimer

Mark Jonathan Harris Award-winning documentary filmmaker Mark Jonathan Harris earned an undergraduate degree from Harvard University. After graduating, he moved to Chicago, where he worked as a reporter for wire services, including the Associated Press. He began making documentary films in 1964. Among his early documentaries is *Huelga!* (1967), which depicts the beginning of the Delano grape strike, an event that led to improved benefits and labor organization for farm workers. Harris's film *The Redwoods,* made for the Sierra Club, contributed to efforts to set aside land designated as a redwood national park in California. In addition to bringing about environmental change, *The Redwoods* won an Academy Award in the short documentary category in 1968.

Harris moved to Los Angeles in 1973. Over the next several years, he made educational films and began a decades-long career teaching filmmaking, starting out at the California Institute of the Arts. Since 1983, Harris has taught filmmaking at the University of Southern California's School of Cinema-Television. He chaired the film and television production department there from 1990 to 1996.

Chronology of Events Relating to *Into the Arms of Strangers*

January 30, 1933: Adolf Hitler becomes leader of Germany.

September 15, 1935: Nuremberg Laws, passed in Germany, strip Jews of citizenship and deprive them of other rights.

November 9–10, 1938: *Kristallnacht* takes place throughout Germany and Austria.

November 21, 1938: The British Parliament approves the Kindertransport program.

December 1, 1938: The first Kindertransport leaves from Berlin, Germany.

September 1, 1939: Germany invades Poland; the last Kindertransport leaves from Germany.

Spring 1940: The British government calls for the internment of "enemy aliens," or refugees, including Jews and others escaping persecution, from Germany, Austria, and other enemy nations.

May 8, 1945: V-E Day; World War II ends in Europe.

2000: Mark Jonathan Harris and Deborah Oppenheimer release the documentary *Into the Arms of Strangers: Stories of the Kindertransport.*

Harris has made several acclaimed documentary films that focus on the period before, during, and after World War II (1939–45). *The Homefront* (1985), on which Harris worked as co-producer, documents the dramatic changes to American society brought on by the war. He returned to that era in 1997, writing and directing *The Long Way Home,* a film that addresses the period directly after the end of World War II. In this film, Harris documented the struggle of the many thousands of refugees left without families or homes after the Holocaust. The film reveals the indifference of many nations around the world to the refugees' plight as well as the heroism and compassion of those who worked to improve the situation. Harris particularly highlights the efforts to establish the Jewish state of Israel, which became successful in 1948. *The Long Way Home* earned much critical praise and several important awards, including the 1998 Academy Award for Best Feature Documentary. In 2000 Harris once again chose the World War II era, particularly the Holocaust, as the subject of a documentary film. He wrote and directed *Into the*

Arms of Strangers: Stories of the Kindertransport, also co-authoring, with Deborah Oppenheimer, the accompanying book. In 2001 *Into the Arms of Strangers* earned Harris his third Academy Award for documentary filmmaking.

In addition to his films, Harris has written articles and essays for newspapers like the *New York Times,* the *Los Angeles Times,* and the *Washington Post.* He has written several short stories that have been published in literary journals, and for many years he served as contributing editor of *New West* magazine. Harris is also the author of several novels for young adults, including *With a Wave of the Wand, Confessions of a Prime-Time Kid* (1985), and *Come the Morning* (1989).

Deborah Oppenheimer Deborah Oppenheimer has spent much of her professional career working as a producer for television shows and movies. She has been the producer of such series as *Norm,* starring Norm MacDonald, and *The Drew Carey Show.* She has also worked on several miniseries and television movies. But her mother's death in 1993, and a chance encounter two years later, inspired her to create a completely different kind of work.

Growing up, Oppenheimer had known that her mother, Sylvia, had been part of the Kindertransport program. In 1939, at the age of eleven, Sylvia Avramovici had left her home and her parents in Germany, traveling by train and boat to England. She spent the next several years living in group homes and with families, longing to be reunited with her own family. Once the war was over, Sylvia learned that her parents had died in a Nazi concentration camp. She eventually moved to the United States, where she met and married Eric Oppenheimer. Deborah Oppenheimer's father had also escaped the Holocaust, leaving Europe with his family months before the war broke out. Throughout her life, Oppenheimer knew few details of her mother's experiences in England during the war. She understood the subject was extremely painful and difficult to speak of for her mother, so she did not pursue it.

When Oppenheimer's mother died of breast cancer at age sixty-five in 1993, Oppenheimer mourned her loss. She felt certain that all information about her mother's childhood had died with her. Two years later, however, she happened to

attend a dinner honoring a man who, it turned out, had also participated in the Kindertransport program. When a few minutes of film footage from that period were shown, Oppenheimer recalls in an essay in the book *Into the Arms of Strangers,* "I desperately peered into the faces, searching for my mother, wondering if I would recognize her young features." Oppenheimer then decided to research the Kindertransport program in an effort to establish a link with her mother's past. Over a period of several years, she met numerous Kindertransport survivors, known as *Kinder,* and learned many details about her mother's life in England during the war.

As a tribute to her mother, and to the many other *Kinder* that she had come to know, Oppenheimer decided to make a documentary film about the Kindertransport. She felt a need to educate people about this extraordinary but often overlooked program. Oppenheimer became involved in many aspects of the film's production, from raising the financing dollars to finding the film's onscreen participants to selecting

Kurt Fuchel, left, whose memoir is one of those featured in the film *Into the Arms of Strangers: Stories of the Kindertransport,* with the movie's producer Deborah Oppenheimer, center, and its writer/director Mark Jonathan Harris at the film's premiere in 2000.
Reproduced by permission of AP/World Wide Photos.

the music that would accompany the interviews. Her passionate involvement was rewarded by the critical acclaim and many awards the film received. On a personal level, the film brought her closer to her late mother and to the grandparents she never knew; she states in the *Into the Arms of Strangers* book that her research into her mother's past resulted in "a relationship with [my mother] and my grandparents that is profound, nurturing, and comforting."

Historical Background of *Into the Arms of Strangers*

In January 1933, Germany had a new leader, a man who was both admired and feared. Adolf Hitler (1889–1945) had achieved leadership with the promise of a strong, powerful government that would pull Germany up from the depths of economic depression and would control the elements of society that were to blame for all of the nation's problems. According to Hitler, those elements—primarily the Jews but also Roma (Gypsies), political opponents of his Nazi Party, homosexuals, and many others—had weakened Germany and polluted what he described as the master race. He believed that white, Christian Germans belonged to the superior Aryan race, and if that race were purified and strengthened, then Germany would rise to its former position as a leading world power. Soon after taking office, Hitler began his program of turning Jews into outcasts and depriving them of their rights. Relentlessly portraying Jews as beastlike, diseased creatures, he encouraged an atmosphere of hostility and discrimination.

Over the next several years, the German government passed several laws limiting the rights of Jews to pursue certain careers, attend schools and universities, and live where they chose. The Nuremberg Laws of 1935 defined the Jewish people as a separate race defined by bloodlines, rather than as a religious or cultural group defined by practices or beliefs. These laws prevented Jews from marrying non-Jews and stripped them of their German citizenship. Hitler's intention in the early years of his reign was to create conditions that were so inhospitable to the Jews that they would leave Germany voluntarily, and more than a hundred thousand did. Others remained, hoping the persecution would end and re-

luctant to leave behind their homes, friends, and careers. Those who did try to leave Germany faced many obstacles, including the difficult task of finding a new country that would accept them. Immigration laws in most Western nations set strict quotas, allowing only a certain number of immigrants in each year, and as the 1930s came to a close, the number of people seeking refuge far exceeded those quotas.

The refugee problem increased enormously after Germany annexed, or took over, Austria in March 1938. Treatment of Jews in Germany and Austria quickly worsened, prompting ever greater numbers of people to try to leave. In the summer of 1938, U.S. president Franklin D. Roosevelt called for a multinational conference to discuss the refugee crisis resulting from Hitler's policies. Delegates from thirty-two nations—including the United States, Great Britain, France, other European countries, several South American countries, Australia, and New Zealand—met in Evian, France. The conference resulted in expressions of regret and sympathy for the mostly Jewish refugees, but not one country other than the tiny Dominican Republic offered to expand immi-

The swastika served as a powerful symbol of anti-Semitism and hatred during Hitler's Nazi regime.
Reproduced by permission of AP/Wide World Photos.

Chiune Sugihara

Amidst the horror and misery of the Holocaust, a time when unthinkable acts were committed against the Jews and others, some courageous people accepted great risk to help the victims of the Holocaust. A Japanese diplomat named Chiune Sugihara went against the direct orders of his government, risking his career and possibly his family's safety, in order to help save the lives of thousands of Jewish refugees.

In 1940 Sugihara represented the Japanese government in Lithuania, a country that was controlled by the Soviet Union at the time. In August 1940, just a few weeks before he and his family were to re-locate to Berlin, Sugihara was approached by desperate Jewish refugees from Poland. Forced to leave their own country after the Nazi invasion, the refugees had to run for their lives, but they had nowhere to go. They begged Sugihara to give them transit visas, documents that would allow them to travel to other countries, so they could safely leave Lithuania before the Nazis invaded that country, too.

Moved by their situation and longing to help, Sugihara asked the government in Japan if he could issue thousands of transit visas to the refugees. Japan ordered him not to do so. After careful con-

gration quotas to allow more refugees to cross its borders. Most nations cited economic difficulties that already strained resources for citizens, making it difficult to provide needed services for additional immigrants. Anti-Semitism, or hatred of Jews, while not necessarily openly acknowledged, also played a role in the rejection of these refugees.

The events of November 1938 known as *Kristallnacht* signaled to the Jews living under Hitler's regime and to the entire world that the Nazis' treatment of the Jews went beyond harassment and isolated acts of violence. The organized, government-encouraged riots on November 9 and 10 made it clear to the world that the situation for the Jews was grave. While governments were reluctant to change their immigration policies, many citizens' groups—including religious agencies both Jewish and non-Jewish—began lobbying lawmakers to take a humane approach to the problem. In Great Britain, these groups acted swiftly and persuasively, obtaining approval from the House of Commons (a branch of Parliament,

sideration, and with the support of his wife and children, Sugihara decided to defy his government and issue the visas. He realized he would probably be punished by his government, but he also knew his visas might provide the only chance the refugees would have to escape. With only weeks to go before his departure for Berlin, Sugihara spent long hours writing as many visas as he could. He later estimated that he issued more than 3,000 visas, enabling thousands of Jews to travel to distant lands, far from the Nazis' grasp.

Years later, upon returning to Japan, Sugihara was forced to resign from his government position for defying orders in Lithuania. He did not return to government service. In the 1960s, he began hearing from some of the grateful survivors whose lives had been saved by the visas he issued. He was later named one of the "Righteous Among Nations," an honor given to heroic non-Jews who helped save Jewish lives during the Holocaust. And in 1992, several years after Sugihara died, a monument to him was built in his hometown. A dedication ceremony was attended by several "Sugihara survivors" as well as officials of the Japanese government.

Britain's lawmaking body) for children under age seventeen to be transported to England for temporary refuge. The agencies would provide funding for the transports and for the children's eventual return to their home countries, and they would also attempt to find foster families or organizations that would care for the children. This program came to be known as Kindertransport. (Similar legislation, in the form of the Wagner-Rogers bill, was introduced in the U.S. Congress in February 1939, but fears about the cost of the program, the wish to avoid an increase in the immigrant population, and a reluctance to get involved prevented its passage.)

With the help of organizers from Britain and Germany, the first Kindertransport left Berlin, Germany, on December 1, 1938, less than a month after *Kristallnacht*. Over the next nine months, trainloads of children—70 percent of whom were Jewish—left Germany, Austria, Czechoslovakia, and Poland for the safety of Britain. Thousands of distraught parents made the painful decision to part with their children in the hopes that they would be safe and that the separation would be temporary. Few could have imagined what was in store for the Jews remaining in Nazi-controlled nations. While they knew the circumstances were terrible, most did not yet know of the horrors of concentration camps, and the Final Solution—the systematic mass murder of the Jews—was years away from being implemented. The 10,000 children who were sent to England as part of the Kindertransport program knew they were being taken away from their families, friends, and homes; they did not know that most of them would never see their parents again.

The Kindertransport ended in September 1939. The sponsoring agencies ran out of money at the end of August, but even if funding had been unlimited, the outbreak of war between Britain and Germany, and other nations as well, on September 3 effectively ended the program. While the refugee children in England shared certain difficulties adjusting to life in a new culture, their individual experiences varied widely. Some quickly found loving foster homes, a few were taken advantage of and forced to work as servants for their new families. Many children lived in group homes, some of which were provided by wealthy English citizens like Baron James de Rothschild, member of an important European Jewish family. After the war broke out, amid fears of bombing raids by the Germans, thousands of British children, including many of the Kindertransport refugees, were sent to the countryside where it was thought to be safer. In the summer of 1940 the older Kindertransport children suffered an additional hardship. Britain's government decided that all refugees between the ages of sixteen and seventy who had come from the countries with which Britain was at war, considered "enemy countries," would be forced to reside in internment camps, or prisonlike compounds. Some, including several hundred *Kinder,* were sent to such camps in Canada or Australia for several months.

By the spring of 1942, news reports reached England about the deportations of Jews to camps in Poland. Soon it became clear that these camps were facilities for mass murder, and many of the refugee children in England feared the worst. For most, their fears were realized at the end of the war when they discovered that their families had perished at the hands of the Nazis. Very few *Kinder* were reunited with their parents after the war, and those few who were soon realized that the parents they had longed for had become strangers in the intervening years. The transition to living with their parents again was difficult, especially for those who had formed attachments to their foster families. The vast majority of refugees, however, had to cope with the loss of their parents rather than becoming reacquainted with them. Some six million Jews, and millions of others, were killed by the Nazis during the Holocaust. Included in the number of Jewish victims were 1.5 million children, a number that would surely have been increased by thousands if the Kindertransport had not existed.

Subject Matter of *Into the Arms of Strangers*

Through interviews, photographs, music, and narration (provided by actress Judi Dench), *Into the Arms of Strangers* tells the story of the Kindertransport as experienced by the *Kinder* themselves. The film proceeds chronologically, beginning with the participants' childhoods, moving on to their experience in Britain, and concluding with their lives in the decades following the war's end. Most of the twelve survivors interviewed for the film recall peaceful, happy childhoods enriched by the sense of security and love their parents provided. As the 1930s progressed and the Jews of Germany became increasingly restricted by anti-Jewish laws and harassed by anti-Semitic Germans, a shadow fell across their lives. The survivors recall a growing awareness among the adults of the danger for Jews in Germany, and an increasing sense among the children of their new roles as outcasts in their own country. Forbidden from playing in parks, gathering in public places, and, in some cases, from attending their regular schools, the Jewish children felt the pangs of suddenly being excluded. Survivor Ursula Rosenfeld remembers the excitement of getting ready for a birthday party and the extreme disappointment when none of the guests arrived. Another survivor, Jack Hellman, tells of being beaten by some boys from his school who threw him through a plate-glass window.

While some families felt determined to stay in their native countries, others tried desperately to emigrate. They faced numerous obstacles, including finding a sponsor in a new country, securing work there, obtaining travel visas and exit permits, and coming up with the money needed to begin again elsewhere. After the brutality of *Kristallnacht*, the sense of desperation increased, as did the difficulties in leaving. When the government of Great Britain agreed to take in refugees under the age of seventeen, many Jewish parents faced a difficult choice: to stay together as a family and endure the risks of life under the Nazis, or to send their children away to a distant country where they could be safe. Franzi Groszmann, mother of *Kinder* Lore Segal, describes her reluctance to let her daughter go, and her husband's insistence that it was the best decision. "I saw in the end that he was right," she recalls. "But the hurt is unbelievable. That cannot be described." When told they would be sent away, the children also experienced tremendous pain, as well as confusion over why it had to happen, and why they had to go alone.

The time between the decision to send a child and the actual departure was frequently very brief. In that time, parents had to decide what essential items to pack for their child, excluding jewelry, money, and other valuables, which the government forbade emigrants from taking with them. They also had to provide comfort, reassurance, and years' worth of advice and loving supervision. As survivor Eva Hayman recalls, "Both mother and father were trying to give the instructions, the guidance that they hoped to have their whole life to give." Parents sent their children away amid promises that they would soon join them; perhaps most sensed these promises to be false, but none knew exactly what awaited them. As German Jewish organizer Norbert Wollheim states, "I did not realize, and I could never realize, that only a year and a half later, from the same railway station, trains would go in the other directions to Hitler's slaughterhouses."

Upon arrival in England, frightened and alone, the children of the Kindertransports faced a difficult transition to a new language and culture. Those who hadn't already been placed in foster homes were sent temporarily to summer camp facilities where, once a week, prospective foster families would come to select a child. The young and attractive children were the first to be chosen; older children who had been left behind were sent to live in hostels, dormitory-like facilities where they lived with other children. Some foster families provided a stable, loving environment; others were less tolerant of the young immigrants living in their homes; still others forced the refugees to act as servants for the household. In all cases, the *Kinder* struggled to adapt and to cope

with the separation from their parents. Many of the children worked tirelessly to bring their parents to England, searching for job opportunities and the money to guarantee the family's eventual re-immigration to their home country. Very few were successful in their efforts; most were not.

When World War II began in September 1939, many of the *Kinder* experienced further upheaval. Some were sent, along with British children, to live away from the large cities, which were thought to be likely targets for German bombing raids. Some, like Alex Gordon, were detained along with other "enemy aliens" and sent to internment camps. In addition, the war made emigration from German-controlled territories nearly impossible for Jews; by the fall of 1941, Jewish emigration was illegal. The children's fear for their parents' safety intensified, particularly after news began reaching England of Jews being deported to concentration camps and death camps. Cherished hopes of being reunited someday with their parents were crushed. Many of the older *Kinder*,

In order to escape persecution or even death, thousands of Jewish children from Austria, Germany, Poland, and Czechoslovakia were sent to Great Britain. Some went to orphanages or group homes, and some ended up with foster families, like that seen here. *Reproduced by permission of the United States Holocaust Memorial Museum.*

having reconciled themselves to living in England for what might be a long time, decided to contribute to the war effort. Some joined the British military, others worked in hospitals.

When the war ended in the spring of 1945, millions rejoiced that the fighting had stopped. But for many of the refugee children who had left their families behind, the end of the war also brought confirmation of their parents' deaths. Many learned that their entire families had been wiped out, and that their homes and communities had been destroyed. Survivor Eva Hayman recalls her reaction upon hearing of her parents' deaths: "Suddenly the future which we had always painted wasn't there. There was no future. There was just an emptiness." Like all of those whose lives had been affected by the Holocaust, the *Kinder* had to learn how to move on and build new lives that were very different from those they had imagined as children. They struggled with a terrible sense of guilt that they had survived when so many others had perished, but many found—in their work and in their children— reasons to look toward the future. Alex Gordon, in reflecting on his losses and on the many hardships he had faced during his childhood and as a refugee in England, reached this conclusion: "I was meant to survive, not because of myself, but [because] the Jews would survive, and I would bring up another generation and they would live. And I look at my children, and my grandchildren, and I know there was a purpose to my life."

Style and Themes in *Into the Arms of Strangers*

Into the Arms of Strangers tells the story of the Kindertransport in a straightforward style, presenting details primarily through the words of twelve surviving *Kinder*. Accompanied by photographs of family members and film footage shot around the time of World War II, the survivors' interviews are intimate and touching without being overly sentimental. The interview subjects sit fairly close to the camera, giving viewers the chance to see the survivors' emotions in all their complexity. The decision to explore the Kindertransport program through the memories of those who participated emphasizes the impact that hatred and prejudice can have on the lives of individuals; through the first-person stories of the *Kinder,* audiences are better able to grasp the tragedy of the Holocaust.

The soundtrack includes a number of children's songs from the period, sung by children in the languages the *Kinder* spoke when they were young. The carefree simplicity of the songs reminds the audience of all that was lost to the *Kinder*: childhood, innocence, security.

Into the Arms of Strangers explores a number of themes in addressing the Kindertransport, a generous but flawed humanitarian effort that had intricate and lifelong consequences for those involved. The film examines the significance of choices, including those made by the parents of the *Kinder* and those made by the English families who took the refugee children into their homes. The parents, knowing at the very least that their children would have a difficult and painful adjustment—and perhaps sensing that they would not be reunited for years or possibly ever—had to put their young children on a train and say goodbye. In addition to thoughts of their children's difficulties, the parents had to cope with their own loneliness and constantly reassure themselves that they had made the right decision. The foster families in England also made difficult choices. They agreed to temporarily adopt children who were complete strangers to them, without knowing the consequences for their own households. With the possibility of war looming ahead, these families took on an additional financial and emotional burden, sacrificing a great deal in order to do what they felt was right.

The choices made by the parents and foster parents involved in the Kindertransport had complicated repercussions for the children. Upon arriving in England, the children struggled to fit in with those around them. They spoke a different language, wore different clothes, and came from a different culture. As they learned more and more English, many of them forgot their native language. As time passed, memories of their childhoods began to fade. They were becoming more English in terms of speech, manners, and pastimes, but they continued to have strong emotional and familial ties to their German, Austrian, Czech, or Polish culture. The tension between past and present resulted for many children in a confused sense of identity.

The vast majority of the refugee children also had to cope with the loss of their parents and other family members. Many of the survivors spoke of the difficulty of learning their parents had died, but not having details about how or where they died. Ursula Rosenfeld recalled the unreal sense she had when she heard of her mother's death: "We had no grave really, no parting, no end, no funeral. It's that sort of faint feeling in the air of hope, and that hope suddenly fading." The *Kinder* also dealt with another kind of loss: the loss of their own childhoods. For many, the carefree innocence of their youth vanished when they were taken from their homes. Suddenly aware of the devastating consequences of hatred and discrimination, they could no longer see the world in the same way. Removed from the care and unconditional love of their parents, the children were forced to take on the responsibility and self-sufficiency of adulthood.

While *Into the Arms of Strangers* exposes much of the suffering endured by the *Kinder,* it also explores the courage and compassion of the participants, their parents, and the foster families. At a time when many chose not to get involved, thousands of foster families made sacrifices to care for a young refugee. While governments around the world turned away from the refugee crisis resulting from Hitler's rule, Britain saved the lives of 10,000 children. The number is alarmingly small compared to the 1.5 million children who died in the Holocaust. But to those who were rescued, the mercy and compassion of the English people meant the difference between life and death, and made possible the lives of their children and grandchildren.

Research and Activity Ideas

1) Imagine that you are leaving home for an indefinite period. You cannot take any money, jewelry, or other valuables, and your remaining belongings must fit into a small suitcase and a backpack. What would you take to remind you of home and give you comfort in your new life? What practical items would you bring?

2) Study the circumstances that led England to detain "enemy aliens"—including those seeking refuge from Nazism—in internment camps in 1940, and compare that action to the Japanese internment camps in the United States beginning in 1942. How were these internment camps justified by the authorities? Examine the racism and prejudice in both England and America that led to such actions. How were these internment camps similar to and different from the concentration camps in Nazi-held territories?

3) Research the Wagner-Rogers bill, the 1939 legislation that would have allowed for some 20,000 children from Nazi-controlled territories to immigrate to the United States. Analyze the reasons why this bill never passed, examining in particular the conditions and feelings in the United States that resulted in anti-immigrant sentiment. What were the motivations of those groups opposing this bill, and how were they able to succeed?

Where to Learn More About ...

Mark Jonathan Harris, Deborah Oppenheimer, and *Into the Arms of Strangers*

Davis, Ivor. "The Story of Kindertransport." *Jewishfamily.com.* http://www.jewishfamily.com/culture/films/kindertransport.txt (accessed on December 18, 2002).

Harris, Mark Jonathan, and Deborah Oppenheimer. *Into the Arms of Strangers: Stories of the Kindertransport.* New York and London: Bloomsbury, 2000.

Into the Arms of Strangers: Stories of the Kindertransport. http://www2.warner bros.com/intothearmsofstrangers/ (accessed on December 18, 2002).

"Mark Jonathan Harris." *Filmbug.* http://www.reellife.com/people/H/mark_jonathan_harris.html (accessed on December 18, 2002).

Soulsman, Gary. "Kindertransport: Lifeline out of Nazi Germany." *Delaware Online: The News Journal.* http://www.delawareonline.com/newsjournal/local/2001/holocaust/children_side4.html (accessed on December 18, 2002).

Chiune Sugihara

Mochizuki, Ken. *Passage to Freedom: The Sugihara Story.* Illustrated by Dom Lee. New York: Lee & Low Books, 1997.

The Kindertransport

Abraham-Podietz, Eva, and Anne Fox. *Ten Thousand Children: True Stories Told by Children Who Escaped the Holocaust on the Kindertransport.* Springfield, NJ: Behrman House, 1998.

Drucker, Olga Levy. *Kindertransport.* New York: Henry Holt, 1995.

My Knees Were Jumping: Remembering the Kindertransports [videorecording]. Anthology Film Archives and the National Center for Jewish Film, 1998.

Schindler's List

Directed by Steven Spielberg

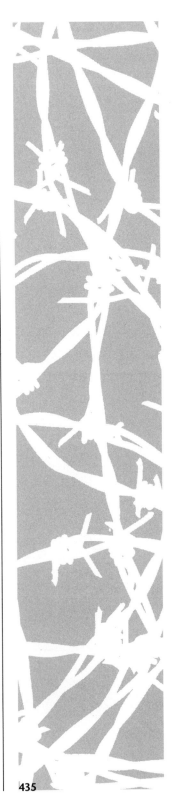

*S*chindler's List, a feature film based on a true story, depicts events that took place during the Holocaust. The Holocaust was the systematic murder of millions of Jews and other people by German leader Adolf Hitler (1889–1945) and his ruling Nazi Party during World War II (1939–45). In the beginning of the film the audience is introduced to the title character, Oskar Schindler (1908–1974), a charming but dishonest Austrian-German businessman who has joined the Nazi Party and befriended powerful Nazi soldiers as a way of furthering his business interests. Schindler owns and operates a factory in Poland, producing materials needed for the war effort. He hires a number of Jewish workers because they are cheap labor; the Jews have been stripped of their rights, their property, and their ability to make a living by the Nazi government, and Schindler knows his profits will soar if he hires them.

Initially intent on making as much money as possible from the war to fund his tastes for food, women, fine clothes, and fancy cars, Schindler at some point begins to sympathize with his Jewish workers. As brutality toward the Jews increases and as the Nazis transport Jews by the thousands to certain

Oskar Schindler, a German industrialist who saved the lives of more than one thousand Jews. *Reproduced by permission of Archive Photos, Inc.*

death in such "extermination" camps as Auschwitz-Birkenau, Schindler realizes that the Jewish workers he employs will escape such a fate if he can convince the authorities that these people are essential for the production of war goods. With the help of his Jewish factory manager, Itzhak Stern, Schindler uses bribery and deceit and manages to save the lives of more than 1,100 Jews. Oskar Schindler died in 1974, and, as he had requested, he was buried in Israel. Some of the people Schindler had protected, who call themselves *Schindlerjuden,* or "Schindler's Jews," appear at the end of the movie, visiting the gravesite of the man who helped to save them.

Awards: Academy Awards, 1993, for Best Picture, Directing, Art Direction, Cinematography, Film Editing, Music (original score), Set Decoration, Writing (screenplay based on material previously produced or published). Golden Globe Awards, 1993, for Film (Drama), Director, Screenplay. Los Angeles Film Critics Association Awards, 1993, for Best Film, Cinematography. New York Film Critics Circle Awards, 1993, for Best Film, Best Supporting Actor (Ralph Fiennes), Best Cinematographer.

Rating: R, for graphic violence, strong language, nudity. *Schindler's List* contains many scenes of graphic and disturbing violence. It also includes several instances of nudity, some of which occur in concentration camp settings and some of which are in a sexual context.

Biography of Director Steven Spielberg

Born on December 18, 1947, in Cincinnati, Ohio, Steven Spielberg showed an interest in film at a very early age. Encouraged by his father, Arnold, an electrical engineer, and by his mother, Leah, a former concert pianist, Spielberg start-

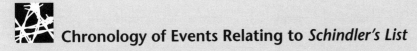

Chronology of Events Relating to *Schindler's List*

April 28, 1908: Oskar Schindler is born in Zwittau, a city in what is now the Czech Republic.

September 1, 1939: Germany invades Poland.

January 1940: Schindler opens his factory in Krakow.

June 1942: First large-scale deportation of Jews, witnessed by Schindler, from Krakow ghetto to death camps.

March 13, 1943: Final liquidation of Krakow ghetto begins. Workers are sent to nearby Plaszow labor camp; others are killed or sent to Auschwitz.

Autumn 1944: Schindler creates a list of more than one thousand of his workers who are to accompany him to the rela-

tive safety of a factory in Brunnlitz, Czechoslovakia.

May 8, 1945: World War II ends in Europe.

April 28, 1962: Schindler is honored by Yad Vashem, the Martyrs' and Heroes' Remembrance Authority, which designated Schindler one of the "Righteous among the Nations of the World."

October 9, 1974: Schindler dies in Frankfurt, Germany. He is buried in Jerusalem, Israel.

1982: Author Thomas Keneally publishes his book about Schindler, which is initially titled *Schindler's Ark*.

1993: Director Steven Spielberg releases his film, *Schindler's List,* which wins the Academy Award for Best Picture.

---

ed out by filming family vacations and other events in his life. By age twelve Spielberg had turned from using his camera to capture everyday happenings to making a movie that told a story, based on a script he wrote and starring his friends. The Spielbergs moved from city to city as Steven grew up, and the Jewish family often settled in primarily non-Jewish neighborhoods. Spielberg encountered many instances of anti-Semitism, prejudice against Jews, during his youth.

Spielberg longed to study filmmaking at the prestigious University of Southern California (USC) or University of California, Los Angeles (UCLA), but his poor grades in high school prevented him from gaining admittance. Instead he attended California State College, making movies on his own and learning firsthand about the film industry through a bold and unusual step. During a tour of Universal Studios in the summer of 1966,

Spielberg slipped away from the rest of the tourists, sneaking onto the backlot to see how a big studio film was made. He repeated this act several times that summer, each time dressed in a business suit and pretending that he was an employee of Universal. In the years ahead, that goal became a reality.

While still in college Spielberg made a short film called *Amblin',* which was shown at the Atlanta Film Festival in 1969. This film grabbed the attention of a Universal executive who signed the twenty-year-old Spielberg to a seven-year contract as a television director. Spielberg directed episodes for numerous television programs, and in 1971 he directed his first professional movie. *Duel* is a made-for-television movie that tells the story of a traveling businessman hunted by a mysterious and violent 18-wheel truck. *Duel* earned rave reviews in Europe and the United States, announcing the arrival of the talented young director. A few years later, Spielberg found himself in charge of a major motion picture that faced technical difficulties, rising costs, and an extended shooting schedule. In spite of such problems, that movie, *Jaws,* was released in 1975 to overwhelming success with moviegoers and critics alike. It eventually earned $260 million, breaking box-office records and establishing Spielberg's unique ability to connect with and entertain people.

While not every Spielberg movie has been a blockbuster on the scale of *Jaws,* the director, producer, and screenwriter has had numerous substantial hits and eventually became Hollywood's most commercially successful director ever. Films like *Raiders of the Lost Ark* (1981), *E.T.—The Extraterrestrial* (1982), and *Jurassic Park* (1993) scored huge successes at the box office. But while Spielberg's thrilling and adventurous films attracted the devotion of moviegoers and even positive reviews from the critics, they were never considered the work of a serious, substantial director. In 1993, however, Spielberg applied his directorial talents to a devastatingly serious subject: the Holocaust. *Schindler's List* tells the true story of a dishonest but ultimately heroic man, Oskar Schindler, who went to great efforts to employ more than 1,100 Jews in his wartime factory, thereby saving them from certain death in Nazi concentration camps.

Millions of moviegoers, as well as many critics and Holocaust scholars, praised Spielberg's film as a painful, mov-

Movie poster for *Schindler's List.* *Reproduced by permission of the Kobal Collection.*

ing representation of one of the modern era's most horrifying events. Spielberg finally achieved widespread recognition as a serious director, winning the Academy Award for best director; the film also won the Best Picture award. Many people have criticized Spielberg, however, for what they consider an oversimplified, sentimental treatment of a complex and dark period in history. They argue that any fictional representation of the Holocaust, even one based on fact, raises difficult issues because such movies are using the destruction of millions of people as a kind of entertainment and to gain profit for the filmmakers. Spielberg quieted some critics by donating the money he had earned from *Schindler's List* to organizations designed to record and document the stories of survivors, and rescuers, of the Holocaust.

Spielberg took a short break from filmmaking after *Schindler's List,* in the meantime acting as executive producer on many films and co-founding the production company DreamWorks, which produces movies, music, television, and more. Spielberg continued his interest in weighty subjects with *Amistad,* his 1997 film about a slave revolt that took place in 1839, and *Saving Private Ryan,* his highly praised World War II drama. In the twenty-first century, Spielberg continued to bring his considerable skills to a number of films, including *Minority Report* and *Catch Me If You Can.*

Historical Background of *Schindler's List*

Schindler's List depicts the actions of a complex and extraordinary man, Oskar Schindler, in the face of the horror and tragedy of the Holocaust. Taking place throughout Europe during World War II (1939–45), the Holocaust was the Nazi government-sponsored killing of approximately eleven million people. The single largest target of the Nazis, who were led by Adolf Hitler, was the Jewish population of Europe; six million Jews were killed during the Holocaust. Hitler openly blamed the Jews both for Germany's defeat in World War I (1914–18) and for the country's economic weakness— widespread unemployment, poverty, food shortages—in the years following. And from the moment he and the Nazi Party came into power in 1933, persecution of the Jews became part of the nation's laws.

Hitler began depriving German Jews of basic rights, calling for a nationwide boycott of Jewish-owned businesses and denying Jews the opportunity to work in certain professions and attend school. He then stripped them of their German citizenship and forced them to sew yellow six-pointed stars, the Jewish symbol known as the Star of David, to their clothing so all who passed them would know they were Jews. By the late 1930s, Hitler's power had grown, his plans for world domination had taken shape, and his actions toward the Jews took a decisive, violent turn. On November 9 and 10, 1938, groups of Nazis charged through Germany's Jewish neighborhoods, destroying homes and businesses, stealing property, setting fire to synagogues (Jewish places of worship), and attacking and arresting tens of thousands of Jews. Many of those arrested were sent to concentration camps, large Nazi-run labor prisons built to hold Jews, political prisoners, and other so-called enemies of the Nazi government. This destruction of Jewish neighborhoods came to be known as *Kristallnacht,* or "Night of Broken Glass," referring to the thousands of windows and storefronts that were shattered that night. No one who had witnessed the horror and violence of *Kristallnacht* could deny that the intent of the Nazis went far beyond simply making life unpleasant for the nation's Jews.

Germany invades Poland and establishes Jewish ghettos

Not satisfied with rebuilding Germany and being its all-powerful ruler, Hitler had long planned to conquer as much of the world as possible, eliminating Jews and other enemies along the way. First in Austria, then in Czechoslovakia, Poland, and other nations, Hitler's armies invaded, took over the governments, and began attacking the Jewish citizens of those nations. When Germany invaded Poland in September 1939, an act that prompted England and France to declare war on Hitler's nation, the Nazis terrorized the Polish Jews in the same ways they had done with the German Jews. They destroyed Jewish homes, businesses, and synagogues, harassed them on the streets, and denied them basic rights. (The Nazis also attacked, harassed, and killed many non-Jewish Poles, believing that most Poles, because they are of Slavic descent rather than Aryan, were of an inferior race. By the end of the war, nearly three million non-Jewish Poles had been murdered by the Nazis.) Eventually the Nazis began rounding up Polish Jews, executing many and forcing the rest to live in crowded ghettos in Poland's cities. The ghettos, located in the cities of Warsaw, Krakow, Lodz, and others, were neighborhoods surrounded by barbed-wire fences or concrete walls that served to keep all the Jewish citizens trapped in one place before they could be transported to concentration camps. (The wall of the Krakow ghetto was made of gravestones that had been removed from the Jewish cemetery.)

The living conditions in Poland's Jewish ghettos were extremely difficult. Usually consisting of only a few city blocks, the ghettos eventually became the temporary homes of tens of thousands of people. The largest, the Warsaw ghetto, held 450,000 Jews. The Lodz ghetto contained 165,000 Jews, while the Krakow ghetto had 18,000 inhabitants. Jews were brought from the countryside and surrounding communities to live in the ghettos, where most ended up living five, ten, or more people to a room. Latecomers were even less fortunate, sleeping in hallways or outside. The Nazis had stolen nearly everything the Jews owned; in the ghettos Jews had little or no money, few possessions of any value, and minimal warm clothing to help them survive the long winters. The Nazis cleverly enlisted a few residents to be part of the *Judenrat,* or Jewish council. The members of the *Judenrat,* believing they were securing their families' safety, assisted the Nazis by making work, food, and housing assignments for other residents.

The Nazis guarding the ghettos distributed food rations to those inside, but quantities were never sufficient and the quality of the food was poor; often the food was lacking in nutritional value or even rotten. Inhabitants had little access to clean drinking water, and it wasn't long before the plumbing broke down. Conditions quickly became unsanitary, and the ghettos became breeding grounds for disease. Already weakened by lack of food and insufficient protection from the cold, many residents of the ghettos became infected by diseases like typhus, which killed more than 15,000 people in the Warsaw ghetto within a few weeks. The Jews were given little access to medicines or health care beyond what they could provide for each other.

Seeing an opportunity to take advantage of the Jews to accomplish necessary tasks, the Nazis forced those who were strong and healthy enough to work as slave laborers. Some went to factory jobs within the ghetto, while others were escorted by Nazi guards to factories and other work sites nearby. The Jewish workers performed a variety of tasks, including the production of weapons, ammunition, and other goods used in the war effort. They were forced to work extremely long hours, often performing tasks requiring great physical exertion. Without sufficient food and suffering from illnesses, many workers collapsed on the job; no longer of use to the Nazi overseers, such workers were usually immediately

shot. Those with unusual physical strength and specialized skills had the best chances of survival.

Oskar Schindler comes to Krakow

The Polish city of Krakow was the administrative center, something like the capital city, of Poland's government general, a term that referred to the German-occupied region of Poland (the Soviet Union occupied another area of Poland during World War II). Oskar Schindler, a Catholic businessman of Austrian-German descent, moved to Krakow soon after the German invasion in September 1939. He, like many other businessmen at the time, hoped to take advantage of the war to make money; wars generate a massive need for goods used by the army, and wars can also result in cheap labor when the citizens of occupied countries are forced to work for their captors. A member of the Nazi Party, Schindler immediately began befriending the Nazi officers in Krakow, using all of his resourcefulness and charm to shower them with gifts and secure their loyalty. He set his sights on owning a factory located on the outskirts of Krakow; this factory had once been owned by Jews, but the Nazis had forbidden Jews to own businesses, and Schindler wanted to buy it at a low price.

To buy the factory, Schindler needed investors. He contacted a Jewish accountant, Itzhak Stern, to help him locate people who would give him money to buy the factory. While most Jews in Krakow had no money, a very few had managed to hide some of their assets from the Nazis. Some of these Jews agreed to invest in Schindler's factory in exchange for the assurance that they could work there. From the beginning it was clear that those with secure jobs had a far better chance of surviving life in Nazi-occupied Poland. While non-Jewish Polish laborers worked for very low wages, Jewish labor was even cheaper, with a small sum being paid directly to the Nazis rather than to the workers. Over time Schindler hired more and more Jews to work in his factory, eventually employing hundreds of people.

The Krakow ghetto was officially established on March 3, 1941. While thousands of people in the ghettos died over time from disease or starvation, or directly at the hands of the Nazi guards, by 1942 the Nazis had devised methods of destroying the Jews at a faster pace. They had built concentration camps, where thousands of Jews were imprisoned and forced to work for the Nazis. They had also built extermination camps, sometimes called death camps, which were designed for the sole purpose of killing as many Jews as possible. Some of the concentration camps were converted at some point into death camps.

As horrible as the conditions were inside the ghettos, life there was still preferable to the alternative: being deported to one of the camps. In the summer of 1942, the Nazis began deporting Jews from the ghettos. These *aktions* involved the brutal roundup of thousands of ghetto residents. Those who expressed their panic and fear, or those who dared to try to hide or resist, were shot immediately. The rest were herded into railroad cars and sent away, heading toward almost certain death. The Jewish workers deemed essential to the war effort—workers in factories like Schindler's, for example, who produced enamel pots and pans as well as ammunition used by German soldiers—were allowed to stay in the ghettos for the time being.

Beyond the Krakow ghetto

When Schindler first began operating his factory, his primary goal was to make money. As he began to know his Jewish workers, though, and as the fate of the Jews in Krakow became clear, Schindler had perhaps begun to sympathize with their plight. In June 1942 he witnessed from a distance one of the violent *aktions* in the Krakow ghetto; he could no longer doubt that government policies dictated the murder of all Jews. In Thomas Keneally's book *Schindler's List,* the inspiration for Steven Spielberg's film of the same name, the author quotes Schindler as saying, "Beyond this day, no thinking person could fail to see what would happen [to the Jews]. I was now resolved to do everything in my power to defeat the system." Schindler increased his efforts to protect as many Jewish workers as possible as the *aktions* continued, depleting the population of the Krakow ghetto. When the final liquidation of the Krakow ghetto began in March 1943 (an event that emptied the ghetto completely), the residents were

Group of women workers standing outside one of Oskar Schindler's factories.
Reproduced by permission of the United States Holocaust Memorial Museum.

The Nuremberg Trials

Every war involves the taking of human life, and during World War II, millions of people died in battle. The Nazis responsible for the murder of millions of Jews and other victims in the ghettos and camps of Eastern Europe, however, had killed people who were not soldiers, who had no weapons, and who had never consented to engage in warfare. The Nazis enslaved and attempted to destroy the entire population of European Jews, committing an act known as genocide. For this act, many individuals would be held responsible in an international court of law, charged with such violations as war crimes (crimes committed during a war that violate wartime customs) and crimes against humanity (atrocious acts committed with the intention of destroying a large group of people).

Of the many war crimes trials that occurred after the war ended, the best known are those that took place in Nuremberg, Germany, between October 1945 and November 1946. During that year, the International Military Tribunal (IMT) put on trial twenty-two Nazi leaders, including Hermann Göring, a high-ranking advisor to Hitler who ran the air force and formulated economic policies, and Hans Frank, who had acted as governor-general of German-occupied Poland. Twelve of the defendants were sentenced to death, three to life imprisonment, four to imprisonment ranging from ten to twenty years, and three were acquitted. In an effort to remove all traces of Nazism from Germany, the IMT also tried and condemned several organizations, including the Gestapo (the Nazi se-

divided into two parts: about 2,000 "essential workers," including Schindler's employees, who were moved to Plaszow, a labor camp built nearby; and about 2,300 other people who were deported to the infamous concentration camp known as Auschwitz.

As the Russian army advanced toward Krakow in the fall of 1944, Plaszow was liquidated and shut down. The workers formerly described as essential were now to be transported to Auschwitz. Schindler bribed the leader of Plaszow, a cruel and barbaric man named Amon Goeth, to let him take his workers to a new factory he wanted to open in the city of Brunnlitz in Czechoslovakia. Schindler indicated that the factory would produce Hitler's secret weapons, which would be used to win the war. Goeth agreed to spare Schindler's workers, and at this point the famed list was created. Schindler's list

cret police), the SA (an armed branch of the Nazi Party also known as "Storm Troopers"), and the SS (the elite Nazi security force that protected Hitler and ran the concentration and death camps).

A later series of twelve trials at Nuremberg, running from late 1946 through 1948, examined the actions of many different people and groups who had a role in the Holocaust. One case tried members of the medical community who had performed inhumane medical experiments on concentration camp prisoners as well as committing other crimes. Other cases examined the actions of German companies that had used Jews as slave laborers. One trial judged members of the *Einsatzgruppen,* the mobile killing squads that had shot masses of Jewish civilians when Germany invaded the Soviet Union. Numerous people were found guilty, several were executed, and many more were sent to prison.

Additional trials were held throughout the years in various locations, including Poland and Israel, as the efforts of Nazi hunters led to the capture and trial of a number of Nazis who had fled at the end of the war were found. In addition to punishing the guilty, these trials helped educate the public about the atrocities that the Nazis committed during World War II. The horrifying testimony of the accused became a permanent part of the historical record, providing further evidence of the extent of Nazi inhumanity.

named more than 1,000 Jewish workers that he declared critical to his factory's success. He later brought nearly 100 additional workers to his factory from a nearby labor camp. The workers were sent by train to Brunnlitz, which was just beyond Auschwitz, and on the way 300 women and children were mistakenly sent to the concentration camp. Schindler traveled to Auschwitz, bribed the necessary guards, and obtained the release of the women. (Historians have pointed out some uncertainty about whether these women went to Auschwitz or to a concentration camp in eastern Germany, but in any case Schindler did rescue hundreds of his workers from a camp, according to the survivors' testimony after the war.)

For the remaining months of the war, Schindler's workers lived in Brunnlitz, working at his factory that many have claimed was rigged to produce faulty ammunition for the German army. While food was scarce and conditions were less than ideal, the situation protected the workers long enough for them to survive the Holocaust. According to her memoir, *Where Light and Shadow Meet,* Schindler's wife Emilie worked tirelessly to obtain food for the workers. After the war ended in Europe on May 8, 1945, the Schindlers went to Germany and then moved to Argentina in 1949, where they lived together for nearly ten years. In 1958 Schindler abandoned his wife and returned to Germany, and in 1961 he traveled to Israel. While there Schindler was honored by Yad Vashem, the Martyrs' and Heroes' Remembrance Authority, which designated Schindler one of the "Righteous among the Nations of the World," an honor given to non-Jews who worked to save Jewish lives during the Holocaust in spite of the risks. In his final years Schindler was an alcoholic and had no source of income. He was first supported by the *Schindlerjuden,* the survivors he had helped, and later he received a small pension from the German government. He died in 1974 and was buried in Israel according to his wishes.

Plot and Characters in *Schindler's List*

At the beginning of Steven Spielberg's film *Schindler's List,* viewers meet Oskar Schindler (played by Liam Neeson), a new arrival in the city of Krakow in German-occupied Poland. A member of the Nazi Party, Schindler immediately launches his campaign to befriend the high-ranking German officers in Krakow. He attends a fancy Krakow nightclub, observes a table of powerful Nazis, and strategically begins buying drinks and food for them. Turning on his considerable charm, Schindler successfully entertains the officers; the people who had never heard of Oskar Schindler at the beginning of the evening came to consider him an important man and fine friend by evening's end.

Having succeeded in the first step, Schindler the businessman then establishes contact with a man he believes will help him assume ownership of a formerly Jewish-owned factory. This man, Jewish accountant Itzhak Stern (played by Ben Kingsley), eventually does help Schindler by putting him in touch with the few Jews who have managed to hold on to some money. These investors enable Schindler to buy the fac-

Oskar Schindler, standing second from right, saved over one thousand Jews, like these survivors, from almost certain death. *Reproduced by permission of the United States Holocaust Memorial Museum.*

tory, and in return Schindler agrees to provide them with pots and pans made in the factory, which the Jews can then sell or trade for food or other goods. The factory, with Schindler as director and owner, eventually opens, staffed by hundreds of Jewish workers.

Throughout the film, the audience sees many examples of the manipulations, bribery, and deceit practiced by nearly everyone in Krakow: Schindler sends lavish gifts to Nazi officers so they will help his business succeed; Stern arranges for unskilled workers to be listed in the factory's records as skilled workers so their lives will be spared; and many Jews inside the ghetto engage in black-market, or illegal, exchanges with the Poles living outside the ghetto, trading whatever goods they can obtain for food or other valuables that will help them survive.

In the winter of 1942, a new labor camp, called Plaszow, is constructed outside Krakow. A young officer named Amon Goeth (played by Ralph Fiennes) has been brought to

Krakow to oversee the camp. In the space of a few scenes the audience learns that Goeth is a dangerous, cruel man who wields his power like a maniac, shooting point blank any Jew that irritates him. Goeth delivers a speech to his men about the long history of Jewish life in Krakow and his plans to erase that history by eliminating the city's Jews. The following scene depicts the liquidation of the Krakow ghetto, an event of horrifying violence that emptied the last of the Jewish residents of the ghetto. During the liquidation, which is witnessed by Schindler and his mistress as they ride horses on the hilltops over the town, hundreds of Jews are brutally murdered while others are ordered to march out of the ghetto onto waiting railroad cars that will take them to death camps. The only Jews allowed to stay in Krakow are those who have been declared "essential workers" in the factories producing war goods; these workers are moved to the Plaszow camp.

Schindler bargains with Goeth to have several hundred of the Plaszow inmates assigned to work specifically for him; Schindler thereby retrieves many of his former workers from the general population in Plaszow. A Jewish woman living as a Christian outside the camp comes to visit Schindler. She tells him that it's widely known that his workers are kept safe, and she asks him to bring her elderly parents, imprisoned in Plaszow, to work for him so they will not be killed. Schindler reacts angrily, asserting that he only hires workers who can perform the necessary tasks. He swears he is not in the business of saving Jews, but he nevertheless arranges for the woman's parents to join the ranks of his workers.

Meanwhile, Goeth's ruthlessness is established in scenes where he randomly shoots inmates of the camp, sometimes for target practice, sometimes on a whim. His behavior toward his young Jewish maid, Helen Hirsch (played by Embeth Davidtz), alternates between obvious attraction and unprovoked abusiveness. In one chilling scene, he visits Helen in her room. Drawn to touch her and wishing to be physically intimate with her, Goeth suddenly remembers that she is a Jew, and, in his mind, less than human. Appalled by his attraction to her, Goeth blames Helen for "seducing" him and viciously beats her.

As the war nears its end in spring 1944, more and more people are sent from Plaszow to death camps. Eventual-

ly Goeth tells Schindler that Plaszow will soon be shut down and all remaining inmates will be sent to Auschwitz-Birkenau, a concentration camp where more than one million Jews met their deaths during the Holocaust. Schindler decides to leave Krakow, satisfied with the huge sums of money he's made and convinced he can do nothing more to help his Jewish workers. At the last minute he has a change of heart; he approaches Goeth offering to give him money in exchange for his workers, who he wishes to transport to a new factory location in Czechoslovakia. With the help of Stern, Schindler creates a list of more than one thousand workers he will take to the new factory. In a final act of bargaining and gambling, Schindler secures a space for Goeth's maid, Helen, on his list.

After greeting trainloads of his workers at the new factory, Schindler realizes that hundreds of women and children were mistakenly routed to Auschwitz. He travels to the concentration camp with a bag full of loose diamonds, and once there negotiates for the release of his workers. He succeeds, and the

Scene from the three-hour-long movie epic *Schindler's List*. Oskar Schindler, played by Liam Neeson, oversees the work of Jewish accountant Itzhak Stern, played by Ben Kingsley. *Reproduced by permission of the Kobal Collection.*

women and children get back in the train cars heading for Czechoslovakia. For the next several months, the last months of the war, Schindler goes to great expense to feed and care for his workers. Determined to only produce ammunition that malfunctions, Schindler spends the last of his fortune covering up his attempt to sabotage the German war effort. Finally the war is over and the *Schindlerjuden* are free. Schindler and his wife, fearing that they will be punished for being Nazis by the Soviet and American soldiers who have won the war against Germany, dress as labor-camp prisoners and carry a letter from the workers describing their efforts to save them. As he is about to depart, Schindler breaks down, overcome by remorse that he didn't do more to save Jewish lives.

The final scene of the movie takes place in the present day, showing a long line of the surviving Schindler Jews, and their descendants, walking toward the grave of the man who helped save their lives. Following a Jewish custom, each of the survivors, accompanied by the actors who portrayed them in the movie, place a small stone on the grave of Oskar Schindler. The film ends with words on the screen explaining that fewer than 4,000 Jews live in Poland today, while the descendants of the Schindler Jews number more than 6,000.

Historical accuracy of *Schindler's List*. The movie *Schindler's List* closely follows the text of the book of the same name on which it was based. The book's author, Thomas Keneally, describes his work as a novel, though it is primarily based on fact. Keneally conducted extensive research, interviewing dozens of the Holocaust survivors known as Schindler Jews. He also visited the sites in Poland where the book's events took place, including the building that once housed Schindler's factory in Krakow and the remains of the concentration camp Auschwitz. In spite of its reliance on actual people and events, Keneally chose to categorize the book as a novel because he felt that, as explained in the author's note at the beginning of the book, "The novel's techniques seem suited for a character of such ambiguity and magnitude as Oskar." He further explains that while he had to create a few of the conversations from his imagination, most of the book's dialogue comes from the remembrances of people who knew Schindler. He says that he tried "to avoid all fiction" in writing *Schindler's List*.

Because Steven Spielberg's film portrays people and events as presented in Keneally's book and in historical documents, it is considered by many to be historically accurate. Most of the characters—Oskar Schindler, Itzhak Stern, Amon Goeth—actually existed. And many survivors have claimed that Spielberg accurately depicts life in a Nazi-controlled Jewish ghetto.

Some events have been left out or shortened for dramatic effect and to keep the film at a reasonable length. For example, in the movie Schindler witnesses the liquidation of the Krakow ghetto that took place in March 1943; his horrified reaction to this violent, murderous event marks a turning point for him in the film. According to the book, Schindler actually witnessed an earlier *aktion*, one that took place in June 1942.

Some critics, while agreeing that Spielberg sticks to the facts for the most part, nonetheless attack the filmmaker for producing a movie that fails to grasp the enormity of the Holocaust, an event unparalleled in its inhumanity. They criticize Spielberg's slick production, which some think is inappropriately exciting and adventurous. They argue that Spielberg reduced the complexity of the Nazis to cartoonish depictions of evil. Some have pointed out that the inmates of the death camps were, in reality, starving, pale, and close to death, while many of Spielberg's actors appear plump and healthy.

Some commentators also claim that Spielberg's characterization of Schindler, who rapidly moves from being a selfish businessman to a selfless hero, ignores the true complexities of Schindler's personality. Schindler's decision to save the Jewish workers, some critics suggest, may have been motivated by self-interest. By the time Schindler began actively trying to save lives, it was clear that Germany was losing the war, and Schindler may simply have been trying to avoid punishment for war crimes, such as employing slave labor, by the Allied victors (including the United States, Soviet Union, and Great Britain). Historians also point out that Spielberg did not address Schindler's behavior after the war. He cheated on and eventually abandoned his wife, struggled with alcoholism, and accepted the financial support of some Schindler Jews rather than earning an income on his own. Many of the

Schindler Jews, however, have argued that his motives, and his sometimes immoral behavior, don't matter as much as the fact that more than 1,100 people survived because of him.

Style and Themes in *Schindler's List*

Schindler's List, shot mostly on black-and-white film, looks gritty and realistic. Much of the filming was done with a handheld camera, capturing its subjects at close range. This technique draws the audience into the story, making the events seem immediate and sometimes unbearably close. On the other hand, director Steven Spielberg deliberately altered the film to look like an old newsreel, at times giving the viewer the sense of watching a documentary movie.

Aside from the opening scene of a Jewish family observing Sabbath rituals and the closing scene showing survivors of the Holocaust visiting Oskar Schindler's grave, the film contains only one instance of color interrupting the stark black and white. Schindler looks on from a hilltop as the brutal Nazi soldiers empty the Krakow ghetto, herding out the Jewish residents, who will later be sent to death camps, and shooting anyone who tries to escape or hide. A small child in a red coat catches his eye, and he watches as the child wanders through the ghetto alone, seemingly unaware and untouched by the madness taking place around her. The sight of this little girl suddenly jolts Schindler into a more complete awareness of the horrors perpetrated by the Nazis; she symbolizes the widespread destruction of all Jews, particularly children, during the Holocaust. Later in the movie the audience catches another glimpse of the red coat, which now covers the girl's lifeless body.

While *Schindler's List* addresses many elements of the Holocaust—the cold, brutal, and systematic destruction of the Jews, the struggle for survival in the desolate conditions of the ghettos—the film is mainly about one man's complex personality and his discovery of his own humanity. At the beginning of the movie, Schindler seems almost proud of his passionate desire to make money in any way possible. While the exact moment of the change in his beliefs is difficult to pinpoint, it is clear that by the end of the film Schindler has taken great risks, and spent large amounts of money, to behave like a decent, even heroic, human being.

Without attempting to reach any conclusions, *Schindler's List* explores the enormity of the Nazi hatred toward the Jews and the incomprehensible wickedness of Adolf Hitler's plan to destroy every Jew in Europe. The film also examines, by focusing on the example of Schindler, the admirable actions of those who risked their lives to help save others.

Research and Activity Ideas

1) Oskar Schindler goes from being a man who is only interested in his own pleasure to someone who risks everything to save the lives of his Jewish workers. What do you think caused this change? What do you think was his first step toward helping the Jews? Explain whether it matters if he was motivated, even at the end, by his own interests, or if he truly wished to perform heroic acts.

2) Describe the complicated relationship between the Jewish accountant Itzhak Stern and Oskar Schindler. Stern's actions are performed behind the scenes, in a quiet way, as opposed to Schindler's more flamboyant, outward behavior. Describe the ways in which Stern acts to save his fellow Jews, and the steps he takes to encourage Schindler to do the right thing.

3) The Nazi leader of the Plaszow labor camp, Amon Goeth, struggles with his attraction to his young Jewish maid, Helen Hirsch. He feels drawn to her, but he also firmly believes, as he tells her one night, that, by being a Jew, "she is not a person in the strictest sense of the word." He refers to the description of Jews by anti-Semites (those who hate or discriminate against Jews) as rats or vermin, a word that refers to fleas and other creatures that are often exterminated. Research the history of anti-Semitism, exploring the ways in which some people classify Jews as less than human to justify treating them badly.

Where to Learn More About ...

Schindler's List

Blake, Richard A. "Schindler's List." *America* 170 (February 12, 1994): p. 20.

Bromwich, David. "Schindler's List." *The New Leader* 77 (February 14, 1994): p. 20.

Bruning, Fred. "Schindler's List." *Maclean's* 107 (April 25, 1994): p. 9.

Dirks, Tim. "Schindler's List." *The Greatest Films*. http://www.filmsite.org/schi.html (accessed on December 18, 2002).

Fensch, Thomas. *Oskar Schindler and His List: The Man, the Book, the Film, the Holocaust and Its Survivors*. New York: Paul S. Eriksson, 1995.

Schindler's List Teaching Guide. http://www.tulane.edu/~so-inst/slindex.html (accessed on December 18, 2002).

Oskar Schindler and the Schindler Jews

Brecher, Elinor J. *Schindler's Legacy*. New York: Plume, 1994.

Keneally, Thomas. *Schindler's List*. New York: Simon and Schuster, 1994. Originally published as *Schindler's Ark,* 1982.

Roberts, Jeremy. *Oskar Schindler: Righteous Gentile*. New York: Rosen Publishing, 2000.

Schindler, Emilie. *Where Light and Shadow Meet*. New York: W. W. Norton & Company, 1997.

Holocaust Music

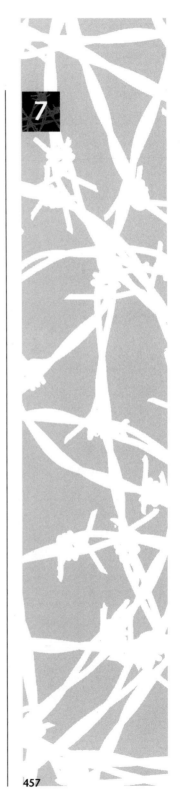

7

Music was an important part of life for those who suffered under the Nazi brutality of the Holocaust, Adolf Hitler (1889–1945) and his Nazi government's systematic murder of six million Jewish and five million non-Jewish men, women, and children. In addition to killing Jews, Hitler attempted to destroy all traces of Jewish culture, including art and music. Jews in ghettos and concentration camps preserved their cultural identity through the singing of traditional religious and folk songs. New songs, often combining new words sung to old tunes, were written to reflect the people's experiences of camp and ghetto life. These songs provide a historical record of this time when traditional means of documenting events, through books, records, concerts, was impossible. As is true of music regardless of the time or place, music during the Holocaust also served as a temporary diversion from suffering for those who created it, performed it, or heard it.

The term "Holocaust music" refers not just to the music that was sung or composed during World War II (1939–1945), but also to music that was written afterward, in response to the horrific tragedy. Some composers wrote music in memory of specific individuals who died; others wrote to express sorrow and mourning for the multitude of victims, as well as anger and frustration with a world that ignored the vulnerable during their time of greatest suffering.

Music under Nazi rule

When he first came to power in Germany in 1933, Hitler had a goal to get rid of the Jews and their influence on German culture and to acknowledge only the cultural heritage of what he called the Aryan people, white Christians of Germanic ancestry. The Nazi government began to outlaw any music or art that did not meet standards for official approval. Above all else, this decree included any music composed or performed by Jewish musicians. It also included music that the Nazis described as "degenerate," meaning lower in quality than traditional German music and harmful to the general population. The music that fell under this category included contemporary, experimental-sounding music as well as jazz, which they objected to because of its close association with black people—what the Nazis called "non-Aryan Negroid" culture. Among the musicians who left their homelands and immigrated to the United States in order to escape Nazi persecution were conductor Otto Klemperer (1875–1973) and composers Paul Hindemith (1895–1963) and Arnold Schoenberg (1874–1951).

Music became a significant tool in Hitler's efforts to gain total control, first over Germany and then over all of Europe. Folk music and anthems that praised the superiority of Germany and its people were used to arouse patriotic feelings among Germans during large public rallies. Marching songs filled with anti-Jewish sentiments were written to be sung by the children and young adults in Nazi youth groups such as the Hitler Youth. The government allowed orchestras to perform only music by traditional German composers; one of Hitler's favorites was Richard Wagner (pronounced VAHG-ner; 1813–1883), a prolific composer of operas that suited Nazi leaders' taste for works that glorified Germany.

The Nazis used music for a twisted purpose in the concentration and death camps, where millions of Jews were forced into back-breaking labor or murdered outright. Prisoner orchestras, made up of any available assortment of musicians and instruments, were made to perform daily for various purposes. In her memoir *Inherit the Truth,* Holocaust survivor Anita Lasker-Wallfisch remembers her time as the cellist in the orchestra at Auschwitz, where the prison orchestra played marches every morning and evening as thousands of other prisoners were taken to and from local factories. She writes of performing Sunday concerts and recalls that "we also had to be ready to play for any SS personnel [members of an elite Nazi unit who were in charge of the concentration and death camps] who came into our block [a section of the prison] for light relief after their exhausting work of determining who should live and who should die."

Music of the ghettos, camps, and resistance organizations

Music had always been an important part of Jewish cultural life in Europe, and its significance continued—and perhaps even increased—as Nazi laws and persecution made life more and more difficult for Jews. Traditional songs became lessons for children when organized classrooms were outlawed. While performing daily tasks, adults sang songs to raise their spirits, restore a sense of community, and express hope for the future. Songs were written to convey feelings of anger and calls for resistance, to document the experiences of life under Nazi control, and to preserve the traditions and cultural identity of the Jews under extraordinary circumstances. Typical themes of ghetto and concentration camp songs included hunger, which was a dominating force in their daily lives; a longing for freedom; criticism of government and local authorities; calls for resistance against the oppressors; and traditional prayers.

One of the best-known concentration camp songs, "Dachau Song," was composed in September 1938 by Herbert Zipper, who ultimately survived Dachau and Buchenwald, an-

Jewish composer and professor Paul Hindemith, who left his native Germany in 1937 after the Nazi Party instituted a boycott of his music. *Reproduced by permission of Getty Images.*

other concentration camp. The lyrics were written by the playwright Jura Soyfer, who later died at Buchenwald of typhoid fever. Zipper and Soyfer wrote this protest song as a response to the inscription *Arbeit Macht Frei,* or "work makes one free"; these words appeared on the entrance gates to Dachau, Auschwitz, and other camps. The two men taught the song, a call to courage and dignity, to fellow prisoners shortly before they were transferred to Buchenwald. After being released from Buchenwald, Zipper eventually immigrated to the United States. After World War II ended, he was astonished to discover that "Dachau Song" had made its way from one concentration camp to another throughout the war, taught from person to person as a small but important form of resistance.

Cultural life in the Jewish ghettos—small, walled-in areas of cities where Jews were forced to live before being transported to concentration or death camps—sometimes included theater and music productions created by and for members of the community as a diversion from the hardships of daily life. The Vilna ghetto theater was organized in January 1942 to perform classics of Yiddish and European drama and original shows that included plays and music based on ghetto experiences. A well-known song from one of those productions was "Yisrolik," which tells the story of a child in the ghetto who peddled goods on the streets in order to survive. The lyrics were written in Yiddish by Leyb Rozental, with music by Misha Veksler, neither of whom survived the war. However, Chayela Rosenthal, younger sister of the lyricist, first sang "Yisrolik" in the Vilna ghetto and went on to record the song after the war, in Paris, before embarking on a successful acting career. "Yisrolik" still represents independence and courage in the face of hard times.

Another famous Yiddish song from the Holocaust was inspired by the Warsaw ghetto uprising in April 1943, during which Jews used guns, hand grenades, and other weapons they had secretly collected to fight against their Nazi captors. The Nazis had the military power to crush the resisters, but the Jews managed to kill a number of their oppressors before being captured or murdered. When he heard news of the events in the Warsaw ghetto, poet and resistance fighter Hirsh Glik, who lived in the Vilna ghetto, wrote "Zog nit keynmol az du geyst dem letstn veg," or "Never Say That You Have

Herbert Zipper, left, who formed a secret orchestra in the Nazi concentration camp Dachau to raise the spirits of other prisoners, survived the Holocaust and went on to become a world-renowned conductor.
Reproduced by permission of AP/Wide World Photos.

Reached the Final Road." Set to the tune of a march, the song was sung in the Vilna ghetto and beyond. It became the official anthem of Jewish partisans, resistance fighters who lived in the woods and conducted secret attacks on the Germans.

Music from Terezin

Terezin, also known as Theresienstadt, was a concentration camp in Czechoslovakia that was designed to deceive the rest of the world about conditions inside Nazi camps. Many well-known Jewish artists and musicians were sent to Terezin rather than being sent directly to one of the death camps. These artists were sent to Terezin, which was sometimes referred to as the "model ghetto," not because Hitler valued their lives or cultural contributions, but because he feared the international reaction if such prominent citizens disappeared into the murderous machinery of a death camp. While Hitler maintained that his vicious campaign against the Jews was not only legal but moral, he also felt that such activities had to be kept secret from the world at large in order to proceed without interference from other nations.

The Nazis made Terezin look like a resettlement area rather than a concentration camp, preserving that image just long enough to persuade observers from the International Red Cross that the Jews were being treated well and given opportunities to pursue cultural activities such as music and theater. In truth, however, conditions at Terezin were horrible just as in other concentration camps, and most of the musicians, actors, and artists whose work was displayed to outsiders were eventually sent to Auschwitz. In spite of the miserable conditions, and because the population of the camp included so many talented musicians, a number of well-known musical works were created at Terezin, placing the camp in a category of its own in the field of Holocaust music.

One of the most famous pieces of music from Terezin was a children's opera called *Brundibar, the Organ Grinder*. It was composed in 1938 by Hans Krasa in Prague, Czechoslovakia, several years before he was transported to Terezin. Krasa's story of children who triumph over the selfish acts of a boastful organ grinder was designed to criticize Hitler without directly mentioning the German leader. Its first performance took place secretly on November 27, 1941, at a children's orphanage in Prague. By that time, Jews were not allowed by law to perform in concerts or plays or to assemble in large gatherings, so staging such an event was an act of defiance against the Nazis.

In 1942 Krasa and the other Jews of Prague were rounded up and taken to Terezin. During his first year there, Krasa rewrote the entire production of *Brundibar* in order to give the imprisoned children a diverting task and to allow them to continue to tell the story. On September 23, 1943, the rewritten *Brundibar* was performed at Terezin for the first time. Fifty-four more performances followed, using a variety of children as cast members. One performance of the opera was initiated by the Nazi guards to impress the Red Cross observers, who accepted the performance as evidence that children were being well cared for at Terezin. Nothing could have been further from the truth. In October 1944, shortly after the Nazi-approved performance, the composer and most of the actors were sent to Auschwitz. Only two of the children who performed in the Terezin opera survived the Holocaust.

Music as a response to the Holocaust

In the years following World War II, composers and poets of many nationalities drew upon their own experiences and the testimony of survivors to respond through music to the unspeakable tragedy of the Holocaust. Some compositions were written in memory of loved ones. Some were written as affirmations of hope in the midst of despair. Some were religious texts set to music, such as the Kaddish, a prayer recited for the dead. Excerpts of letters, diaries, poems, and other works written by Holocaust victims were also incorporated into songs by composers for whom music seemed the most effective way to share these stories with a world that was reluctant to hear them.

Famous Jewish composer Arnold Schoenberg, who fled his native Austria in 1933, after Hitler seized power in Germany.
Reproduced by permission of the Catholic University of America.

In 1947 composer Arnold Schoenberg wrote *A Survivor from Warsaw,* an eight-minute work dedicated to the memory of the brutal deportations of Jews from the Warsaw ghetto. The discordant sounds of the orchestra and men's chorus depict the growing violence and horror in the lives of the Warsaw Jews. The music reaches an emotional end with the text of the Shema, a central Jewish prayer declaring a belief in and love for one God. Schoenberg escaped from Austria in 1933 when Hitler came to power. He eventually settled in the United States, where he lived the remainder of his life. *A Survivor from Warsaw* was first performed in the United States on November 4, 1948.

In 1978, Canadian composer Ben Steinberg (1930–) wrote *Echoes of Children,* a cantata based on a variety of sources, including a nineteenth-century Jewish folk song, scripture texts from chapter thirty-seven of the biblical book of Ezekiel, and the writings of children who died during the Holocaust. The cantata for orchestra and chorus was written in memory of the millions of children who died during the Holocaust. It has been performed for television audiences in both Canada and the United States.

The United States Holocaust Memorial Museum (USHMM) maintains a growing collection of printed music, recordings, and documentation about music's role during the Holocaust. The collection covers the spectrum of Holocaust music, including songs from the ghettos, camps, and partisan organizations; music that was banned by the Nazis; music that emerged from the Terezin concentration camp; anti-Nazi songs from World War II; and compositions, performances, and recorded commentary from survivors, as well as works written by composers who were murdered during the Holocaust. The USHMM Web site, available at www.ushmm.org, provides online links to recorded archives featuring performances of music from and about the Holocaust.

Representative Books about Music in the Holocaust

Cummins, Paul F. *Dachau Song: The Twentieth Century Odyssey of Herbert Zipper.* New York: Peter Lang, 1992. *This biography addresses the life of Herbert Zipper, who wrote "Dachau Song." Zipper survived both Dachau and Buchenwald concentration camps and immigrated to the United States, where he pursued a long career as a composer, conductor, and music educator.*

Fenelon, Fania. *Playing for Time.* New York: Atheneum, 1977. *Translated from French by Judith Landry, this autobiography recalls the life of a Paris cabaret singer who survived Auschwitz and Bergen-Belsen concentration camps as one of "the orchestra girls."*

Kalisch, Shoshana, and Barbara Meister. *Yes, We Sang!: Songs of the Ghettos and Concentration Camps.* New York: Harper & Row, 1985. *This collection contains more than two dozen songs with piano accompaniment, plus background information about the songs, their composers, and life in the Nazi concentration camps.*

Lasker-Wallfisch, Anita. *Inherit the Truth: A Memoir of Survival and the Holocaust.* New York: St. Martin's Press, 1996. *This book relates the story of a young cellist who survived the Holocaust in part because of her musical abilities. The author tells about her experiences as a member of the infamous Auschwitz-Birkenau "Lager Orchestra," or camp orchestra.*

Mlotek, Eleanor, and Malke Gottlieb, compilers. *We Are Here: Songs of the Holocaust.* New York: Workmen's Circle and Hippocrene Books,

1983. *This collection of music of the Holocaust contains singable translations of the original songs, with an introduction written by Holocaust survivor Elie Wiesel.*

Representative Online Resources about Music in the Holocaust

"Music of the Holocaust." *A Teacher's Guide to the Holocaust.* http://fcit. coedu.usf.edu/holocaust/arts/music.htm (accessed on January 15, 2003). *This Web site provides lists of Holocaust-related music as well as links to sound files, photographs, and additional Web sites of interest to students and teachers researching the subject.*

"Music of the Holocaust: Highlights from the Collection." *The United States Holocaust Memorial Museum.* http://wlc.ushmm.org/museum/ exhibit/online/music/ (accessed on January 15, 2003). *This Web site includes background text, music files, photographs, and other features related to Holocaust music.*

Rubin, Ruth. "The Story of Yiddish Folksong." *The Music of the Holocaust.* http://www.remember.org/hist.root.music.html (accessed on January 15, 2003). *This 1979 article provides background information about songs that were sung during the Holocaust in concentration camps, ghettos, and elsewhere.*

Representative Recordings of Music from the Holocaust

Berman, Karel, and Pavel Haas. *Composers from Theresienstadt.* Channel Classics, 1985. *This compact disc features music written by Pavel Haas, who died at Auschwitz in 1944, and Karel Berman, who survived the Holocaust.*

Hear Our Voices: Songs from the Ghettos and the Camps. HaZamir, 1994. *This recording contains more than two dozen songs, including "Yisrolek" and other music from Terezin, Vilna, Vishnetz, Sachsenhausen, and Pryztik, performed by the Zamir Chorale of Boston.*

Krasa, Hans. *Brundibar.* Channel Classics, 1993. *This compact disc recording of the Terezin children's opera* Brundibar, the Organ Grinder *also includes "Czech Songs for Children's Chorus and String Quartet."*

Partisans of Vilna: The Songs of World War II Jewish Resistance. Flying Fish Records, 1989. *Twelve songs sung in Yiddish celebrate the spirit of the Jews who resisted their oppressors. The collection includes the famous Partisan anthem, "Never Say That You Have Reached the Final Road."*

Remember the Children: Songs for and by the Children of the Holocaust. The United States Holocaust Memorial Museum, 1991. *This collection features Adrienne Cooper, a well-known interpreter of Yiddish stories and songs.*

Rise Up and Fight! Songs of the Jewish Partisans. The United States Holocaust Memorial Museum, 1996. *This recording contains eighteen songs, sung in a variety of languages, and includes a performance by singer, activist, and actor Theodore Bikel. The CD includes a booklet with English translations of each song.*

Terezin: The Music 1941–1944. Romantic Robot, 1991. *This two-disc set includes performances of works by Terezin victims Pavel Haas, Gideon Klein, Hans Krasa, and Viktor Ullmann.*

Representative Recordings of Music in Response to the Holocaust

Cohen, Michael. *I Remember.* Newport, 1999. *This recording includes works of chamber music based on Anne Frank's* The Diary of a Young Girl.

Davidson, Charles. *I Never Saw Another Butterfly.* Music Masters, 1990. *This song cycle, composed in 1968, was based on the collection of poetry and artwork by children of Terezin.*

Penderecki, Krzysztof. *Dies Irae* (Dedicated to the Memory of Those Murdered at Auschwitz). Conifer, 1989. *This work was first performed on April 16, 1967, at Auschwitz-Birkenau, during the dedication of a memorial at the site of the Nazi death camp.*

Senator, Ronald. *Holocaust Requiem: Kaddish for Terezin.* Delos DE, 1994. *English composer Ronald Senator introduced this work at Canterbury Cathedral in his home country in 1986. The English text is based on poems and diaries of children who died at Terezin.*

Shostakovich, Dmitri. *Symphony No. 13.* Decca, 1984. *This symphony, also known as "Babi Yar," was written to commemorate the massacre of tens of thousands of Jews at a ravine near Kiev, Ukraine. The text comes from the poem "Babi Yar," written by the Russian poet Yevgeny Yevtushenko.*

Bibliography

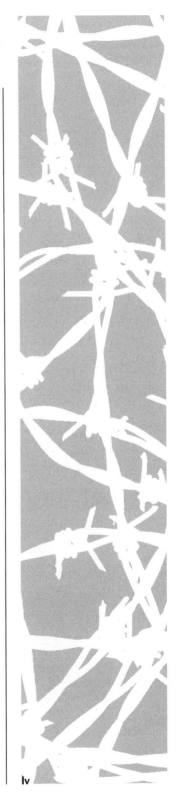

The following list of resources focuses on material appropriate for middle school or high school students. Please note that the Web site addresses were verified prior to publication, but are subject to change.

Books

Adler, David A. *We Remember the Holocaust*. New York: Henry Holt, 1989.

Bachrach, Deborah. *The Resistance*. San Diego: Lucent Books, 1998.

Bachrach, Susan D. *Tell Them We Remember: The Story of the Holocaust*. Boston: Little, Brown, 1994.

Boas, Jacob. *We Are Witnesses: Five Diaries of Teenagers Who Died in the Holocaust*. New York: Henry Holt, 1995.

Chaikin, Miriam. *Nightmare in History: The Holocaust 1933–1945*. New York: Clarion Books, 1987.

Dolan, Edward F. *Anti-Semitism*. New York: Franklin Watts, 1985.

Drucker, Malka, and Michael Halperin. *Jacob's Rescue*. New York: Yearling Books, 1994.

Friedman, Ina R. *Escape or Die: True Stories of Young People Who Survived the Holocaust*. New York: Lippincott, 1982.

Gelissen, Rena Kornreich. *Rena's Promise: A Story of Sisters in Auschwitz.* Boston: Beacon Press, 1995.

Glatstein, Jacob, Israel Knox, and Samuel Margoshes, eds. *Anthology of Holocaust Literature.* New York: Atheneum, 1978.

Greenfeld, Howard. *The Hidden Children.* New York: Ticknor & Fields, 1993.

Grossman, Mendel, and Frank Dabba Smith. *My Secret Camera: Life in the Lodz Ghetto.* San Diego: Gulliver Books, 2000.

Holliday, Laurel. *Children in the Holocaust and World War II: Their Secret Diaries.* New York: Pocket Books, 1995.

Landau, Elaine. *The Warsaw Ghetto Uprising.* New York: Macmillan, 1992.

Laska, Vera, ed. *Women in the Resistance and in the Holocaust: The Voices of Eyewitnesses.* Westport, CT: Greenwood Press, 1983.

Lewy, Guenter. *The Nazi Persecution of the Gypsies.* Oxford: Oxford University Press, 2000.

Marrin, Albert. *Hitler: A Portrait of a Tyrant.* New York: Viking, 1987.

Meltzer, Milton. *Never to Forget: The Jews of the Holocaust.* New York: HarperCollins, 1991.

Meltzer, Milton. *Rescue: The Story of How Gentiles Saved Jews in the Holocaust.* New York: Harper & Row, 1988.

Moore, Bob. *Victims and Survivors: The Nazi Persecution of the Jews in the Netherlands, 1940–1945.* New York: Arnold, 1997.

Pettit, Jane. *A Place to Hide: True Stories of Holocaust Rescues.* New York: Scholastic, 1993.

Rashke, Richard. *Escape from Sobibor: The Heroic Story of the Jews Who Escaped from a Nazi Death Camp.* Boston: Houghton Mifflin, 1982.

Resnick, Abraham. *The Holocaust.* San Diego: Lucent Books, 1991.

Rittner, Carol, and Sondra Meyers, eds. *The Courage to Care: Rescuers of Jews during the Holocaust.* New York: New York University Press, 1986.

Rosenberg, Maxine B. *Hiding to Survive: Stories of Jewish Children Rescued from the Holocaust.* New York: Clarion Books, 1994.

Stadtler, Bea. *The Holocaust: A History of Courage and Resistance.* West Orange, NJ: Behrman House, 1994.

Suhl, Yuri, ed. *They Fought Back: The Story of the Jewish Resistance in Nazi Europe.* New York: Schocken Books, 1975.

Tito, E. Tina. *Teen Witnesses to the Holocaust: Liberation.* New York: Rosen Publishing Group, 1999.

Web Sites

A Cybrary of the Holocaust: Remember.org. http://remember.org/ (accessed on February 13, 2003).

The History Place: A Holocaust Timeline. http://www.historyplace.com/worldwar2/holocaust/timeline.html (accessed on February 13, 2003).

The Holocaust Chronicle. http://www.holocaustchronicle.org/ (accessed on February 13, 2003).

The Holocaust History Project. http://www.holocaust-history.org/ (accessed on February 13, 2003).

Holocaust Memorial Center. http://www.holocaustcenter.org/ (accessed on February 13, 2003).

Holocaust Survivors. http://www.holocaustsurvivors.org/ (accessed on February 13, 2003).

Holocaust Teacher Resource Center. http://www.holocaust-trc.org/ (accessed on February 13, 2003).

Jewish Virtual Library: The Holocaust. http://www.us-israel.org/jsource/holo.html (accessed on February 13, 2003).

Museum of Tolerance: A Simon Wiesenthal Center Museum. http://www.museumoftolerance.com/mot/index.cfm (accessed on February 13, 2003).

Survivors of the Shoah Visual History Foundation. http://www.vhf.org/ (accessed on February 13, 2003).

A Teacher's Guide to the Holocaust. http://fcit.coedu.usf.edu/holocaust/default.htm (accessed on February 13, 2003).

United States Holocaust Memorial Museum. http://www.ushmm.org/ (accessed on February 13, 2003).

Women and the Holocaust: A Cyberspace of Their Own. http://www.interlog.com/~mighty/ (accessed on February 13, 2003).

Yad Vashem: The Holocaust Martyrs' and Heroes' Remembrance Authority. http://www.yad-vashem.org.il/ (accessed on February 13, 2003).

Index

Note: *Italic* type indicates volume number; **boldface** indicates main entries and their page numbers; (ill.) indicates photos and illustrations.

F

G

H

I